WOMEN EMPOWERMENT
THROUGH CAPACITY BUILDING

About the Author

Christabell, P.J. is a lecturer in the Department of Economics, Government College for Women, Thiruvananthapuram, which is affiliated to the University of Kerala. Earlier, she was a faculty in Economics in ICFAI National College, Thiruvananthapuram and Gondar University, Ethiopia. She has to her credit a number of research papers published in journals of international and national repute. She has also participated in various seminars and conferences.

Women Empowerment Through Capacity Building
The Role of Microfinance

Christabell, P.J.

CONCEPT PUBLISHING COMPANY, NEW DELHI-110 059

Cataloging in Publication Data—DK
Courtesy: D.K. Agencies (P) Ltd. <docinfo@dkagencies.com>

Christabell, P. J.
Women empowerment through capacity building : the role of microfinance / Christabell, P.J.
p. cm.
Study conducted at Ulloor Panchayat in Thiruvananthapuram District, Kerala, India.
Includes bibliographical references (p.).
Includes index.
ISBN 13: 9788180694455
ISBN 10: 8180694453

1. Microfinance—India—Ulloor (Panchayat) 2. Self-help groups—India—Ulloor (Panchayat) 3. Poor women—Employment—India—Ulloor (Panchayat) 4. Women in economic development—India—Ulloor (Panchayat) 5. Women in politics—India—Ulloor (Panchayat) I. Title.

DDC 332.095 483 22

The Indian Council of Social Science Research gave the financial support towards the publication of this work. However, the responsibility for the contents of the book—facts, opinions, conclusions, etc.—is entirely that of the author and not of the ICSSR

ICSSR Consultant: **Dr. R.S. Deshpande**

ISBN-13: 978-81-8069-445-5
ISBN 10: 81-8069-445-3

First Published 2009

Published and Printed by
Ashok Kumar Mittal
Concept Publishing Company
A/15-16, Commercial Block, Mohan Garden
New Delhi-110 059 (INDIA)

Phones . 25351460, 25351794
Fax : 091-11-25357103
Email : publishing@conceptpub.com

PROF. MRIDUL EAPEN
MEMBER
STATE PLANNING BOARD
THIRUVANANTHAPURAM
E-mail: meapen@keralaplanningboard.org

Foreword

'Women' during the 1970s were emerging as a recognized constituency in the development effort. The growing evidence on their marginalisation focused attention on ways of gendering the development process which would improve the position of women in society. Lack of adequate credit was identified as a major constraint in transforming women's lives, in particular, poor women. The failure of the formal banking system in meeting the financial needs of the rural poor despite its tremendous growth created the context for the emergence of micro finance. With the setting up of poverty targeted Micro Finance Organizations (MFO) like the Grameen Bank and others in the 1980s, and their reasonably successful experience of meeting the credit needs of poorer women through micro loans, micro credit became a critical policy tool for poverty allieviation. Its spread was rapid through Self Help Groups (SHGs), primarily of women and hence its potential for empowering women also came to be projected as a major objective in encouraging its growth. Substantive literature has emerged and is continuing to emerge in this area as also its praxis in the form of a tremendous growth of micro finance institutions with an infusion of credit, poor households would be able to break out of the vicious circle of poverty. Such households need many more financial services such as savings and insurance, besides other social and economic support; and hence one talks of micro *finance* and not of micro *credit* now.

Since poverty alleviation or empowerment cannot be assumed to be automatic outcome of micro finance programmes, more serious studies have focused on understanding the path through which finance links up with poverty reduction and empowerment. This, needless to state, helps in designing more effective poverty reduction programmes and also throws up more appropriate indicators for impact evaluation. A major issue faced by micro finance organizations, still being grappled with, is the need to upscale their activities and promote livelihoods beyond minimum levels of sustenance. Some questions still remain unanswered: whether micro finance through self help groups and largely based on self-employment is the most effective way of providing livelihoods and reducing poverty or is creation of wage employment a better policy option? Perhaps, the latter which gives certainty of a wage at the end of the day would be a preferred option of the poor. It would be more difficult for women to undertake self-employment ventures. There could be many reasons for this: (a) on an average, women have had less access to training for modern skills than men; and (b) access to information on new products and markets too is more difficult for women. But they appear to be more willing, given the flexibility in working hours it provides, which enables them to combine household work with an income earning activity, however small the remuneration. State policy, at least in India, does not appear to have taken adequate note of this huge burden that women carry daily to sustain lives and livelihoods.

The issue of empowerment of women through micro finance programmes has generated considerable debate which continues—whether bringing women together has resulted in more transformatory outcomes enabling women to challenge the existing patriarchal structures within and outside the household. Much of the controversy has been on account of differences in perceptions on 'empowerment' which could be defined narrowly in terms of individual capacity building or in the more transformative sense in which feminists would define empowerment (From the point of view of feminists the problem is female subordination defined in terms of the unequal relations between men and women within the social process which work to the detriment of women based as they are on the sexual division of labour along lines of gender; empowerment would necessarily call for challenging the inequitous gender relations). What needs to be emphasized in my view is that social change is slow and the very fact that micro finance activities have brought together women in such large numbers out of the household (though largely in its proximity) is an achievement and if maintained on a fairly sustained basis, could constitute a platform for action, in particular for addressing the many ways in which gender inequities operate.

This book on Women's Empowerment and the Role of Microfinance based on the experience of a cluster of SHGs organized by an MFO in a district of Kerala, is a welcome addition to the literature on micro finance. Against the background of over two decades of the functioning of MFOs which has allowed for a continuous process of adapting to lessons learnt in practice, it guards against certain pitfalls and uses a rather innovative concept of 'empowerment' which while seemingly narrow in its perception, subsumes a certain 'relatedness' to others which broadens its scope. The emphasis is on "democratic capacity building" of women and "economic capacity building" as two major indicators.

The late 1990s was the period when the Left Front government of Kerala launched the 'People's Plan Campaign (PPC) for Decentralized Planning' (coinciding with the 9th Five Year Plan) and the first local body elections had been held as per the direction of the 73rd and 74th Constitutional Amendments mandating a 33 percent representation of women at all three levels of the Local Self Governing Institutions (LSGIs). The 'feminisation' of political leadership at the local level opened up considerable space for addressing women's needs and priorities. This was buttressed by a conscious attempt to incorporate gender issues into the *process* of planning. It was further strengthened by providing for a Women Component Plan (WCP); the LSGIs were advised (later mandated) to set apart 10 percent of the plan grant-in-aid (devolved from the State Plan resources) for preparing projects that directly benefit women.

Hence it was expected that decentralised governance, with broad-based democratic involvement would act to strengthen the synergy between efficient implementation of development interventions and broader goals of gender equity and social justice. Neighbour Hood Groups (NHGs) and Self Help Groups largely of women (which had come up under the PPC) were viewed as a sub-system of the LSGIs which would facilitate more democratic functioning and larger community involvement to be able to fight gender discrimination even while exploring avenues of economic empowerment.

This study of a single MFO, *Samatha Vanitha Swayam Sahaya Sangham* (Samatha for short) and its group of SHGs in a panchayat area though rather 'micro' in its approach, does throw up certain larger issues that merit attention given the range of issues discussed, interspersed with brief case studies, within one of the earlier though still very relevant framework of Linda Mayoux. [Linda Mayoux, "Participatory Learning for Women's Empowerment in Microfinance Programmes: Negotiation, Complexity, Conflict and Change" IDS Bulletin 29 (4)]. About 163 groups of 20-25 women each were formed, the majority of them belonging to the low income group and covering the entire geographical spread of the panchayat. Of these groups, a sample was selected for an indepth study of their activities and performance and from each of the selected SHGs, an adequate number of women were selected for the beneficiary survey, both through responses to detailed questionnaires and focus group discussions.

Groups, of course, were started with the objective of encouraging women to save; the groups' linkage to banking enables them to avail of formal credit if the need arose which would also free them from dependence on money lenders. The MFO was to facilitate the groups in procuring the loan which was given directly to the groups by the banks. So Samatha's role was primarily promotional in nature. The book provides an insightful review of the literature on micro finance, the

Indian experience and its own findings throw up interesting observations on the role of micro finance in capacity building of women, both economic and democratic.

There is an interesting discussion on the issue of subsidy dependence of SHGs and the need to make the groups independent of it; another is the need to target the really poor an issue which evades all efforts to make programmes 'inclusive'. A question we raised earlier is perhaps relevant here—would wage employment programmes, despite their poor track record, still remain a better alternative for the really poor being self-targeting? However, the problem here is the need to design schemes which provide 'quality' employment to the poor, whose character is to some extent changing over time with growing literacy and not to condemn them to a low wage for ever (very often even the minimum wage is not paid to workers).

Surprisingly, only one-eighth of the SHGs under study used micro credit for investment in income generating activities; and the larger number used it for repaying borrowings from sources with a higher rate of interest, like money lenders and other private lending institutions. The enterprise ventures did provide earnings to its members; they were rather meagre varying between Rs. 500 and Rs. 1500 per month—the highest being Rs. 3000. Intra SHG loan was not adequate as start-up funds and the larger number of groups supplemented it by loans from banks and money lenders. Dependence on money lenders persisted in trading activities such as fish and vegetable vending since money was needed on a daily basis. While policy rhetoric emphasizes the readiness of banks to give micro credit to SHGs, in reality it was not easy to access bank loans. The experience of the women was quite bitter; banks continued to insist on collateral security and procedures were very cumbersome. However, it is also possible that some groups had not reached the necessary level in terms of own savings and hence were not eligible for loans.

The study's observations on shortcomings in respect of the operations of the MFO, its failure to sustain training/skill development programmes to enable women to access new opportunities are analysed; network of the groups themselves to avail of economic inter linkages and build up their democratic capacity, which could have resulted in better outcomes, throw fresh light on what is fairly well known that one has to go beyond micro credit to allieviate poverty and build up democratic capacity of women. However, what really needs emphasis and is largely missed out in most studies is that policy attempts to infuse micro finance through SHGs of women for poverty reduction and empowerment have to recognize women's work load and frame concomitant policies for its reduction in terms, for instance of provision of child care support, fuel and drinking water.

24 September, 2007 **Mridul Eapen**

Preface

The disadvantages faced by poor women in developing countries are due to relative lack of assets. Their economic participation is both a reward on its own and a major influence for social change in general. As employment opportunities all over the world are decreasing, entrepreneurship is seen as one way to lift women out of poverty. Capital derived from credit and savings is a key asset that allows poor people to seize market opportunities. Since formal credit institutions rarely lend to the poor, special institutional arrangements such as microfinance have been promoted as a key strategy for reducing poverty in all its forms by agencies all over the world. Several studies brought to light that microcredit managed and utilised by women borrowers themselves has the greatest impact on poverty reduction. This work is an attempt to analyse a case study of a microfinance organisation (MFO) from Kerala, the south-western state of India, *Samatha Vanitha Swayam Sahaya Sangham* (SVSSS) in capacity building among women.

I am thankful for the financial support given by the Indian Council of Social Science Research (ICSSR) to publish the book.

The University of Kerala, Thiruvananthapuram has given permission to publish my Ph.D. thesis. I am grateful to the University of Kerala.

I am deeply indebted to my supervising teacher Dr. M. Kunhaman for his gifted academic counselling and guidance.

I owe my sincere gratitude to my teachers in the Department of Economics, University of Kerala, Dr. G. Karunakaran Pillai, Dr. B. Alwin Prakash, Dr. M. Saralamma and Dr. A.K. Prasad. I thankfully remember the support and encouragement extended to me by former Head of the Department Dr. S. Uma Devi during the early stages of the research. I express my deep felt gratitude to Dr. P.R. Gopinathan Nair, former Head of the Department of Economics, University of Kerala who patiently went through my draft and gave useful comments and suggestions.

I am thankful to Dr. Mridul Eapen, Member, Kerala State Planning Board for giving comments and timely support.

I do convey my gratitude to Dr. V.C.V. Ratnam, former Head of the Department of Economics, Scott Christian College, Nagercoil for providing research materials, suggestions, encouragement and assisting to complete my work.

I do thankfully remember the co-ordinators, group leaders and members of *Samatha Vanitha Swayam Sahaya Sangham* for their patience and helpful mentality while conducting the field-work.

I am also thankful to my colleagues in Government College, Nedumangad and Government College for Women, Thiruvananthapuram for their support.

I gratefully remember all the members of my family for their moral support to me in this work.

Christabell, P.J.

Contents

List of Tables

List of Figures

Abbreviations

ADDs	Agricultural Development Divisions
ADS	Area Development Society
AKRSP	Aga Khan Rural Support Programme
ARDRS	Agricultural and Rural Debt Relief Scheme
ASA	Association of Social Advancement
BAAC	Bank for Agriculture and Agricultural Cooperatives
BancoSol	Banco Solidario S.A.
BKK	Badan Kredit Kecamatan
BPL	Below Poverty Line
BRAC	Bangladesh Rural Advancement Committee
BRDB	Bangladesh Rural Development Board
BSS	Bharat Sevak Samaj
BRI	Bank Rakyat Indonesia
CAD	Command Area Development
CBs	Cooperative Banks
CBNP	Community Based Nutrition Programme
CDS	Community Development Society
CRR	Cash Reserve Ratio
DDP	Desert Development Programme
DLDB	District Land Development Bank
DPAP	Drought Prone Areas Programme
DRDA	District Rural Development Agency
DWCRA	Development of Women and Children in Rural Areas
DWCUA	Development of Women and Children in Urban Areas
DYD	Directorate of Youth Development
EAS	Employment Assurance Scheme
ESII	Efficiency and Subsidy Intensity Index

FIAM	Foundation for Integrated Agricultural Management
FUNDELAM	Fundacion' de la Mujer Campesina
FWP	Food for Work Programme
FWWB	Friends of Women's World Banking
GA	Group Animator
GB	Grameen Bank
GKY	Ganga Kalyan Yojana
HADP	Hill Area Development Programme
IADP	Intensive Agricultural Development Programme
IFAD	International Fund for Agricultural Development
IGVGD	Income Generation for Vulnerable Group Development
IRDP	Integrated Rural Development Programme
JLLIs	Joint Liability Lending Institutions
JRY	Jawahar Rozgar Yojana
KRP	Key Resource Person
KSSP	Kerala Shastra Sahitya Parishad
LDBs	Land Development Banks
LIC	Life Insurance Corporation
LPS	Lower Primary School
MACS	Mutually Aided Cooperative Societies
MC^2	Mutuelle Communautaire de Croissance
MFAL	Marginal Farmers and Agricultural Labourers
MFI/Ps	Microfinance Institutions/Programmes
MFO	Microfinance Organisation
MWS	Million Wells Scheme
MYRADA	Mysore Resettlement Development Agency
NABARD	National Bank for Agriculture and Rural Development
NBFC	Non Banking Finance Companies
NGO	Non Governmental Organisation
NHG	Neighbourhood Group
NRY	Nehru Rozgar Yojana
NSS	Nair Service Society
OBC	Other Backward Class

PACS	Primary Agricultural Credit Societies
PASSS	Pazhakulam Social Service Society
PKSF	Pali Karma Shahayak Foundation
PMIUPAP	Prime Minister's Integrated Urban Poverty Alleviation Programme
PMRY	Prime Minister's Rozgar Yojana
PPC	Peoples' Plan Campaign
PRI	Panchayat Raj Institutions
PRODEM	Fundaci'on Para la Promoci'on Desarollo de la MicroEmpresa, or Foundation for the Promotion and Development of Microenterprises
PSBs	Public Sector Banks
PTA	Parent Teacher Association
RASTA	Rural Agency for Social and Technological Advancement
RBI	Reserve Bank of India
RCTP	Rural Credit and Training Programme
RD 12	Rural Development-12
RFA	Rural Friends' Association
RFIs	Rural Financial Institutions
RLEGP	Rural Landless Employment Guarantee Programme
RMK	Rashtriya Mahila Kosh
ROSCAs	Rotating Savings and Credit Associations
RRBs	Regional Rural Banks
SACA	Small Landholders Agricultural Credit Association
SC	Scheduled Castes
SDI	Subsidy Dependence Index
SEWA	Self Employed Women's Association
SFDA	Small Farmers Development Authority
SGSY	Swarnajayanthi Grama Swarozgar Yojana
SHARE	Society for Helping and Awakening Rural Poor Through Education
SHG	Self help group
SHPI	Self Help Promoting Institutions
SIDBI	Small Industries Development Bank of India
SJSRY	Swarna Jayanti Shahari Rozgar Yojana

SLDBs	State Land Development Banks
SLR	Statutory Liquidity Ratio
SNDP	Sree Narayana Darma Paripalana Sangham
ST	Scheduled Tribes
SVSSS	Samatha Vanitha Swayam Sahaya Sangham
TADP	Tribal Area Development Programme
TRDEP	Thana Resource Development and Employment Programme
TRYSEM	Training Rural Youth for Self Employment
UBSP	Urban Basic Services for the Poor
UPS	Upper Primary School
USEP	Urban Self Employment Programme
UWEP	Urban Wage Employment Programme
VGD	Vulnerable Group Development
WCP	Women Component Plan
WOCCU	World Council of Credit Unions
WWF	Working Women's Forum
ZP	Zila Parishad

1

Introduction

Poverty is a multi-dimensional concept implying lack of income, lack of resources, deprivation of the means of livelihood and vulnerability to economic shocks. The inadequacy of traditional definitions of poverty, based on incomes and consumption was widely acknowledged and modern thinkers elucidated the new concerns of sustainable livelihood approach and concept of social exclusion in the spectrum of poverty. The sustainable livelihood approach to the study of poverty has particularly emphasised the need for local participation. In this approach, each community can define criteria of well-being and the key elements of deprivation as they appear in the local context. In the 1970s, the concept of social exclusion came into the literature of poverty to analyse the condition of those who are not necessarily income-poor—though many are that too (UNDP, 1997).

Amartya Sen defined poverty as lack of entitlements and capabilities. Entitlements refer to the set of alternative commodity bundles that a person can command in society using the totality of rights and opportunities that he or she faces. On the basis of this entitlement, a person can acquire some capabilities and he/she may fail to acquire some other capabilities. Capability is thus a kind of freedom, the substantive freedom to achieve alternative functioning combinations (Sen, 1999).

Women and men experience poverty in different ways. Of the 1.3 billion people living in poverty, 70 per cent are women. In developed countries like USA, more than half the women-headed households are poor. The number of rural women living in absolute poverty rose by nearly 50 per cent over the past two decades (UNDP, 1995; p. 36). In short, women constitute the poorest all over the world. This phenomenon is often referred to as feminization of poverty.

Women face a wide range of biases in society against them—unequal opportunities in education, employment and asset ownership. The lingering poverty among women is linked to their unequal situation in the labour market, unfair treatment meted out to them under social welfare systems and their subordinate status as well as lack of power in family. Economic institutions influence the resources to which women and men have access, the activities they can undertake, and the way in which they can participate in the economy. It pertains to markets and hierarchies that have sets of rules governing transactions and influencing decision making about consumption, savings, investment, work and reproduction. The economy determines the opportunities that people have for improving their standard of living.

Despite considerable progress achieved in recent decades in developing women's capabilities, their participation in economic and political decision making remains limited. In no developing region do women enjoy equal rights with men. In many countries, women still lack independent rights to own land, manage property and run business.

In most of the low income third world households, women have a triple role. Triple role of women relates to gender divisions of labour within the household. Women's work includes reproductive work, productive work and community managing work. The reproductive work comprises of childbearing/childrearing responsibilities and domestic tasks undertaken by women, required to guarantee the maintenance and reproduction of the labour force. It includes not only biological reproduction, but also the care and maintenance of the workforce (husband and working children) and the future workforce (infants and school-going children).

The productive work comprises work done by both women and men for payment in cash or kind. It includes both market production with an exchange value, and subsistence/home production with an actual use-value, but also a potential exchange value. For women in agricultural production this includes work as independent farmers, peasants' wives and wage workers. The community managing role comprises activities undertaken primarily by women at the community level as an extension of their reproductive role. This is to ensure the provision and maintenance of scarce resources of collective consumption, such as water, health care and education. It is voluntary unpaid work, undertaken in 'free time' (Moser, 1993).

Poverty resulting from declining rural production, male migration, desertion, divorce or widowhood also impels women to join the waged labour force. In the formal wage sector, women's earnings are lower than that of men. Patterns of job segregation exist in all societies. In all economies women predominate at the lower levels of the labour market. Sex-segregated jobs based on gender hierarchy keep women into lower paid and lower skilled jobs (Reskin and Hartmann, 1991). New areas of employment create new forms of women's work and perpetuate women's subordination. For example, Free trade zones which are characterized by low employment costs with higher levels of productivity. In addition, sexual harassment in the workplace that makes working conditions unpleasant and dangerous reduces workers' morale and productivity.

In most of the developing countries, a large number of workers are beyond the reach of formal regulations. They work in informal sector, generally in family enterprises or in small and unregistered firms. The size of the informal sector tends to be larger in less developed countries and women are predominantly employed in the informal sector. Laws and regulations affect small-scale self-employment. Credit institutions that require traditional forms of collateral security exclude women as borrowers. Difficult procedures for starting a business, non-availability of credit and lack of political contacts prevent women from registering enterprises. Within the informal sector more government restrictions could trigger to shift to even more hidden enterprises, making it harder to monitor gender disparities. Situation is not better for women in self-employment and family run enterprises. Small scale 'petty commodity production' within the so-called informal sector is both dependent and involuntary in nature. Its relationship to large-scale formal sector production is exploitative in terms of issues such as access to credit, markets and raw materials (O'Connell, 1994).

Women work in subsistence economy too. While women work on subsistence food production, men produce cash crops. This results in high level of invisibility of rural women's work. Wide wage gaps remain between females and males. Female employees earn about three-quarters of what men earn. Gender differences in education, work experience, and job characteristics are the reasons. Women remain greatly underrepresented in high paying jobs, including administrative and managerial jobs (Hunter College Women's Studies Collective, 2005).

There is a terrible deficit of women in substantial parts of Asia and North Africa, which arises from sex bias in relative care. According to Sen (1992), the number of missing women in China is 44 million, in India 37 million and the total exceeds 100 million worldwide. Gender bias in the provision of food and health care, as well as violence against females causes deprivation of the world of millions of women. In China, selective abortion of female fetuses and other son-selection methods have skewed the male to female birth ratios from 1.07 in 1980 to 1.4 in 1993. It is also estimated that the One Child Policy in China has resulted in the deaths of more than one million first born girl infants.

From an early age, girl children are socialized into very specific gender roles. In most of the societies, there is differential treatment between male and female children. In addition, freedom of association, communication and contact is surrounded by limits and prohibitions. There are marked differences within regions and within countries. Agarwal (1988) points out that where women's labour participation in agriculture is low and dowry demands are high as in Northwest India, girls are more likely to be seen as economic liabilities. On the contrary, where women's economic productivity is high or where there is a demand for female labour in agriculture as in some parts of South India, discrimination against women and girls is less prevalent. Extreme poverty and scarcity of resources have cruel and dangerous implications for girls, but discrimination is not limited to poor families. High status gives boys priority access to the best food and boys eat better than girls even in richer households.

Throughout the world, more male children are immunized and treated by hospitals than females. In 30 developing countries, death rates for girls between the ages of one and four years have been found to be higher than or equal to those for boys, whereas in industrialized countries death rates for boys are generally higher than for girls. Female infants and children are generally less susceptible to infections and malnutrition than males, due to certain biological advantages, but this trend can be reversed by external factors such as exposure to risk and the kind of care received. From an early age the pressure on girls to assist household work is far higher than boys. For example, withdrawal from education to take care of their younger siblings (O'Connell, 1994).

In short, gender inequalities undermine development. So, improving gender equality has to be a part of any sustainable strategy for development. Inequalities in rights, resources and political voice disadvantage women; they also disadvantage the rest of the society and impede development. The costs of gender inequality are felt strikingly in low-income countries. Although poor women often bear the brunt of gender disparities, men and future generations cannot escape the consequences. Unequal rights to own land or apply for credit deprive women of resources for their livelihood and for security in old age, leaving them more dependent on male relatives. Wider gender disparities in schooling produce correspondingly different abilities for women and men to acquire and process information and to communicate. The gender imbalances in resources and power have consequences for relative autonomy of women and men and their influence in household decision-making. The resulting dependence and stereotyping are a common source of oppressive anxiety and helplessness for both men and women (World Bank, 2001b).

Women are vastly underrepresented at all levels of government, limiting their power to influence governance and public policy. They hold less than ten per cent of seats in Parliament in all regions except East Asia. In no developing region do women hold more than eight per cent of ministerial positions. There is very low representation of women in parliaments and in ministerial positions across the world's regions, developing or industrial (UNDP, 2000). According to a recent survey by the Inter-Parliamentary Union (2000) of 187 women holding political office in 65 countries, about nine-tenths of respondents believe they hold different view of politics and society than their male counterparts. The survey data suggest that women's greater presence and positions in politics have altered the traditional male approach to social welfare, legal protection and transparency in government and business.

Despite the greater prominence of gender issues in the development debate, the importance of bringing a gender perspective to policy analysis and design is still not widely recognized, nor have the lessons for development been fully integrated by policymakers or the donor community.

Context of the Study

Women and Determinants of Poverty

The peculiar disadvantages faced by women are due to relative lack of assets—human, natural, physical, social and financial. Distribution of human assets such as the capacity for basic labour, skills and good health is heavily biased against women. They work longer hours than men in every country. Women carry 53 per cent of the total burden of work in developing countries and 51 per cent in industrial countries. Most of their work remains unpaid, unrecognised and undervalued. Women's labour force participation has risen by only four per cent in 20 years from 36 per cent in 1970 to 40 per cent in 1990 (UNDP, 1995; p. 4). Women normally receive a much lower average wage than men. All regions in the world record a higher rate of unemployment among women than among men.

In the developing countries, ownership of natural assets such as land has tended to be heavily biased in favour of the male members of the family. Land is a very important asset, but women and men do not have equal rights to land in most settings. Women's use rights to land are generally guaranteed through customary channels, but norms against women owning land mean that women are generally denied title to land. Even where local norms give women strong rights to use land, women acquire those rights through men—so these rights are precarious, contingent on a woman's martial status. Some customary laws give sons the exclusive right to inherit, while wives and unmarried daughters have the right to be maintained, and married daughters have no claim on their deceased father's property (Quisumbing *et al.*, 1999).

Access to physical assets such as infrastructure is restricted by institutional barriers. Social assets, such as networks of contacts and reciprocal obligations that can be called in times of need, and political influence over resources are also low for women. Lack of access to financial assets such as savings and to formal credit is another stumbling block to their progress (Sen, 1999). Across developing regions, female-run enterprises tend to be less capitalized than those run by males. Throughout Sub-Saharan Africa, female farmers have poorer access than male farmers to machinery, fertilizer and extension information. Female-managed enterprises (farm and non-farm) continue to have poorer access to credit and related financial services.

Effects of Economic Participation of Women on Society

Rising household incomes can lead to more equal human development for females and males. The expansion of economic opportunities reduces gender disparities. It depends on the availability of the income generating activities and their organization (World Bank, 2001b). Greater employment opportunities for women may increase national output. Employment outside the home will lead to a substitution of unrecorded female labour within the home for recorded female labour in the formal economy that is captured in standard national income accounting. This will enhance the visibility of women's labour and increase measured output, even if true output is unchanged. This substitution leads to increase in productivity and actual economic output.

It is widely accepted that economic participation of poor women is the solution for many of the problems they face. Economic participation of women is both a reward on its own and a major influence for social change in general. First, women's earnings increase the aggregate income levels of poor households. The National Family Health Survey conducted throughout India in 1997 has revealed that 43 per cent of working women contributed at least half the total earnings of their families and that the earnings of 18 per cent of the working women formed the sole source of income of their families. Second, women contribute a much larger share of their earnings to basic family maintenance than men do. On an average, women spent 98 per cent of their earnings toward family maintenance whereas men contributed only 78 per cent. The men kept the balance for their personal use (Mencher, 1988).

Increases in women's income translate directly into better health and nutrition for children. A study of six villages in the semi-arid regions of Andhra Pradesh and Maharashtra found that the children of those mothers who participated in the daily-wage-labour market had significantly higher intake of certain key nutrients than other poor children. This suggests that children's nutritional status tends to be much more positively linked to the mother's earnings than the father's. Kumar (1978) found that among the landless and marginal farmer households in Kerala in which the mother was in the wage labour force, it was her own wages that primarily accounted for the positive household wage-income effect on child nutrition; where the mother was not in the wage-labour force, an increase in household wage income showed no incremental effect on child nutrition. Hence, in the short-term, women's earnings have an immediate positive effect on the incidence and severity of poverty at the household level. In the long-term, there are important inter-generational effects on the quality of human capital (Bennet, 1992).

Economic participation of women also leads to their better position in the family. A study of 40 agricultural labour and cultivator households in a semi-arid and agriculturally backward region of Andhra Pradesh found that women who worked for wages had a greater role in household decision making—particularly over the allocation of food (Bidinger *et al.*, 1986). This suggests that women's employment not only brought more income into the family, but also gave women more control over its disposal.

Women's income is vital to the well-being of children. For example, child nutrition has been shown to correlate positively with the size of the mother's income. Income not earned and/or not allocated by the woman is not automatically directed towards children's nourishment. In Brazil, additional income in the hands of women has a greater positive impact on child survival and nutrition than does additional income in the hands of men. Increases in household income are associated with improvements in child survival probabilities and in child height-for-weight and height-for-age measure. Additional income in the hands of women enlarges the share of the household budget devoted to education, health and nutrition-related expenditure (World Bank, 2001b).

The above empirical works have brought out clearly that "the relative respect and regard for women's well-being is strongly influenced by women's ability to earn an independent income, to find employment outside the home, to have ownership rights and to have literacy and be educated participants in decisions within and outside the family" (Sen, 1999; p. 191).

Need for Financial Assets to Women

As employment opportunities all over the world are decreasing, entrepreneurship is seen as one way to lift women out of poverty. Experience shows that most of the poor women invest money wisely and make sound decisions to maximise returns. Access to savings and credit facilities helps poor women to make comparatively larger investment and allows them to take advantage of profitable business opportunities and to increase their earning potential.

Capital derived from credit and savings is a key asset that allows poor people to seize market opportunities—such as investing in a small business or using farm inputs. Only two to five per cent of the 500 million poorest households in the world have access to institutional credit (UNDP, 1997; p. 62). Women receive a disproportionately small share of credit from formal banking institutions. In Latin America and the Caribbean, women constitute only seven to ten per cent of the beneficiaries of credit programmes. A study of 38 branches of major banks in India found that only 11 per cent of the borrowers were women. In Zaire, women formed only 14 per cent of borrowers from commercial banks. In Africa, of the total rural agricultural workers, women received less than ten per cent of the credit to small farmers and one per cent of the total credit to agriculture (UNDP, 1995; p. 39).

Most of the banks require the borrowers to be wage/salary earners or property owners who can provide acceptable collateral security. Limited education, complicated loan procedures and long distances to the nearest bank further constrain women's access to institutional credit. As a result, women constitute a very small proportion of borrowers from formal financial institutions.

Microfinance: An Innovative Financial Arrangement for the Poor

Since formal credit institutions rarely lend to the poor, special institutional arrangements become necessary to extend credit to those who have no collateral security to offer. Microfinance, by providing small loans and savings facilities to those who have been excluded from commercial financial services, has been promoted as a key strategy for reducing poverty in all its forms by agencies all over the world. Microcredit has been defined as "programmes that provide credit for self-employment and other financial and business services (including savings and technical assistance) to very poor persons" (Micro Credit Summit, 1997). Now-a-days, microfinance represents something more than microcredit—it also refers to savings, insurance, pawns and remittances, in sum to a much wider range of financial services (Tankha, 1999). Thus microfinance refers to the entire range of financial and non-financial services, including skill upgradation and entrepreneurship development, rendered to the poor for enabling them to overcome poverty.

Access to these facilities is seen as a way of providing the poor with opportunities for self-reliance through entrepreneurship, cushioning the poor against economic shocks and providing a means of social empowerment for poor women in their communities. In most cases, microcredit programmes offer a combination of services and resources to their clients in addition to usual credit for self-employment. Also, this is an effort to provide a bridge between formal financial markets and the informal groups in the formal microfinance initiatives.

The basic idea of microfinance is that poor people are ready and are willing to pull themselves out of poverty if given access to economic inputs. The success model of the Grameen Bank (GB) of Bangladesh attracts the attention of people from all over the world. Following the example of the Grameen Bank, many developing countries use the model of microfinance for financing the poor. Banco Solidario S.A. (BancoSol), a NGO converted into a commercial bank in Bolivia and Bangladesh Rural Advancement Committee (BRAC), a NGO in Bangladesh, are examples.

Self Help Groups

The basic unit of microfinance is a group of persons called Self Help Group (SHG). Self help groups are small informal associations created for the purpose of enabling members to reap economic benefit out of mutual help, solidarity and joint responsibility. These small and homogeneous groups involved in savings and credit activities are capable of taking care of the risks through peer monitoring. The credit fund, if it comes from an outside source, is disbursed to individual members according to agreed criteria and the group undertakes joint liability for debts of each member. Thus, the joint liability provides incentives or compels the group to undertake the burden of selection, monitoring and enforcement that would otherwise fall on the lender (Rajasekhar, 1997).

Microfinance and Women

Many Microfinance Institutions/Programmes[1] (MFI/Ps) have targeted women who live in households having very little or no assets. These MFI/Ps have significantly increased women's security, autonomy, self-confidence and status within the households by providing opportunities for self-employment. Microcredit managed and utilised by women borrowers themselves has the greatest impact on poverty reduction. Over a decade of banking with the Grameen Bank, women as loan managers are less likely to remain poor, as most of them (eight out of ten) will be out of poverty after a few loan cycles. Partnership of women with their spouses or other adult household members in loan utilisation and management, on the other hand, is also more likely to move them out of poverty, with a probability of six in ten (Todd, 1996).

Statement of the Problem

The Government of Kerala launched the 'People's Campaign for Decentralised Planning' (PPC) on 17th August 1996. The Campaign envisaged a development programme by ensuring the involvement of people right from delineating local developmental problems, financial participation and project formulation to the implementation and evaluation of programmes. For this purpose, several local level institutional arrangements were made. They include ward committees (*grama sabhas*), beneficiary committees, neighbourhood groups (*ayalkoottams*) and self help groups (*swayam sahaya sanghams*). Through these institutions, political and democratic processes among people were envisaged.

The women self help groups were set up primarily as a sub-system of the People's Plan Campaign (PPC). It was envisaged that through these groups, the discriminations faced by women in Kerala would be attended to, to some extent. Besides, the SHGs would form the training ground for women to take part in the political process. These groups were also meant for enhancement of the resource base of the women at the local level. In most panchayats, the Women Component Plan (WCP) was the major factor behind the constitution of such groups. The present study is an investigation into the performance of these local level institutional arrangements in the fulfilment of the objectives of the PPC.

The women self help groups constituted by the local bodies in Kerala may be seen from the larger context of microfinance. The groups follow the same pattern and directions put forward by National Bank for Agriculture and Rural Development (NABARD). The present study.aims to add insights to the functioning of various types of microfinance institutions.

The *Samatha Vanitha Swayam Sahaya Sangham* (SVSSS—means *Samatha* Women Self Help Group) of Ulloor panchayat in Thiruvananthapuram district is one of the earliest experiments launched under Peoples' Plan Campaign (PPC) in Kerala. It started functioning in the panchayat as early as in 1997. Following the example of this experiment, women SHGs were constituted in almost all the panchayats in Kerala. The study also intends to assess the stability of such groups and their impact at the micro level.

Objectives

The major objective of the enquiry was to understand the contribution of microfinance to the well-being of poor women in terms of mobilisation of microsavings, utilisation of microcredit and organisation, management and performance of income generating activities. It also tried to assess the role played by microfinance in building up economic and democratic capacity building of women and thereby enhancing empowerment. The study was intended to evaluate the performance of self help groups and to identify the factors which contribute to their successful performance and sustainability. It studied the level of participation of women in self help groups and examine the group dynamics that influence their participation. It assessed the extent of participation of the poor in the microfinance institutions.

Hypotheses

It is hypothesized that microfinance helps to enhance the resource base of women and microfinance institutions can effectively act as a sub-system of local bodies and commercial banks for conferring inputs and services on the poor.

Design of the Study

In order to gain a background understanding of microfinance institutions and programmes, major Non-Governmental Organisations like Shreyas, RASTA (Rural Agency for Social and Technological Advancement), BSS (Bharat Sevak Samaj), MALAR and Santhidan were visited. Functionaries in charge of Kudumbashree—the Kerala State Poverty Eradication Mission; NABARD and a few selected commercial banks were also consulted. Discussions with experts and activists in this field revealed that three models of SHG-Bank linkage have emerged. In the first model, commercial banks directly link SHGs without intervention of any microfinance institutions or NGOs or other promoting agencies. In the second model, banks provide credit to SHGs where NGOs act as Self Help Promoting Institutions (SHPIs), performing only promotional role. Under the third model, NGOs act both as SHPIs and financial intermediaries for channelising credit from banks to SHGs.

In Kerala, a large number of NGOs and other agencies are engaged in microfinancing. Most of them help in the promotion as well as financing SHGs. However, the second SHG model is not common. The self help groups formed in the background of PPC follow the second model. In these cases, volunteers, panchayat members or Key Resource Persons (KRP) play the role of facilitators.

The *Samatha Vanitha Swayam Sahaya Sangham* (SVSSS) in the Ulloor panchayat in Thiruvananthapuram district is another typical example of the second SHG model. It was formed by volunteers of the *Kerala Shastra Sahitya Parishad* (KSSP), a well-known NGO in the state. Here, only three or four members of the NGO initiated the SHGs. Hence, the self help groups are found to be quite independent. Each group has its own byelaws and mode of functioning. They are mostly suited to the local situations and the needs of the members in the group. The group members themselves perform the financial and economic roles of the groups. It is in this context that this organisation (SVSSS) was selected for case study.

Pilot Study

In order to understand the structure, functions and variations of SHGs under SVSSS in the Ulloor panchayat, the researcher visited a few units in different wards. Following that, a chart was prepared for choosing samples, with details such as names of the groups, year of their formation and number of members in each group. Discussions with facilitators were also held in order to select appropriate samples and cases.

Study Area

Ulloor panchayat is a special grade panchayat[2] situated in the outskirts of Thiruvananthapuram Corporation. It has a total area of 16.67 sq. km. and a total population of 47,005. In this panchayat, economic participation of women is low. Indebtedness is the major problem of the poor households. Women fell prey to moneylenders who lent money at exorbitant rates of interest.

Samatha Vanitha Swayam Sahaya Sangham (SVSSS)

The Microfinance Organisation (MFO), *Samatha Vanitha Swayam Sahaya Sangham* (SVSSS), was formed by a few KSSP volunteers in 1997 with the goal of inculcating the importance of saving in the minds of poor women, to save them from the clutches of moneylenders and to initiate a process of developing microenterprises among them. The organisation, therefore, formed SHGs all over the panchayat. Each SHG consists of 20 to 25 women in a neighbourhood, the majority of them belonging to low-income groups.

Sources of Data

Besides the primary data collected through field investigations, secondary data are used for the study, wherever found appropriate. The major sources of secondary data used are Decennial Censuses, NSSO, Directorate of Economics and Statistics (Government of Kerala), NABARD and the print and electronic media.

Methodology

Data were collected using two-stage sampling. In the first stage, SHGs were chosen and in the second stage, members were selected from the SHGs. Primary data were collected through an extensive fieldwork by the researcher. Two different schedules were used in the primary data collection and the data were processed mechanically. Qualitative methods such as case study, focus-group discussions and observation method were also used. In the analysis of data, both qualitative and quantitative methods were used.

Method of Sampling

Sampling Technique Used for Selecting Self Help Groups

At the first stage, details of all the 163 SHGs under SVSSS were collected. From the list, 34 SHGs were randomly selected using the lottery method giving a representation of groups from 15 wards spread across the panchayat. The number of groups selected from each ward is given in Appendix I.

Sample Beneficiaries

At the second stage, ten members from each SHG were selected for conducting a beneficiary survey using a schedule. Demographic particulars and information on standard of living, level of participation in other organisations and SHGs, personal savings and loan details and the microenterprises initiated by 323 members were collected from them.

Data Collection Instruments

Schedules

Two detailed schedules were prepared for collection of data: one for SHGs and the other for beneficiaries. The first was administered among leaders (secretary and president) of the SHGs (see Appendix II). Data were collected through interviewing them and holding focus-group discussions with all the members in the group. For supplementing the data relating to groups, reports and records of respective groups were checked. In order to maintain uniformity, details such as total savings, total loans of the group members etc. were collected as on March 31, 2001. For collecting data from beneficiaries, a different schedule was used (see Appendix III). Both open-ended and close-ended questions were included in the schedule.

A pre-test had been conducted towards the end of March 2001 before finalising the interview schedule. Data from three SHGs and thirty beneficiaries were collected during this period. A preliminary analysis had also been done. On the basis of the field experience during the pre-test and the preliminary analysis, the schedules were modified and refined.

Interview Guide

Besides the field survey using pre-designed schedules, information was collected through interviews and focus-group discussions with members. For this purpose, an interview guide was used which indicated the topics for further dialogue. Detailed information on members' views about the organisation, group activities and members' participation in the groups was collected. Relevant observations were systematically recorded and an informal approach was followed throughout the discussions.

Fieldwork

The field survey was conducted during May 2001 to August 2001. The information was collected during the weekly meetings of the SHGs and visits to the members' households. Other data related to the organisation were collected from reports and the newsletters published by the organisation and through discussions with the co-ordinators.

Data Processing and Analysis Plan

The statistical data were processed using the SPSS package. Simple tools like percentage, mean and standard deviation were used to interpret the data and draw meaningful inferences. For evaluating the performance of SHGs, a performance rating technique (see Appendix IV) was used. The indicators of the technique were drawn from NABARD and other sources. For capturing the involvement and participation of the poor in the organisation, a poverty index (see Appendix V) was also used.

Limitations of the Study

All the defects that could be raised against discussions based on data from a sample survey are applicable to this study too. In spite of the limitations, it is hoped that this study would bring out the nature and problems of microfinance in general.

Chapter Scheme

Chapter two tries to give a brief review of the microfinance institutions and programmes existing in various parts of the world. This is followed by a review of theoretical and empirical literature in chapter three. After a discussion in chapter four of the efforts of the Government of India to launch microfinance in the country, an attempt to describe the state of microfinance organisations and programmes in Kerala is made in chapter five. The details of the study area and the microfinance organisation studied are furnished in chapter six. The extent to which MFOs have helped women in their attempts for capacity building forms the topic of discussion in chapter seven. Chapter eight is devoted to an appraisal of the emerging issues in the field of microfinance. The summary and conclusions of the study are presented in the final chapter along with a few suggestions for improving the performance of the microfinance system.

NOTES

1. Microfinance institution/microfinance programme/microfinance organisation: In the literature relating to microfinance, these three terms are usually used interchangeably. Even if they sound alike, there are certain differences among them. The term microfinance institution has a broader and larger meaning. Agencies which operate microfinance programmes, such as NGOs, independent cooperatives, local, state and central governments and development-oriented Non Banking Finance Companies (NBFCs) are collectively known as microfinance institutions (MFIs). On the practical side, the business of microfinance is generally conducted by NGOs. For Central and State governments also, microfinance is part of their policies and programmes. Different types of microfinance projects may be grouped into microfinance programmes (MFPs). On the other hand, some of the NGOs or agencies cater to microfinance services only. They may be called Microfinance Organisations (MFOs). In this study, SVSSS (*Samatha Vanitha Swayam Sahaya Sangham*) is referred to as microfinance organisation since it is neither an institution nor a programme, but provides microfinance services to a locality.
2. A special grade panchayat in Kerala means a panchayat having an annual own revenue of Rs. 500,000 or more (Panchayat Act, 1988). Ulloor panchayat, the study area is a special grade panchayat. At present, seven wards out of fifteen wards are merged with the Thiruvananthapuram Corporation.

2

Theoretical and Empirical Issues of Microfinance

The innovative credit delivery system—microfinance—was a breakthrough in the world of finance. It changes the life of the poor, especially women, not only by providing financial services such as microsavings and microinsurance, but also by imparting training in entrepreneurial development. Over the past few decades, microfinance institutions and programmes all over the world have adopted numerous innovative ways of providing credit and savings services to the entrepreneurial poor. These include the provision of small loans to poor people, especially in rural areas, at full-cost interest rates, without collateral security, repayable in frequent instalments. Borrowers are organised into groups, which reduce the risk of default. There are also effective mechanisms which disseminate valuable information on ways to improve the health, legal rights, sanitation and other relevant concerns of the poor.

The world of microfinance is fostered by a number of issues. Researchers have contributed substantially to the conceptual issues and methods of microfinance. The literature abounds with theoretical and empirical studies. The theoretical issues relating to microfinance may be broadly divided into three categories: sustainability of microfinance institutions/ programmes, their outreach to target populations, and their impact. A brief review of the studies is made below:

Sustainability

A financial institution must maintain its sustainability in order to maintain on a continuous basis, its activities and services for meeting its objectives. Sustainability of a microfinance institution means its capability to operate as a development institution for the poor to maximise the expected net present social value (social value *minus* social cost discounted through time) comprising the net gain of users from loans and deposits, the profits or losses of the MFI/Ps and the social opportunity cost of the resources used.

Financial Sustainability

A microfinance institution would be sustainable only if it is financially sound. As microfinance institutions are institutions for development, their financial sustainability is very important. Unsustainable microfinance organisations inflict costs on the poor in excess of gains.

An analysis was done by Khandker *et al.* (1995b) about the financial sustainability of a microcredit programme Rural Development Programme—RD-12 of Bangladesh Rural Development Board (BRDB). The authors analysed the institution's cost structure, and examined whether the cost structure and the cost per unit of principal lent justified the rate of interest that borrowers were being charged. Programme-level information, such as operational cost, lending cost, default cost, and costs of funds, was calculated to find the cost structure. As the programme level data were inadequate, the researchers also used estimates of cost to societies at the sub-district (*thana*) level. As the programme is highly subsidised, it was profitable. But the study concluded that, even though the programme was profitable, it was not cost-effective and that its financial viability was doubtful.

For measuring performance of one of the most profitable rural finance institutions in the world, the Bank Rakyat's Unit *Desa* System (BRI) in Indonesia, financial ratios such as return on equity and return on assets were used (Yaron *et al.*, 1998). The return on equity compares an institution's net income in a given fiscal year with its average equity during that fiscal year. The average annual equity is usually calculated as the sum of the start-of-year equity plus year-end equity, divided by two. When net income was measured against start-of-year equity, it was found that the return on equity of BRI increased to about 90 per cent in 1990 and 1991 and to an astounding 407 per cent by 1995. In competitive financial systems, one per cent return on assets is considered as an indication of sound financial performance. The BRI's pre-tax return on assets reached 6.1 per cent in 1995 as against 2.6 per cent in 1991. The authors consider, therefore, that as the units of BRI earned returns on rural financial intermediation at rates well above those of the banking industry, it was financially sustainable.

Reliance on Subsidy

Many of the microfinance institutions and programmes in the world today are heavily dependent on outside sources of funds for their operation. As most of them receive subsidies, the effect of subsidies on the sustainability of these institutions has to be considered. Economic viability of microfinance institutions is usually measured on the basis of their reliance on subsidy. The major form of subsidy these financial institutions enjoy is concessional borrowing. While an infusion of subsidy shows an improvement in financial performance of an institution, its true performance may be deteriorating. Hence the over-dependence on subsidy is viewed as the inverse of self-sustainability.

The Grameen Bank (GB) receives subsidies on a continuing basis. Despite high repayment rates reported, its performance has been uneven (Morduch, 1999). The revenues generated by the GB from the poorest borrowers (target group) cover just 70 per cent of their full cost. On the other hand, Hashemi and Schuler (1997) noted that the subsidy dependence of GB had declined over the years (from 180 per cent in 1987 to 36 per cent in 1994). If GB were to pay full market rates for the credit fund it received, it would have to raise its interest rate to borrowers by 36 per cent, to an annual effective rate of over 27 per cent to cover all expenses.

To measure the extent of subsidy dependence of MFI/Ps, Yaron (1992) developed an index called Subsidy Dependence Index (SDI). SDI is expressed as a ratio that indicates the percentage increase required in the on-lending rate to completely eliminate all subsidies received in a given year by the MFI/Ps. SDI has a lower bound of 100 per cent but no upper bound. An SDI of zero means that an MFI/Ps has achieved full self-sustainability. An SDI of 100 per cent indicates that a doubling of the prevailing average on-lending interest rate would be required to eliminate subsidies. A negative SDI indicates that a financial institution has achieved full self-sustainability and that its annual profits exceeded the total annual value of any subsidies received by the financial institution and that it could lower its average on-lending interest rate, eliminate all subsidies, and remain self-sustainable.

An evaluation of the subsidy dependence of four public MFI/Ps—Badan Kredit Kecamatan (BKK) and Bank Rakyat Indonesia's Unit *Desa* (BRI) in Indonesia, Bank for Agriculture and Agricultural Cooperatives (BAAC) in Thailand, and Grameen Bank (GB) of Bangladesh—using the index showed that one MFI (BRI) had attained complete subsidy independence and two others (GB and BKK) were moderately subsidy-dependent and one (BAAC) had a high degree of subsidy-dependence (Yaron, 1992).

Many researchers have used SDI to measure subsidy-dependence. But SDI cannot clarify how a subsidy was used—whether it benefited clients or it went mainly to inefficient bureaucracy. Also, increase in subsidy does not always reflect inefficiency or declining viability. It might have been due to increase in membership and borrowers. But it is to be noted that microfinance institutions should be able to minimise subsidy per borrower by increasing the number of borrowers.

While comparing the efficiency and sustainability of formal and quasi-formal microfinance programmes in Bangladesh, Khalily *et al.* (2000) developed a superior index called Efficiency and Subsidy Intensity Index (ESII). Using this index they examined the efficiency of GB and Association of Social Advancement (ASA). The analysis shows that both GB and ASA have been operating with high degree of cost and financial efficiency. ASA being a quasi-formal organisation was more cost-effective and sustainable than GB, a formal organisation. This difference is attributed to low salary base and high lending interest rate of the former. The operation of GB is relatively costly because of high salary based on national pay scale and relatively low lending rate. If ASA had to operate with the average salary of GB, given the present level of operation, it would be worse off. This was evident from a simulation of increase in wage rate. In contrast, GB would be better off at a low salary base such as of ASA.

During the period 1993-97, the degree of ESII declined for both GB and ASA. The positive subsidy intensity of ASA is contrary to the traditional belief that it is a self-sufficient organisation with no subsidy dependency. Consequently, social costs are associated with these two programmes. The study showed that GB would be able to reduce social cost and improve sustainability by improving cost efficiency, increasing loan size and lending rate, and changing portfolio mix without incurring any operating cost. GB was close to achieve sustainability. Similarly, ASA had attained a higher degree of sustainability within seven years of its microcredit operations. It took a longer time for a formal organisation like GB to become sustainable than a quasi-formal organisation like ASA.

Sustainability of microfinance institutions/programmes is the success of these institutions. For achieving sustainability, factors such as autonomy in operational policies, innovative low-cost delivery systems, flexible loan terms and conditions, close monitoring of loan performance and development of domestic savings are essential.

Outreach or Targeting

The major limitation of most formal financial institutions is that they fail to reach the poor. The primary objective of the innovative finance institutions like microfinance is to reach the really needy. Many microfinance institutions/programmes have penetrated into the rural populations in developing countries like Bangladesh, Indonesia and Thailand. The Grameen Bank has 2.06 million clients and provides an estimated 36 per cent of its total credit to poor landless people living in rural Bangladesh. The Bank for Agriculture and

Agricultural Cooperatives (BAAC) serves about 76 per cent (borrowers) of Thai farming households; the Bank Rakyat Indonesia (BRI) provides credit to approximately five per cent (1.90 million borrowers) of all Indonesian households and extends savings facilities to as many as 14.50 million households (Yaron *et al.*, 1997). However, quality of the financial services rendered is reportedly poor. Several studies point out that many of the programmes failed to reach the poorest of the poor for various reasons. The issue of mis-targeting has drawn the attention of several researchers.

Outreach has three dimensions. Firstly, the quality of services delivered by MFI/Ps improves the quality of life and economic contributions of poor people. They should be able to act as both short-term source of liquidity and long-term reserve for emergencies. Their financial services should be available as an ongoing basis. Secondly, MFI/Ps should serve the people in extreme poverty. Thirdly, the scale of outreach should be wide, reaching a large number of people of the target group.

Aspects of Outreach

Outreach is the social value of the output of a microfinance organisation in terms of six aspects: depth, worth of users, cost of users, breadth, length and scope. Depth of outreach is the value that society attaches to the net gain from the use of microcredit by a given borrower. Worth of outreach to users means the cost the borrower is willing to pay for a loan. Cost of outreach to users is the cost of a loan to a borrower. Cost of users includes both price and transaction costs. Breadth of outreach is the total number of users. Length of outreach is the time frame in which a microfinance organisation produces loans. Without length of outreach, a microfinance organisation may improve social welfare in the short-term but it may wreck its ability to do so in the long-term. Scope of outreach is the number of types of financial contracts offered by a microfinance organisation. In short, the term outreach is commonly proxied by the sex or poverty of borrowers, the size or the terms of loan contracts, the price and transaction costs borne by users, the number of users, the financial and organisational strength of the lender, and the number of products offered, including deposits (Navajas *et al.*, 2000).

Mis-targeting

It is the primary duty of microfinance institutions/programmes (MFI/Ps) to provide large numbers of poor people (including the very poor and women) access to quality financial services. But several studies have pointed out that MFI/Ps are not reaching poor households adequately. On the other hand, many better off households (non-poor) are supposed to have been availing their services due to mis-targeting. Even though many checks are instituted in the structure of microfinance, the non-poor continue to exist in the structure. From the studies conducted in various countries, the following factors are cited as the major reasons for failure to reach truly large numbers of poor households with financial services for poverty reduction:

- Lack of or ineffective targeting and consequent inefficient allocation of resources (or leakage to the non-poor);
- Relative lack of attention to organisational financial sustainability;
- A general shortage of funding for deficits;
- Lack of suitable legal identity and lack of adequate regulation of most MFI/Ps working with the poor;
- Inadequate motivation and limited vision of the boards of management of MFI/Ps.

The extent of mis-targeting by the Grameen Bank was estimated around four to six per cent in 1988. It increased to 20 to 30 per cent in 1996. Matin (1998) argues that some people in the target group have graduated to the non-target group. Increasing incidence and severity of mis-targeting are consequences of credit-deepening, i.e., once an increase in the average loan size takes place, it leads to increased incentives for participation by the non-target group.

Many researchers have tried to find out the reasons for the inclusion of non-poor in microfinance programmes and institutions, in spite of targeting techniques in use. Zaman (1998) who examined the mis-targeting of Bangladesh Rural Advancement Committee's (BRAC) RD-12 Programme found out that targeting became less strict with time. Evidence showed that the members selected by BRAC in recent years were not so poor as the members who had joined it at the start of programme's operations. The old cohort of members had smaller areas of land than the later cohorts. The survey which used a composite index of quantity of land owned, value of non-land assets, total savings, proportion of heads of household who are manual labourers, average years of education in the household and dependency ratio, conducted in ten villages of Bangladesh showed that about 32 per cent of the households belonged to the non-target group. On the other hand, 59 per cent of the eligible households in these villages were left uncovered by BRAC. The study concluded that pressures exerted by target group members themselves for inclusion of influential non-target group households might have compelled programme administrators to relax their official targeting criterion. Another argument is that non-poor people have the potential to create employment opportunities for the poorest by setting up small/medium-scale enterprises.

Problems Relating to Targeting and Targeting Techniques

There are two types of targeting—broad targeting and narrow targeting. While the former means the spending on social services like public education and public health care, the latter deals with targeting the poor directly. Microfinance is an example for narrow targeting (van de Walle, 1998). Towards identifying the target group of microfinance, a host of devices like income criteria, acreage equivalents, wealth ranking, key asset ownership and other non-economic criteria have been employed. Successful targeting is assumed to be a proxy for MFI/Ps success. It should be cost-effective also as MFI/Ps have only scarce resources.

The field workers of Grameen Bank use a simple set of asset or wealth indicators to identify poor households at the village level. They are persons with less than half an acre of agricultural land and with total household (including agricultural land) asse.s the value of which is less than one acre of average quality agricultural land in the community. In the case of Bangladesh Rural Advancement Committee's Rural Development Programme, the indicators taken are manual labour as the household's main occupation, and the extent of land owned. Zaman (1998) questions the use of land-based targeting criterion. He argues that it may include the non-poor (such as teachers and shopkeepers) who are 'land poor' and exclude the 'landed poor'. Gailey *et al.* (1999) pointed out that identifying the poor using land index has to be valid in the context in which they are used. For example, the Grameen Bank's half acre of agricultural land would not be valid in the dry, rocky, single-cropped area of the Indian Deccan nor in the dry, upland single-crop areas in Java or Central China. In such places, even two or three acres of agricultural land may be insufficient to provide an income above the poverty line.

Low Participation of Poor Women

Giving women access to credit, it has been argued, is a means by which both the economic standing within the household and the social position within the society of the poor women can be improved. Evidence shows that female membership in MFI/Ps is a more efficient targeting device. Mahmud (2000) who evaluated the data collected from Pali Karma Shahayak Foundation (PKSF) and BRAC feels that the households' demand for the type of credit provided by these programmes is the major factor in the participation decision. Poor households that participate do so because they derive a net positive utility from credit use to the extent that they are willing to suffer some welfare loss in terms of women members' increased workload. The household preference for female membership implies that the households' objective of deriving net utility from credit use coincides with the goal of the programme to target poor households. Thus, the participation of households that prefer to enrol a female family member, serves the poverty reduction goal of programmes better than those which prefer to enrol a male family member.

On the other hand, the participation of women in various MFI/Ps is limited for a variety of reasons. A case study of thirteen MFI/Ps operating in seven developing countries concluded that significant female-male gaps exist in all the countries indicating the unequal economic and social relations between women and men. Such inequality was particularly significant in Bangladesh where women's position was so poor *vis-à-vis* men and where female participation in credit schemes has now reached very high levels—93 per cent. But the extent of women participation varies from 18 to 99 per cent across the 13 MFI/Ps. It is interesting to note that the percentage of credit to women is lower than the percentage of female borrowers. In Bangladesh Rural Advancement Committee (BRAC), only 67 per cent of the total credit is controlled by 74 per cent of female borrowers. Also the coverage of women from vulnerable groups such as widowed/divorced/female-headed households, the disabled and the old and the infirm is significantly low in most of the institutions (Hulme and Mosley, 1996).

In another study, the outreach and participation of poor women in the microfinance institution Mutuelle Communautaire de Croissance (MC^2) in Cameroon were examined (Bomda, 1999). The study concluded that the participation of women in MC^2 activities has been increasing (from eight per cent in 1992 to twenty per cent in 1998). Though women were very active in savings activities, the share of loans granted to them was low. The problem of offering collateral security for loan was the main handicap that limited women's access to credit.

Ineffective Outreach to the Poorest

Since the 1980s credit schemes have been advocated as a device to reduce poverty. Hulme and Mosley (1996) have questioned the effectiveness of such schemes. Using data from microfinance institutions in seven developing countries, they compared increases in borrowers' incomes with increases in the income of control group of thirteen different kinds of institutions. The study found out that the case study institutions have extended the reach of the formal financial sector into upper- and middle-income poor households; they have been relatively ineffective in reaching the poorest. Again it was found that clients above the poverty line did better than the control group, while clients below the poverty line were worse off than the control group. Richer clients generally had larger increase in income than poorer clients. A survey for evaluating the outreach of Banco Solidario S. A. (BancoSol) of Bolivia, a private, fully chartered commercial bank found that although BancoSol's clients are poor, they are not among the poorest of Bolivians (Gonzalez-Vega *et al.*, 1997).

Navajas *et al.* (2000) in their study dealt with three empirical questions: Do microfinance organisations reach the poorest of the poor? Do group loans reach the poorest more than individual loans? Do rural lenders reach the poorest better than urban lenders? The authors selected five microfinance institutions in Bolivia (BancoSol, PRODEM, FIE, Sartawi and Caha de Ahorroy Prestamo) having different lending technologies and geographic market niches. For the purpose, a random sample of 622 borrowers was collected in the urban areas in and near La Paz and in the rural Altiplano near Lake Titicaca. The study came up with five major findings: first, improved social welfare from microcredit depends not only on the depth of outreach but also on its worth, cost, breadth, length and scope. Length matters most since the drive for length leads to incentives that prompt improvements in the other aspects. Second, the lenders in La Paz tended to serve not the poorest but rather those near the poverty line. Most microfinance organisations in the world serve this same niche. The poorest are less likely to be creditworthy and to demand loans while many of the non-poor can borrow elsewhere. Third, since the distribution of demand and creditworthiness on unconditional supply are unknown, it was not clear whether the Bolivian lenders had deep outreach in an absolute sense. Fourth, group lenders in La Paz had deeper outreach than individual lenders. In general, group technologies have more potential for deep outreach since they substitute joint liability for collateral security. Fifth, the rural lenders in La Paz had deeper outreach than the urban lenders in the sense that the typical rural borrower was more likely to be among the poorest.

The major objective of the MFI/Ps is outreach to the poor with financial services in order to reduce poverty. It is evident that sustained delivery of microfinance services to the poor (particularly to women among the poor) results in a substantial proportion of them lifting themselves and their households completely out of poverty. But mere reaching of enough number of poor households seldom does do any good. Efficient targeting and rendering quality financial services are major factors behind the successful functioning of any microfinance institutions/programmes.

Impact

Microfinance programmes and institutions have become important components of strategies to reduce poverty and to promote microenterprise development. Sustainable employment and income generation for the rural poor are indicators of the success and potential of a credit programme. For individual borrowers, the question of viability involves undertaking income generating activities and ensuring regular repayment of loans. Such positive effects indicate the ability of the borrowers to repay their loans on time; and a high recovery rate improves the financial and institutional viability of the credit delivery system. Impact assessment involves evaluation of a microfinance programme or an institution in terms of its income generating capacity and related aspects.

Impact on Poverty and Standard of Living

The effects of microcredit programmes on poverty were examined using data on consumption, savings, asset ownership and net worth to assets of households of GB participants (Khandker *et al.*, 1995a). The study showed an increased caloric intake and better nutritional status of children in the households surveyed. There was evidence of a shift from traditional farm activities to non-farm activities. Increases in overall levels of employment, labour force participation among women and self-employment were also observed. Another study assessed the economic impact of the Grameen Bank on rural households. The study (Hossain, 1988) found that the loans had generated new employment for one-third of the members of the GB. They had remained unemployed before joining GB. The average level of employment for members increased from about six working days to eighteen working days per month. Working capital for Grameen Bank-supported enterprises increased nearly four-fold in 2.25 years. The study also reported increases in per capita food consumption in member households and in investments in housing, education and sanitation.

Pitt (2000) estimated the impact of participation in three group-based microfinance programmes: GB, Bangladesh Rural Advancement Committee (BRAC) and Bangladesh Rural Development Board's (BRDB) Rural Development Programme—RD-12. He measured the impact in terms of gender participation on participating households' mix of agricultural contract that takes the form of own-cultivation as opposed to agricultural wage labour. Pitt found strong evidence of the fact that participation in these group-based microcredit programmes substantially alters the mix of agricultural contract chosen by participating households. In particular, both female participation and male participation induced a significant increase in the area of own-cultivation through sharecropping, in association with a complementary increase in male hours in field crop self-employment and a reduction in male hours in the wage agricultural labour market, consistent with its presumed effects on diversifying income and smoothing consumption.

Impact on poverty of income generating programmes, and thrift and credit societies and women empowerment was were assessed by a study (Oomen, 1999) of all the districts and municipalities of Kerala in which the urban Community Development Societies (CDS) were functioning. The economic status of 56.5 per cent of Neighbourhood Groups (NHGs) investigated had improved and 65 per cent of the members expected the programme to bring to them more economic opportunities. In short, microfinance has contributed indirectly to build the self-esteem and self-reliance of the poor, giving them the confidence and the economic means to move out of the stranglehold poverty and into path of positive change.

Well-being and Empowerment of Women

An empirical study (Todd, 1996) to examine the long-term impact on the poor of two decades of banking by Grameen Bank has demonstrated that credit can fundamentally change the lives of poor women even in the absence of other aid programmes and in an environment hostile to women's autonomy. It showed that the microcredit managed and utilised by women borrowers themselves had the greatest impact on poverty reduction. Women as loan managers are less likely to remain poor, as most of them (eight out of ten) will be out of poverty after a few loan cycles over a decade of banking. Partnership of women with their spouse or other adult household members in loan utilisation and management, on the other hand, is also more likely to move them out of poverty as noted by the above study, with a probability of six in ten. Those women borrowers who acted as conduits of credit to other household members could bring only two out of ten out of below poverty line after a few loan cycles. Thus not only should women be targeted and brought into microcredit programmes, special efforts also have to be made to ensure that loan capital, at least some of it, is utilised and managed by women themselves, to ensure effective poverty reduction.

The impact of credit on women's relative well-being in Grameen Bank's credit programmes was also examined (Osmani, 1998). Well-being was defined in terms of three sets of capabilities, viz., autonomy, control over decision making within the family and relative access to household resources. The combined results of indirect and direct assessment show that by providing access to credit, GB has partially succeeded in improving women's relative well-being. The author cited two reasons for this partial nature of improvement. First, exposure to income-earning activities in a single generation cannot wipe out centuries of cultural conditioning. Second, owing to their low absorptive capacity, i.e., their limited ability to utilise large volumes of credit in the prevailing cultural conditions and in the absence of sufficient economic opportunities, the women borrowers are increasingly depending on their husbands in order to make better use of credit. A kind of joint enterprise is thereby emerging in which the wife provides the credit and the husband provides the entrepreneurship. This implies loss of the woman's independence; her bargaining power within the household might not improve as much as it otherwise might have, had she been running her own enterprise.

Impact on Financial Market

In developing countries, the formal financial institutions are not able to reach the poor and needy effectively. Hence, the poor are often forced to depend on informal sources of borrowings at usurious rates of interest. Evidence shows that in Bangladesh, borrowing from microcredit sources (such as GB, BRAC and RD-12) has reduced the incidence of borrowing from informal sources. As microfinance is cheaper than informal finance, access to microfinance has helped to reduce household borrowing from informal sources. Microfinance also provides an alternative facility for savings mobilisation from the poor. The study also found that there was an increase in mandatory savings as well as voluntary savings of the members. This assures that an appropriate facility of savings can increase the savings rate of a country in which such a facility had not existed. The study also found that the savings impact of MFIs is more pronounced for women than for men (Khandker, 2000).

On the other hand, another empirical research established that increased access to credit from microfinance institutions in Bangladesh has not fully succeeded in substituting for the higher cost informal credit sources. A study of informal credit transactions conducted in a village in northern Bangladesh came out with this conclusion (Sinha and Matin, 1998). MFI lending technology was found insensitive to variations in household conditions. Most MFIs put all households on a treadmill of continuously increasing loan size and insist on a fixed repayment schedule. While an easily accessible loan may seem attractive to a cash-starved poor household, its resource profile and the wider economic and policy environment impose limits on the marginal return to capital. Credit escalation under these circumstances increases the likelihood of cross-financing from informal sources to sustain the MFI's line of credit. Target households, in particular, resort to extensive cross-financing of their loans. It is argued that cross-financing can have a deleterious effect on the household economy in long run if households continuously manage loan repayment without having the ability to repay.

Small Loans and Short-term Impact

The impact of many microfinance institutions and programmes shows a positive note. But the impact of small loans of such institutions sometimes becomes short-term; loans get diverted to purposes other than income generating activities, such as consumption. Coleman (1999) conducted a survey of 445 households in 14 villages in Northeast Thailand that are supported by two Thai NGOs—Rural Friends Association (RFA) and Foundation for Integrated Agricultural Management (FIAM), for studying MFI's success in promoting borrower welfare. The village banks of both the NGOs follow identical banking methodology with six-month loan cycles and identical beginning loans of 1,500 baht and loan ceilings of 7,500 baht. The average wealth of the households surveyed was 529,586 baht, and average household low-interest debt (excluding village bank debt) was 31,330 baht, of which 9,342 baht was held by women. In such an environment, the loans of 1,500 to 7,500 baht had a negligible impact. The women surveyed complained that the size of village bank loans was too small for them to be productive/need-based. These loans, being too small to invest productively because of economies of scale, served primarily as consumption loans.

Fundacion' de la Mujer Campesina (FUNDELAM) (1995), a credit programme in Ecuador, undertook a baseline survey of the population being served for analysing the effect of its credit programme. The study revealed that there was in fact a relationship between credit and family income, although a direct correlation could not be confirmed. Given the precarious and constantly deteriorating incomes within households, the small amount of financial assistance in the form of loans received, was not sufficient to generate a sustained process of capitalisation. However, this credit did enable women to finance part of the cost of productive assets, in particular agricultural equipment, which in turn, generated additional incomes and cushioned households from an overall worsening of socio-economic status. In quantitative terms, the research found that participation in the credit programme produced positive changes, including increase in the percentage of women with paid employment and the nutritional, health and housing conditions of families. In sum, the situation of women who received credit improved in the short-term, though access did not ensure sustained longer-term changes. Reasons for the latter were the smallness of the loans, irregularities in their distribution, and their use for purposes other than those for which they were intended.

The foregoing review of the studies shows that the poorest clients use loans for risk-reducing purposes (consumption and low-risk production technologies). This even points into the fact that while credit may be an effective vehicle for boosting the incomes of the poor, it may be less effective, or even counter-productive, in helping the poorest of the poor to raise their living standards. Thus alternative poverty reduction mechanisms (like more intensive programmes) are advisable for the group.

Complexity of Sustainability, Outreach and Impact

Microfinance, an institutional innovation for rural development is governed by a critical triangle comprising financial sustainability, outreach to the poor, and impact for the poor. Within this triangle, there are trade-offs to be observed while seeking to reduce transaction costs for financial institutions. Reaching more of the poorest with smaller loans increases transaction costs for the microfinance institution. Wide outreach to the poor is costly if they are geographically dispersed. Impact of microfinance may not be achieved without the provision of complementary services (such as training and entrepreneurial development programmes) that in turn increases costs.

The performance of Bank Shita Daya, a private rural bank in Java, was analysed in terms of outreach to the poor and non-poor, financial viability and sustainability, resource mobilisation and sound microfinance practices (Seibel and Parhusip, 1998). The experience indicates that the bank covers their costs and greatly increases the bank's outreach to the poor as a new market segment, but initially adds very little to the bank's overall profitability. The case study shows that viability and sustainability can be attained in banking with the poor. It concludes that only financially viable institutions can sustainably reach the poor in significant numbers.

Debt is not an effective tool for helping the most poor people to enhance their economic condition—be they operators of small farms or microenterprises, or poor women. In most cases lack of formal loans is not the most pressing problem faced by these individuals. It must also be recognised that providing financial services to poor people is expensive and building sustainable financial institutions to do this job requires patience and a keen eye for costs and risks. So it is suggested that financial systems that deal in small transactions efficiently must be developed. Second, innovation is required to assist more poor people to become creditworthy and to have long-term working relationships with formal financial institutions (Adams and von Piscke, 1992).

Apart from the issues of sustainability, outreach and impact, researchers have given attention to some other issues relating to microfinance as well. Transaction cost in the microfinance system, overemphasis on self-employment, low credit absorption among the poor, problems of replication and competition are some of them.

Transaction Cost in Microfinance System

Transaction cost relates to the costs of lenders at all levels. In delivering credit to the poor, interest rates of the banks, service charges of the intermediaries (NGOs) and rates ultimately charged by SHGs to their members need to be taken into account to arrive at the final interest burden to be borne by the borrowers. In other words, for lenders, interest rates must be pitched to cover all the costs plus profits.

The use of NGOs and SHGs as intermediaries by commercial banks significantly lowers transaction costs compared to direct lending to the poor. An analysis of lender transaction costs (Puhazhendhi, 1995) based on a sample of 108 accounts from branches of three banks (one Regional Rural Bank, one public sector bank and one private sector bank) in India showed that costs were the lowest in cases in which banks used SHGs as financial intermediaries and NGOs acted as non-financial intermediaries. Transaction costs included in this study were expenses on identification of the borrower, collection of the application and document verification, pre-approval visit, loan appraisal, loan approval, disbursement and maintaining of accounts, post-approval visit, monitoring and follow up and recoveries. Transaction costs were estimated using the cost-allocation method, multiplying the number of hours spent by bank personnel per loan account by salary and allowances per hour. A constant average loan amount of Rs. 5,000 was used when comparing different models. The estimates showed that bank transaction costs were considerably lower where NGOs and SHGs were involved as financial and non-financial intermediaries than where banks lent directly to the rural poor.

Efficacy of Microfinance and Self-employment

Many researchers feel that the exclusive focus of MFIs on credit and its assumptions that credit affects household welfare is only *via* one path i.e., income. Matin (1997) examined the consequences of developing entrepreneurship by credit in Grameen and Shakti groups. The study found that for Shakti members who were utilising their loan amounts for additional income generating activities, their initial income sources and ability to support weekly instalment in case of any problem, acted as a very important factor behind their participation in the first place. It was also argued that the group-based enterprise model might not be the right template in all cases. For example, the collective responsibility system distributes risk unevenly if a few more enterprising and also more risky borrowers are given loans that are much larger than the average loan size in the group.

For studying the impact of the programme on targeted women, Hasanuzzaman (1996) examined the Income Generation for Vulnerable Group Development (IGVGD) Programme in Bangladesh. During and after the nurturing in the Vulnerable Group Development (VGD) cycle and their consequent involvement in economic endeavours, the women observed have various economic and social changes in their lives. A number of causes and factors have been identified in this study that contributed to their improvement and thereby building within them confidence and self-awareness. Conscientized and properly trained IGVGD women with their practical knowledge and skill were able to manifest their capability in effectively investing credits and savings and engaging themselves in profitable ventures. It was observed that such capacity was possible due to access to credit free of collateral security, group actions on the basis of cooperation and necessary support and subsequent supervision from the organisation. These women, however, were not in total control of themselves or capable of improving their lot on their own. Thus most of them were in a process where they were engaged in income-earning activities but could not go alone and were in need of a pulling hand. In their struggle to become self-supporting, continuous assistance and regular follow up were very important.

Berger (1989) examined the impact of providing credit to self-employed women. She feels that credit cannot be regarded as a panacea to cure the ills of all self-employed women in the informal sector. Other institutional problems like illiteracy, low education and weak management skills also hamper the efforts of women microentrepreneurs to increase their incomes. Training and technical assistance oriented to the informal sector would also be helpful to women. Yet, a woman's economic and household work responsibilities severely limit her time to participate in training. In addition to changes in the financial sector, governments could intervene in other areas to improve the lot of women microentrepreneurs. The current approach overlooks the obstacles to microenterprise expansion posed by government's economic and social policies and by structural barriers that hamper the microenterprise sector as a whole.

Inadequate Demand or Low Credit Absorption of Poor Clients

The basic idea of microfinance is to give small loans to the poor whenever necessity arises. On the other hand, established institutions like Grameen Bank and other MFI/Ps were able to deepen their credit process by giving more loans as well as bigger loans overtime. As far as the poor are concerned, large amounts of loans are essentially a burden. This fact affects the performance of the MFI/Ps as a whole. Matin (2000) feels that effective outreach to the intended target group and good repayment performance are the two important pillars of the current microfinance success. The study on GB shows that both might be in danger due to rapid credit-deepening. The contention is that the success of the simple lending technology (group contract, simple loan size vetting and other standardised practices) used by these institutions might have by now become too simplistic and that it suffers from a homogenised understanding of financial needs of their clients. This has created failures at two levels. One, the failure in maintaining an adequately attractive service for the poorer segment and two, the failure to manage the complexities of large amounts of disbursement per borrower.

Zander (1997) examined the eighteen year experiences of International Fund for Agricultural Development (IFAD) in promoting financial services for the poorest. He feels that the poorest of the economically active poor are also 'bankable'. However, a demand-driven support strategy with the requirements of the ultimate client as the primary focus requires an approach integrating the client and institutional and financial sector issues and options. The failure of many past programmes shows that there are no shortcuts for promoting financial services for the poor. Demand for adequately priced loans for the poor with margins for operating costs and risks for the lending institutions, is not unlimited. The effective demand for credit among the poor could be much less than what is assumed. In addition, if clients' demands are not assessed, support for institutions may not automatically percolate to the intended beneficiaries.

Problems in Replication and Competition

In spite of a number of positive features of microfinance, two factors destroy many microenterprise credit projects. The first is uniformed replication, adopting the form of a relatively successful model without a grasp of the substance that animates and sustains it. The second is that any attempt at innovation contains risks, many of which are not apparent at the outset in credit projects (Adams and von Piscke, 1992).

The replication of the success models is happening all over the world. The replicators give, however, little importance for local conditions and evaluation of earlier programmes. On the other side, co-existence of many programmes and institutions undermines the basic principles of microfinance. Morduch (2000) feels that those interested in replicating the well-known success stories have had only partial and unreliable evaluations on base plans. It is true that the optimism of the 'win-win vision' has generated much energy for the microfinance movement. The socially oriented programmes should have careful economic and social evaluations. Systematic experimentation and evaluation with household level data can be critical along these lines. GB and BRAC are pioneers in this area with a large, comprehensive survey completed in 1991-92. Another aspect is that the role of competition between programmes—some subsidised and some not—must also be taken into account.

Increased competition as a mechanism for improving credit delivery to poor people could undermine the very basis of joint liability lending schemes. Competition among MFI/Ps leads them to undermine repayment incentives for their borrowers. This situation is likely to become more common with time, as several countries now have similar programmes that operate in the same geographic areas. In Bangladesh, for example, GB, BRAC, and Thana Resource Development and Employment Programme (TRDEP) increasingly operate in the same area. Malawi, for example, has two different programmes, Small landholders Agricultural Credit Association (SACA) and a newer replicate of the Grameen Bank called the Mudzi Fund. Buckley (1996b) found that many borrowers who were participants in the Mudzi Fund were those who had been dropped earlier from participation in the SACA programme for not repaying loans. When these two programmes continue to exist side-by-side, they run a real danger of undermining each other. The threat to exclude a defaulter from one programme is less effective if individuals can easily move from one programme to the other.

The foregoing review shows that the 'solidarity methodology' of lending through rural credit delivery system has had significant impact on poverty and income levels of the poor. However, systematic studies on microfinance in all its aspects are non-existent in the Indian context.

3

Microfinance
A Historical Overview

Finance is the lubricant, which oils the wheels of development. All economies rely upon the intermediary function of finance to transfer resources from savers to investors. In market economies, this function is performed by commercial banks, financial institutions and capital markets. In many developing countries, capital markets are at a rudimentary stage, and commercial banks are reluctant to lend to the poor largely because of the lack of collateral security and high transaction costs. The poor would borrow relatively small amounts, and the processing and supervision of lending to them would consume administrative costs disproportionate to the amount of lending. Several studies have confirmed that complicated loan procedures and paperwork, combined with a lack of accounting experience, limit poor people's access to formal sources of credit. Commercial lenders in rural areas prefer to deal mainly with large-scale farmers. The absence of commercial banks in certain areas has led to non-conventional forms of lending.

In order to fill this void, financial institutions such as Rotating Savings and Credit Associations (ROSCAs), cooperatives and credit unions which patterned on traditional models of microlending have emerged all over the world in recent years. These organisations use innovative strategies for serving their clientele. These three types of institutions mobilise savings and lend money to local common groups, professions or neighbourhoods. These institutions which exist in many parts of the world may be considered the models of the present day microfinance institutions. Most of the famous microfinance institutions/programmes (MFI/Ps) in the world have drawn many lessons from these institutions.

The decade of the 1980s saw an unprecedented growth in the number of MFI/Ps all over the world. The pioneer in this field, the Grameen Bank of Bangladesh, was started in 1976. The Bank convinced the world that the poor are able to save and that they are creditworthy. Viewing the success of the institution various poverty alleviation and microenterprise programmes followed the Bank's strategy. The Unit *Desa* System of Bank Rakyat Indonesia (BRI), the Thana Resource Development and Employment Programme (TRDEP) in Bangladesh, the Self-Employed Women's Association (SEWA) in India etc. are the more reputed among them. While many of the programmes used the solidarity group methodology, others lent directly to individual borrowers. But several innovations have been made in repayment strategies, lending techniques, fixation of the periods of loan repayment, collateral security etc. One of the most striking features of these programmes/ institutions is that the majority of their borrowers are women. The repayment levels of loans of these institutions are also very high.

Traditional Models of Microlending

Informal and small-scale lending arrangements have long been in existence in many parts of the world, especially in rural areas. They provide the rural population access to loans within their localities and cushion against the vagaries of economic fluctuations; they also foster a cooperative and community feeling among the rural people. The groups formed among the local people provide joint guarantee to repayment of loans and serve as instruments for spreading information useful for their economic and social progress.

Rotating Savings and Credit Associations (ROSCAs)

In Asia, West Africa, the Caribbean, and the south of the United States, traditional types of lending institutions are in existence.

They are voluntary associations known as Rotating Savings and Credit Associations (ROSCAs). The basic principle upon which the ROSCAs are founded is the same everywhere: "a lump sum fund composed of fixed contributions from each member of the association is distributed, at fixed intervals and as a whole, to each member of the association in turn. Thus, if there are ten members in an association, if the association meets weekly, and if the weekly contribution from each member is one dollar, then each week over a ten-week period a different member will receive ten dollars (i.e., counting his own contribution). If interest payments are calculated by one mechanism or the other, as part of the system, the numerical simplicity is destroyed, but the essential principle of rotating access to a continually reconstituted capital fund remains intact. Whether the fund is in kind or in cash; whether the order in which members receive the fund is fixed by lot, by agreement, or by bidding; whether the time period over which the society runs in many years or a few weeks; whether the sums involved are small or rather large; whether the members are a few or many; and whether the association is composed of urban traders or rural peasants, of men or women, the general structure of the institution is constant" (Geertz, 1963; p. 243).

The ROSCAs provide capital in addition to what is available in a largely traditional society. In India, these rotating credit associations are known as chit funds. Chit funds are established in all parts of the country (places of employment, in neighbourhoods of the city and in peasant villages). The simple chit fund is the more widespread form. The number of members in a group is usually around ten to twenty and they pay small amounts on a weekly or monthly basis. Rotation is by lot, and the winner gets the fund. This uncomplicated kind of fund has no apparent purpose other than the provision of capital to people who find the accumulation of lump sums of money extremely difficult. The members of these groups do not come together nor do chit fund activities enliven the meetings of other formal organisations. The second type of rotating credit fund is the commission chit fund. This incorporates a device for allocating interest and remunerating the organiser by giving the fund each time to the lowest bidder. Under a bidding procedure, the difference between the lowest bid and the total amount of the contributions, minus an allotment to the organiser, is shared by the remaining members, including the organiser, who is a participant member (Anderson, 1966).

The Cooperative Movement

The cooperative movement was started first in Western Europe, later it spread to North America and Asia in the mid-19th century. They are private, self-help organisations. They have great relevance and importance for the people of developing countries, in particular for the rural poor. These organisations put together men and their means for the fulfilment of social ends, otherwise unattainable individually. Cooperation refers to an institutional framework to organise self-help among those who participate in it. In general, such an organisation consists of persons of small means.

It has all along been mainly confined to agriculture, and largely for the supply of credit. Non-agricultural cooperatives, and those located in urban areas have progressed very slowly. Whether organised by farmers or by urban residents, they have usually the lower or the middle ranks—not the lowest ranks—in society as members. They have been started by groups who wanted to join forces to protect their particular interests in the face of what they saw as adverse conditions in the surrounding private markets. While they had to run a business-like operation in competition with others, cooperatives differed from the usual business firm. Their capital came from contributions by equal shares by all members, each one of whom has one vote in running the organisation; policy makers are elected from among the members and major policies are decided by member voting. Profits are distributed either in proportion to purchases or as a return on membership shares. As cooperative activities spread to nearby groups, cooperative federations were formed to supply the primary cooperatives with joint services, operating with the same principles as their member units (Adams and Vogel, 1986).

The global experience in the promotion of rural cooperatives in developing countries has been mixed. The most generally recognised successes on a national scale are of those in Egypt, Taiwan and South Korea. In all these three countries, cooperatives came up as a result of strong and sustained government promotion efforts, conditioned by land reforms that produced agrarian systems with a predominance of small farms in the size of around one hectare.

However, the movement faced a number of shortcomings in its performance in due course. First, it failed to fulfil the main purpose for which it had been launched, namely supply of credit to farmers and rescuing them from the clutches of the moneylenders. Cooperatives provided credit only to a small proportion of the total rural population. Inadequacy of credit and restrictions on its distribution were the major reasons. Second, cooperatives did not have much to show by way of achievement in the field of non-credit activities even productive agricultural activities. The tardy growth of cooperatives in the field of processing of agricultural produce, marketing and distribution of consumer products was also conspicuous. Most of the societies did not provide credit for productive activities undertaken by agriculturalists. In general, consumption loans were not given. Third, the movement had made little headway in urban areas. Fourth, cooperatives did not spread to all areas, particularly to the backward areas of the world.

The Credit Union System

Credit unions are cooperative financial institutions that began operating in developing countries in the 1950s. Credit unions, or savings and credit cooperatives, are base level financial institutions that provide savings and credit services to their individual members. As cooperatives, they are organised and operated according to basic cooperative principles. There are no external shareholders; the members are the owners of the institution, with each member having the right to one vote in the organisation (Magill, 1994).

Membership eligibility in a credit union has traditionally been restricted to groups of people who have some natural affiliation to and a common bond with one another. Restricting membership to persons of a group known to one another reduces credit risks and provides peer pressure to meet loan payment obligations. Historically, two types of bond existed: closed bond based on employment where only employees of a given company are eligible for membership, and associational bonds, where people affiliated with a specific group (such as teachers, members of a church or small employers) are considered eligible for membership.

The credit union system that comes under the World Council of Credit Unions (WOCCU) is made up of four different types of institutions: credit unions, leagues, regional confederations, and the worldwide confederation—each of which has a specific role and purpose. According to statistics maintained by WOCCU, there are currently more than 36,000 credit unions in seventy-nine countries. These credit unions have nearly 78 million members, $232 billion as member-owned savings and deposits, and $178 billion as outstanding loans to members. Most of these unions are concentrated in developed countries. Credit unions in the US, Canada, and Australia, for example, account for 85 per cent of the total membership and 97 per cent of the total savings and loans in the system. It is interesting to note that more than half of the total number of credit unions in the world was in sixty-seven developing countries, these credit unions had, however, only 15 per cent of the total membership, three per cent of the loans and less than 0.5 per cent of member-owned savings (Table 3.1).

Table 3.1: Credit Unions of WOCCU in Developing Countries, 1989

Region	*Countries (No.)*	*Credit Unions (No.)*	*Members (No.)*	*Savings (US $ million)*	*Loans Outstanding (US $ million)*
Africa	25	5152	2343412	539.7	384.5
Asia	7	9157	1168805	118.8	107.7
Caribbean	19	465	806125	548.2	416.1
Latin America	16	2364	4340376	600.0	486.8
Total	**67**	**17138**	**8658718**	**1806.7**	**1395.1**

Source: Magill, 1994.

Credit unions in the developing countries tend to serve low-income and lower middle-income segments of the population. The low-income market niche of credit unions is a result of two different factors. First, many credit unions were established by socially oriented missionary and other groups that had been working with low-income membership base. Second, credit unions provide a basic set of services that low-income members find valuable, because they do not have access to these services through existing formal sector alternatives. But these services are not attractive to more affluent clientele. Credit unions in the developing countries are single-purpose cooperatives that specialise in providing financial services to their members. Savings and relatively short-term instalment credit are the two principal financial services offered by credit unions.

Credit unions follow a "minimalist" approach to credit delivery; very rarely do they provide training, technical assistance, or ancillary services to their members. The credit union movement has developed numerous methods for minimising credit risk. As the members know one another the level of recovery will be high, information cost low and risk quite small. Insistence on a prescribed minimum by way of savings balances and tying of loans to the amount of a member's savings are the other risk-reducing methods followed by the unions. Another method for reducing risk is character-based lending. Although the loans may be used for productive activities, the key to the amount of any loan is the ability of the member to meet the repayment schedule. Maintaining a diversified portfolio is another method followed for minimising risk. Since credit unions lend for a wide variety of purposes, the portfolio risk of specialising in a single type of activity is reduced (Besley *et al.*, 1993).

Several factors constrain the performance of credit unions. First, credit unions tend to be small. Many credit unions have very small membership and make only fifty to one hundred loans a year. The demand for loans often exceeds the supply of savings, creating severe liquidity problems for most of the credit unions. Credit rationing, in one form or another, is the standard practice followed; it is carried out through queuing or limiting the loan to a member to a relatively low multiple of the amount of his/her savings.

The three institutions (ROSCAs, cooperative movement and credit union system) have several things in common. They work among people who have some common characteristics and use their members' own resources for financing the loans. But in most cases, these institutions fail to reach the poor adequately. Hence the emergence of a set of new institutions in recent years for catering to the needs of the poor.

Emergence of Microfinance

Various institutions are involved in the delivery of microfinance services, especially since the dawn of the 1980s. They include formal commercial banks, rural banks, and NGOs. Their methods of doing business range from the Grameen Bank-style of solidarity groups and institutions dealing with individual clients to self-managed self help groups. These institutions provide relatively small loans and their repayment periods are relatively short. Women are the major beneficiaries of MFI/Ps, and the destination of the funds mainly includes agriculture, trading, small craft, processing units and consumption. The administrative structure is, in general, simple and the entire process is participatory in nature (Table 3.2).

Table 3.2: MFI/Ps by Year of Starting and Ownership Pattern

Name of MFI/Ps	*Year of Starting Microfinance Business*	*Type of Ownership*
GB	1976	Shares owned by Bangladesh Government and members
BRI	1984	State owned bank
BancoSol	1987	Commercial bank
TRDEP	1987	Government programme
SEWA	1974	Cooperative bank run by members
SACA	1988	Ministry of Agriculture Department, Government of Malawi

Source: Hulme and Mosley, 1996; Shylendra, 1999.

The interest rates charged by microlending schemes are kept high with a view to covering all the costs. Nonetheless, the rate of repayment of loans is claimed to be quite high, an achievement attributable mainly to the informal participatory structures of the system which create an atmosphere in which debtors honour their obligations. The prominence given to microcredit in recent times owes much to the success of a few microcredit programmes/institutions and the saga of their remarkable growth. The Grameen Bank of Bangladesh, the most prominent of the success cases, now reaches over 23 lakh persons, with a cumulative lending of $2408.3 million. Similar examples of success are known also in Latin America (e.g. Banco Solidario in Bolivia) and Africa (e.g. the Kenya Rural Enterprise Programme). Some institutions have gone beyond credit to offer insurance and other financial services. Institutions such as the Grameen Bank (GB) and the Bangladesh Rural Advancement Committee (BRAC) offer non-financial services, such as retail outlet facilities for products of their clients.

It is easy to spot several such successful institutions/ programmes in different parts of the world today. A thumbnail sketch of six microfinance institutions/programmes from all over the world is presented below:

Grameen Bank—The Pioneer

The pioneer institution of microfinance was the Grameen Bank of Bangladesh launched in 1976 by Professor Muhammad Yunus, an Economics professor at Chittagong University, mainly for the purpose of providing loans to the landless poor, in a manner acceptable to them, both culturally and organisationally. The guiding principles have been to bring the bank to the people in the villages, to replace collateral security by group liability and to give borrowers a free hand in the use of loans, though group supervision is exercised over processing and repayment.

The bank grants individual and group loans secured by a system of group guarantee. Every borrower is expected to repay the loan in weekly instalments over a period of one year.

The members are also asked to deposit at least one taka a week as personal savings and to contribute to an emergency insurance fund against sickness, defaults and other contingencies. Most of the loans are used for small-scale trading and shop keeping, food-processing and livestock raising. The level of repayment is close to 95 per cent (Egger, 1986).

As a special bank for the poor, the Grameen Bank has been remarkably successful. There are a number of factors for success of the Grameen Bank. They are: (a) clear basic concept and guiding vision of the institution, (b) strong institutional identity, (c) charismatic and conscientious leadership (of Prof. Muhammad Yunus), (d) disciplined staff with a clear understanding of the norms of organisation and its clientele, (e) simple and transparent procedures, and (f) two-tier system of borrower group. In spite of all these factors, the presence of a highly motivated, socially cohesive target group plays a very important role.

The clients come from relatively homogeneous traditional communities with strong social control mechanisms. Women, in particular, are economically and socially tied to their families and communities, lacking viable opportunities to live elsewhere; they are highly susceptible to social pressure. Also, in case of prospective borrowers, they know one another and therefore, are in a position to screen out individuals whom they perceive as credit risks. To a large extent, individuals screen themselves out, fearing negative consequences if they fail to repay loans. Lack of alternatives, sense of honour and relative social cohesion of their communities help the borrowers to pressurise one another to ensure repayment. Factors such as grant of loans for activities selected by borrowers, weekly repayments and availability of subsequent loans helped prompt repayment. Loans are kept small to avoid burdening of borrowers with debt burdens beyond their capacity to repay. Breaking loan repayment into small weekly instalments pre-empts the need to raise a large amount of money at one time. Weekly repayment also facilitates monitoring of repayment by the group (Hashemi and Schuler, 1997).

From its inception, the Grameen Bank had some very innovative features that helped its success. First, no collateral security was required from the poor. Individuals were asked to organise themselves into groups of five. The individuals in the group gave collective guarantee/group guarantee for one another so that loan repayment became a collective responsibility. Second, credit was provided to the rural poor who owned less than half an acre of land; 94 per cent of these were women. Third, the loans were small (an average $100 each) and carried no interest subsidy. In fact, they were given at a much higher interest rate than bank loans in the market, reflecting the extra administrative cost of small loans. Fourth, the poor were required to set aside some saving—at least one taka (US 2.5 cents)—a week. This encouraged the habit of self-reliance among the poor. Fifth, the bank went to the poor, without waiting for the poor to come to the bank.

The Grameen Bank is a semi-government institution; 40 per cent of its shares are held by the member-borrowers, landless men and women; the rest are held by the state. The bank has over 2,334,780 members, of whom 2,210,160 (more than 95 per cent) are women. It has disbursed over $2,408.30 million of credit and has accumulated borrowers' savings of nearly $176.90 million. Although it reaches only a fraction of the total landless households in the country, it has demonstrated the effectiveness of its approach—a clear commitment to poverty alleviation based on stringent conditions for membership. The bank operates through a network of village branches each of which is run by a manager with the assistance, usually of five bank workers.

Grameen Bank's continuing expansion clearly shows that the poor are creditworthy and that they can use loans productively. It has dispelled doubts about their promptitude and reliability as customers of commercial and public banks if services were made available to them under similar institutional arrangements with proper follow up.

BRI—The Agricultural Credit Institution Turned into Village Banks

Bank Rakyat Indonesia (BRI), one of the five state-owned commercial banks in Indonesia, has the special assignment of providing banking services to the rural areas, with particular emphasis on agricultural credit. BRI has a nationwide network of small village banks known as the BRI Unit Banking (Unit *Desas*) System. It was started in Yogyakarta in 1969 as part of a pilot project for the national rice intensification programme, BIMAS (Naisbitt, 1996). More than 3,600 Unit *Desas* were established during 1970—1983 throughout the country to service BIMAS credit; most of them were located in the capital towns of sub-district (*kecamatan*), each serving on an average eighteen villages.

BIMAS credit was provided primarily in kind, to farmers certified as efficient by the Agriculture Department's extension workers. While BRI, in principle, retained authority for loan approval, under severe pressure from agricultural development officers in the local administration who had to achieve lending targets, many loans did not receive proper financial scrutiny. Unit *Desa* overdue rates, which did not exceed ten per cent during 1970-1976 rose to 54 per cent in 1984. The system losses, which were not above Indonesian Rupiah two billion till 1978 rose to Indonesian Rupiah 25 billion in 1984. The number of farmers participating in the scheme fell by 60 per cent between 1975 and 1983 (Mosley, 1996c).

Following the financial crisis in 1983, Indonesian government liberalised the financial system. Thus the objectives of the BRI were stipulated as the following: to replace directed agricultural credit with broad-based credit for any type of rural economic activity; to replace subsidised credit with positive on-lending rates with spreads sufficient to cover all financial and operational intermediation costs; and to provide a full range of financial services (savings as well as credit) to the rural population (Yaron *et al.*, 1997).

Thus BRI set its own borrowing and lending rates. It also introduced new financial instruments for both savings (SIMPEDES) and lending (KUPEDES) through the Unit *Desas*. The distinguishing feature of the latter is that the Unit *Desas* may lend for any productive purpose, and agricultural lending now forms only a small part of their portfolio. The repayment period for BRI working capital loans is three to twenty-four months, while for investment loans it is three years. Loans are granted for any productive enterprise and it is allowed after the assessment of the business plan. The repayment term is monthly and the collection is made at branch office in sub-district (*kecamatan*) principal town. The BRI Unit *Desas* do require collateral to the extent of the loan: however, collateral security does not have to be offered in the form of land. Many applicants use house plots, motorcycles or even consumer durables as collateral security. Twenty-four per cent of the total beneficiaries are women. The Unit *Desa* System has been highly profitable since 1987 and has accounted for more than 30 per cent of the BRI's net income (Mosley, 1996c).

BancoSol—An NGO turned Bank

Banco Solidario S.A. of Bolivia, popularly known as BancoSol, is the first non-governmental institution in the world to convert itself into a deposit-taking bank. It aims to lend exclusively to low-income people and has a high repayment rate. With a per capita income of $620, a life expectancy of sixty years and under-five mortality rate of 126 per thousand, Bolivia is not only poorer than any other country of Latin America, but also poorer than the average for a less developed country of the world. Bolivia's banking system, even more than other parts of the economy, was characterised during the pre-1985 period by extreme inefficiency and inability to reach the small borrower.

Though quasi-formal institutions like credit unions had existed, they did not contribute to filling the credit market vacuum for small rural and urban enterprises. BancoSol's predecessor was PRODEM (Fundaci'on Para la Promoci'on Desarollo de la MicroEmpresa, or Foundation for the Promotion and Development of Microenterprises). It was established in late 1985, in order to establish a microenterprise-lending programme in Bolivia. A Bolivian businessman, Fernando Romero, persuaded a group of Bolivian businessmen to invest in PRODEM. Thus was born the BancoSol (Mosley, 1996a).

BancoSol lends to individuals within 'solidarity groups' of four to seven members. It uses intensive loan collection methods, which have been never experimented by commercial banks or specialised farm credit institutions. The default rates are consistently low. The MFIs charge market interest rates, which reflect local financial market conditions. The interest rate for loans at BancoSol is four per cent a month, with effective rate of 55 to 57 per cent a year. BancoSol's minimum loan is $80 and its maximum $5,000. BancoSol insisted on a compulsory savings deposit (in its case, five per cent of the value of the loan), not returnable until the loan was fully paid up.

The method by which BancoSol makes loans is also interesting. Officers undertake extensive fieldwork, survey local neighbourhoods, and get to know potential clients. Once clients have been identified, a credit evaluation is conducted for each client. At BancoSol, the solidarity group acts as the key screening mechanism and is a substitute for collateral security; community members choose to be in a group with others who are creditworthy and on whom they can rely to make timely loan repayments. BancoSol imposes no maximum income requirement (Glosser, 1994). Loans would be given to an existing business and to persons above eighteen years of age willing to form a group. In BancoSol, the majority of loan recipients are women (71%).

BancoSol's achievements during its short life are remarkable. In an atmosphere of national financial turmoil, an institution was created which aimed squarely at the urban poorest while charging commercial interest rates. It has grown faster than any other institution of this type in Latin America, and has now diversified into deposit taking and rural lending.

TRDEP: The Rolling Programme

The Thana Resource Development and Employment Programme (TRDEP) was initiated by the Government of Bangladesh in 1987, to reproduce and adapt the Grameen Bank experience and methods. It is a project overseen by country's Ministry of Youth and Sports and run by the Directorate of Youth Development (DYD) in Dhaka. In 1986, the programme was started with an initial budget of Tk 20 million ($0.5 million).

TRDEP has over 10,000 members spread over fourteen branches and village centres (*kendras*). Each branch has about sixty members and has approximately twelve staff members, five or more of whom are group animators carrying out the savings and loan operations in the *kendras*. TRDEP is a three to four year 'rolling programme', approximately 15,000 people had received their maximum permissible limit of four loans. About 71 per cent of the members of TRDEP are men. Procedurally, TRDEP *kendras* consisting of thirty to fifty members from the target group are organised into five to seven member sub-(joint liability) groups. The programme officially stipulates a 'youth' age limit of thirty-five years. TRDEP encourages the sub-groups to be family-based. The membership of the same sub-group ensures peer pressure, and reduction of that a single family may represent. At first, TRDEP assumed that such a stipulation would ensure the participation of women in the programme.

The credit delivery procedures effectively allow for substantial injections of capital into families and households. Even though the loans are individually taken and listed for each sub-group member, they can be pooled in one family-group enterprise if taken simultaneously. Additionally, the four loans which each member is permitted to take occur in quick succession; on repaying their first loans, members become immediately eligible to apply for the second loan, and so on. Successive loans can become, in principle, increasingly large (Tk 2,000→Tk 2,500→Tk 3,000→Tk 4,000). In this manner, TRDEP's lending procedures theoretically allow a household or family to borrow nearly Tk 60,000 over a four year period, progressively reinvesting in an enterprise, thereby greatly enhancing the potential for the programme's overall aim, the clientele's graduation out of poverty (Montgomery *et al.*, 1996).

In fact, savings are a minor part of TRDEP's operations; members have to save Tk one per week, which after one year constitutes only two per cent or three per cent of the value of their first loans of approximately Tk 2,000. Each loan is of fifty-two weeks duration, and is offered at an interest rate of 16 per cent. The only other direct cost to the borrower is a five per cent deduction from the loan principal which is a forced deposit into the branch Provisional Fund. TRDEP provides a short but supposedly intensive induction course for new members. This includes issues of family planning, health and hygiene, immunisation, the advantages of savings, and credit procedures; but TRDEP is a short process. In addition, TRDEP has a skill-training and institution-building provision. A single group animator (GA) oversees a centre during its lifetime and conducts weekly meetings to collect savings and loan instalments.

The formation of family-based groups which can pool loans is a procedure capable theoretically, of overcoming the constraints of microcredit, a constraint mentioned by several analysts of Bangladeshi schemes lending small amounts to individuals. In reality, loan pooling amongst TRDEP's clientele is much less prevalent than it was expected. Family-based groups seem to be not common. Even where there are kin relations amongst a group, this does not ensure loan pooling. Additionally, a husband and wife may feel it less risky to invest in several small-scale activities, rather than go for larger enterprises.

SEWA—An Indian Experience

In India, the Self-Employed Women's Association (SEWA), which followed a different way, was also successful. It was formed in Ahmedabad in 1972 as a trade union of women working in the informal sector. Any self-employed woman in India may become member of this organisation by paying Rupees five per year as the membership fee. The organisation covers three categories of self-employed women workers:

(a) Small-scale vendors, traders and hawkers;
(b) Home-based producers such as weavers, potters, *beedi*-makers, milk-producers and garment-stitchers; and
(c) Agricultural labourers, construction workers, washerwomen, cooks and cleaners.

SEWA has empowered these women by combining the strategies of trade unions and cooperatives. SEWA has organised its own cooperative bank and a group life insurance scheme so that its members could become self-reliant. It has also started several skill-training courses to enhance the income-earning potential of its members as well as providing legal services to enable indigent women to obtain the benefits of national labour legislation that had been denied to them. The objective of the union is to safeguard the interests of the self-employed women workers through the following three-pronged strategy:

(a) Direct action by conducting meetings, processions, demonstrations and writing to the government employees concerned against injustice on self-employed women workers;
(b) Dealing with government departments by registering a complaint using the legal structures;
(c) Organisation of self-employed women to influence policy-decision making and to bring about changes in labour laws so as to respond to the needs of self-employed women. This includes looking into their financial needs and thereby providing working capital to free them from the stranglehold of private moneylenders (Bhatt, 1989).

The experience of SEWA with the self-employed women has shown that the major problem they face is that of managing working capital. Borrowing from a nationalised bank is difficult for them, as it needs scrupulous following of certain procedures unfamiliar to them. Moreover, the banks want security in the form of assets which poor women seldom possess. Initially SEWA had mediated with the nationalised banks to secure loans for poor women. In the process, the organisation realised that neither the actual capital needs of women nor their small financial emergencies could be met with the existing structure of the banking system. This realisation motivated the organisation to have its own bank on a cooperative basis.

Within a period of six months, 4,000 women contributed Rupees ten each, towards the share capital of such a bank. Thus the SEWA Bank was started in 1974. The main aim of the Bank is to provide savings and credit facilities to the members of SEWA and in turn help them in taking up livelihood promotion activities (Shylendra, 1999). Though the bank's jurisdiction was confined to Ahmedabad city, it is now being extended to other parts of Gujarat through self help groups. All the SHGs are linked to SEWA Bank of Ahmedabad through their district level federations. In Ahmedabad alone, it has a membership of more than 50,000 working women, who make use of the Bank's services, such as credit, health facilities, life insurance and legal aid. It has 362 producer groups and 84 co-operatives. The present membership in the whole of Gujarat rose to more than 220,000 (Bhatt, 2006).

Highlights of SEWA: It provides all banking facilities to its members/depositors; all procedures of the Bank are designed to suit the illiterate and the poor women; the majority of SEWA loans are unsecured (in 1987 nearly 79 per cent of the loans were unsecured loans); and the bank extends loans to enable the members to recover mortgaged jewellery and land and to improve housing. The experience of SEWA showed the way to a number of NGOs in India and abroad.

SACA—The Farmers' Club

Smallholder Agricultural Credit Administration (SACA) in Malawi is an example of the farmers' club system. Prior to 1958, African farmers had no source of formal credit excluding commercial banks; the only source of agricultural credit was the Farmers' Loans and Subsidies Board, which served only white farmers. For raising smallholder productivity by the provision of input loans, the National Rural Development Programme was started in 1982, when the Government of Malawi created a Central Credit Fund, the precursor of SACA.

SACA was created in 1988. SACA has eight Agricultural Development Divisions (ADDs) in the country, covering all areas. Each of these ADDs has an average of four Rural Development Projects. The Farmers' Club Group Lending System was piloted in Lilongwe in 1993. All groups are voluntary associations and each group consists of at least ten members. In 1993 a typical farmers' club had twenty-six members.

The joint liability of group members was supplemented by a security fund, which was initially considered as a prelude to a rural savings movement. Borrowers were required to pay ten per cent of their loan amount as a deposit into a common group fund that was set up with a commercial bank under the supervision of the administration of SACA. The main function of the farmers' clubs is to obtain seasonal credit for members by accepting mutual liability for the loans obtained for each member. Not only does the group provide the substitute for collateral security but it is also vested with the responsibility of ensuring repayment of the credit packages. This has the effect of encouraging club officials to place importance on the ends rather than the means used to achieve this, namely, suitability of the credit package and its appropriate application. Thus the farmers' club system successfully removes the need for securing loans on collateral security and thereby increases access to credit; it also lowers the administrative and monitoring costs of lending and until recently it ensured high repayment rates (Buckley, 1996b).

SACA also makes available a small number of medium term loans to individuals who may or may not be members in the farmers' club. These loans are usually repayable over five years at twenty per cent per annum and are made in kind for durable items such as farm carts, ploughs and sprayers. Loans are also made for livestock including dairy animals, oxen and poultry. In theory, if one group member defaults then the whole group is ineligible for future loans. In practice, this does not always happen because SACA has a policy of 'exclusion as last resort', essentially because it is believed that a heavy-handed policy would result in too many groups breaking up. Most farmers' clubs function as both supportive and disciplined bodies but the repayment objective is paramount; the exclusion sanction is found most effective in ensuring credit discipline. Until 1991-92, most clubs had avoided defaulting and the repayment rates in all regions of the country were impressive. In the SACA farmers' club, 28 per cent of the total members were women.

An Appraisal of Microfinance Institutions and Programmes

Thus it is found that the reasons behind the emergence and growth of successful MFI/Ps all over the world were varied. The reasons for the successful functioning of these MFI/Ps and similar kinds of institutions and programmes all over the world may now be looked into.

Physical and Socio-economic Environment

The physical and socio-economic environment of the target clientele determines the success of the credit intervention. Factors such as population density, education (of the population and the MFI/Ps staff), the quality of the rural infrastructure etc. are some of them. Most of the successful institutions and programmes are established in developing parts of the world (Asia, Africa and Latin America). In these areas, the population density is high. Credit interventions are likely to be more successful in areas with a relatively high population density because average administrative costs are likely to be lower in such areas. Likewise, the availability of well-educated, low-cost staff with good knowledge of the community would improve the efficiency of MFI/Ps and perhaps lower transaction costs. Most successful institutions such as Grameen Bank, BRI invest heavily in ongoing training. GB selects and trains staff who have thorough knowledge of local conditions. The provision of credit alone is unlikely to draw the very poor out of poverty because they have limited access to markets, networks and skills. Access to non-financial services such as skill-based training, could help to improve the poor's return on their investments (Yaron *et al.*, 1997).

Cultural factors are important for success or failure of MFI/Ps. For example, joint liability groups are more successful in some cultures than in others. In developing countries traditional communities are prevalent. Thus the group and joint liability methodology are found to be appropriate. There are efforts to replicate the experiences of GB and other successful Joint Liability Lending Institutions (JLLIs) in countries such as the US and Canada. Although there has been an increase in the number of peer group programmes in these countries, many programmes have been terminated due to lack of success. One reason for the limited success is that they do not have the advantage of monitoring, peer pressure, mutual insurance and informal transfer that exist in the programmes in the developing parts of the world (Conlin, 1999).

Group-based Savings and Credit Services

Various forms of social intermediation are warranted to make financial services available to socially and economically marginalised members of society. One of the most important kinds of such intermediations for overcoming social barriers is the provision of group-based savings and credit services. Thus microfinance institutions and programmes use solidarity groups and other group-based methodologies like SHGs for their effective functioning. Joint liability-lending is the most important feature of successful microlenders such as GB, BancoSol, TRDEP and SACA (Table 3.3).

Table 3.3: MFI/Ps on the Basis of Borrower Profile as in 1995

Name of MFI/Ps	*Borrower*	*Total Number of Borrowers*	*Women Borrowers (%)*
Grameen Bank	Individual within group of five within centre of thirty	2,334,780	94.67
BRI	Individual who start any productive enterprise	1.9 million	24
BancoSol	Individual within solidarity group of four to seven individuals	62,410	71
TRDEP	Join a Kendra form a five person group attend regularly. Loan must be approved by other sub-group members	10,000 present members, 15,000 past members	30
SEWA	Members of the co-operative members	50,000	100
SACA	Group of small landholders	400,062	28

Source: Hulme and Mosley, 1996; Shylendra, 1999.

The solidarity group methodology adapts elements of the traditional model of rotating savings and credit associations, which are widespread in the developing world. In ROSCAs, members contribute a regular amount every week or month, with group members taking turns for collecting the full contribution of all members. In peer group lending schemes, members receive loans and then make regular weekly or monthly repayments, with group members providing a mutual guarantee for loan repayment (Appendix VI).

The economic logic of joint liability-lending is that it can mitigate some problems that arise in lending to poor people. The central issue of such credit markets is twofold: first, the lender does not know much about the borrower (asymmetric information), and second, the commonly used contractual arrangements for contending with asymmetric information do not work because the borrowers are too poor for the lender to use financial sanctions to achieve repayment of loans. Joint liability can achieve better screening to contend with adverse selection, encourages peer monitoring to reduce moral hazard, gives group members incentives to enforce the repayment of loans, and reduces the lenders' audit costs (Ghatak and Guinnane, 1999).

Importance of Savings

The provision of financial services to rural communities, especially poor communities, has traditionally focused almost exclusively on extension of credit. Savings, insurance and other financial products and services were largely ignored. This emphasis on credit was due partly to the perception that the poor cannot save. Thus, the traditional approach of rural finance has ignored savings mobilisation, the 'forgotten half of rural finance' (Vogel, 1984). Often the need for safe, liquid and remunerative savings facilities take precedence over the need for credit, because savings improve clients' ability to smooth consumption with own resources, and allows them to avoid the burden of debt repayments during income downswings.

One of the most important contributions of microfinance to the world of finance is that the poor are enabled to save. The savings of the poor (especially women) are often minimal. But there are many advantages to savings, both for the borrower and the MFI/Ps. Borrowers see savings as a way to enhance family security. Savings also give borrowers a yardstick for measuring their economic progress. By providing borrowers with a growing stake in their peer-lending group, savings accumulation provides an incentive for borrower insistence on efficient and transparent management of funds.

In some microcredit systems, savings generated by the members of a peer lending group are relevant among the group's members, creating a second loan portfolio whose interest income becomes an additional source of income to the borrower. For the microcredit lending institution, savings can provide an important source of additional collateral security for meeting the risk of non-repayment, and for increasing the supply of available loan capital. Finally, savings as a percentage of total loan portfolios provide a convenient measuring rod of the programme's rates of internal capitalisation and financial self-sufficiency. Access to savings facilities with a positive return would smooth consumption of the poor also (Sarma, 1999).

The GB in Bangladesh stipulates savings and deposits as a precondition to extending credit. Likewise, all the other MFI/Ps mobilise large amounts of savings, and there is little doubt now that the rural poor are able to save. On the other hand, MFI/Ps which have a high share of savings relative to other sources of funds, are found to be more efficient and self-sustainable.

Innovative Loan Instruments, Strategies and Methods for the Poor

The MFI/Ps have innovated lending strategies suitable to local conditions and needs. Each institution has its own instruments, strategies and methods of disbursement of loans and of collection. Though the MFI/Ps follow diverse techniques some common characteristics are observed all over the world (Table 3.4).

Table 3.4: MFI/Ps on the Basis of Loan instruments and Methods

Name of the Institution	*Interest rate*	*Collection method for loans*	*Incentives to repay*	*Collateral requirement*
Grameen Bank	24	Weekly at or near borrowers premises	No	No
BRI	30	Three months to three years at branch office in Kecamatan principal town	0.5% per month premium, refunded twice a month if all payments on time	Yes
BancoSol	60	Fortnightly or monthly on bank premises	No	No
TRDEP	16	Weekly in 52 instalments collected by group animator at village Kendra meeting	Peer group pressure; future loans	None, but a five per cent deduction from loan principle, sub-group joint liability
SEWA	24	Weekly in SHGs	No	None
SACA	18	A single repayment at point of sale of crop	No	No

Source: Hulme and Mosley, 1996; Shylendra, 1999.

The most interesting innovation in the field of microfinance is that it covers all the costs incurred by the MFI/Ps. The interest rates in the MFI/Ps referred to earlier are fairly higher than the rates prevalent in the banking sector of the economies concerned. Likewise, the repayment strategies are also suited to the requirement of the local population. Most of the MFI/Ps collect the loans on weekly, fortnightly or monthly basis. This practice helps borrowers to repay loans on a regular basis and the amounts they have to repay in instalments come down. The place at which the borrower has to repay the loan is also suitable to local population. Most of the MFI/Ps provide mobile banking facilities, repayment facilities in nearby area offices and field staff to collect the loan amounts.

Most of the MFI/Ps do not require collateral security for granting loans. Some insist on collateral security such as landed property, consumer durables or vehicles. TRDEP deducts a five per cent of the loan principal as collateral security. Savings and joint liability of groups are also usually considered as collateral security. MFI/Ps use 'stick and carrot' techniques to ensure proper repayment. 'Stick' means imposition of penalties such as higher interest rates, delaying of second loans, ousting from the group, etc. Giving incentives for repayment of loans is considered 'carrots'. BRI gives 0.5 per cent per month as premium to the borrowers who make all payments on time. These factors lead to the high repayment rates among these institutions and programmes.

Learning from Experiences

It was observed that the microfinance institutions and programmes existing all over the world today were not started simultaneously. They learned the lessons of microfinancing through various experiences and models. Some institutions like Bank Rakyat Indonesia's Unit *Desa* System were started for catering to the credit needs of the agricultural population. When it was found that the poor were excluded from, and more non-poor were coming into the system, the bank innovated its strategies and tried to lend exclusively for the poor.

Most credit programmes for the poor around the world have adopted many lessons from Grameen Bank such as the following:

(a) The use of social rather than economic collateral security through the formation of jointly liable borrowing groups;
(b) The formation of centres or village organisations made up of joint liability groups;
(c) Large field staff and good outreach and disbursement of loans and collection of payments from borrowers' villages;

(d) Provisional savings funds, which are often made up of deductions from loans, are not immediately accessible to group members but the same serve as an insurance mechanism for the programme if defaults occur; and

(e) The use of additional 'insurance' deductions to help the programmes or institutions copes with the high risks of lending to the poor and the vulnerable.

Since the 1970s, peer group lending programmes have grown in number, size and variety of settings. The unprecedented emergence of a number of microfinance institutions and programmes all over the world especially in the developing countries has contributed largely to the local populations of these countries. Similarly, the presence of insurance schemes, microsavings and other characteristics of microfinance shows that there is an unmet demand for a broad array of financial services among the poor.

4

Emergence and Growth of Microfinance in India

The responsibility of meeting the credit needs in the rural areas of India was entrusted primarily with the cooperative banking sector until about the mid-1960s. As the technological developments in the agricultural sector started gathering momentum, it was expected that commercial banks would play an increasing role in the rural credit market through branch expansion and direct lending. One of the major objectives of the nationalisation of Indian commercial banks (in two spurts in 1969 and 1980) was the improvement of the flow of formal institutional credit into rural households, especially to the poor, thus relieving them of the burden of usurious debt.

Although these measures were ambitious and laudable, they did not reach the poor people in adequate measure. A paradigm shift was needed for reaching the poor and the needy with timely and adequate credit facilities at a fair price. It was in this context that microfinance institutions and programmes (MFI/Ps) emerged around the globe and showed the way. Many Non-Governmental Organisations (NGOs) started working in this field. Viewing the success of these experiments, the National Bank for Agriculture and Rural Development (NABARD), the apex bank for rural credit in India, came forward to link the self help groups formed by NGOs with various banks in the country. The Government of India, while launching poverty alleviation programmes in urban (SJSRY) and rural (SGSY) areas also emphasised the need for formation of groups for reaching the benefits of these programmes to the people below the poverty line.

In this chapter, section one deals with the institutional reforms launched by the Government of India since independence and their impact on the Indian economy, especially in the field of credit to the poor people. In subsequent sections, the emergence of microfinance in India, the major players in the field and the various programmes initiated by Government of India for reaching the needy are reviewed.

Institutional Arrangements

In order to reach the people, a multi-agency approach involving cooperatives, Public Sector Banks (PSBs), Regional Rural Banks (RRBs) and development banks was launched in India. Since independence in 1947, Government of India has been concerned to provide affordable credit facility to the rural producer in competition with the private moneylender. To this end, it had taken a variety of measures such as the following:

(i) Created Cooperative Banks (CBs) for short-term finance and Land Development Banks (LDBs) for long-term finance at the state, district and village levels;
(ii) Nationalised twenty major commercial banks, fourteen in 1969 and six in 1980;
(iii) Set up a regulatory framework specifying, *inter alia*, maximum interest rates for particular categories of loan, minimum 'Statutory Liquidity Ratios' (SLR) for assets deposited with the Reserve Bank of India (RBI), and minimum shares of commercial bank portfolios which must go to specified priority sectors, including agriculture;
(iv) Set up a number of lines of credit in favour of rural and urban low-income groups at prices even lower than the statutory minimum interest rates for each sector. The most important of these is the Integrated Rural Development Programmes (IRDP) (Mosley, 1996b) and Differential Rate of Interest (DRI) at four per cent.

Co-operative Banks: Short-term Credit

Soon after independence, a chain of co-operatives was set up in India to serve the poor in rural and urban areas. The village level primary co-operative credit societies are eminently suited to the socio-economic conditions of the Indian villages. The number of primary agricultural credit societies supplying short-term credit has increased considerably during the past few decades. The vast network of such societies (called Primary Agricultural Credit Societies—PACS) throughout the length and breadth of the country has made considerable progress in the provision of agricultural credit.

Under the co-operative system, credit extended to agriculture has increased massively from a mere Rs. 24 crore in 1950-51 to as much as Rs. 15,920 crore in 1998-99. Of this, short-term credit has gone up hugely from Rs. 23 crore to Rs. 12,320 crore during the same period. Co-operative credit occupies a major proportion of total institutional credit (i.e., by co-operatives, commercial banks, and regional rural banks) with its share standing at about 45 per cent.

At least ten persons are required to form a primary agricultural credit society. The working committee, whose members are elected annually, conducts its activities. The capital of the society is drawn from several sources—entrance fee from members, deposits, issue of shares and money received from the government and other institutions. Societies undertake different functions. Credit societies advance short-term and medium-term credit. A part of the profit from the working of societies has to be kept in reserve. These societies are given certain concessions by the government with regard to income tax, registration fee, etc.

During the 1990s, some important changes took place in the co-operative movement which have given it quite a new and progressive approach. Some of the major changes are the following: (a) the scope of cooperative societies, which till recently was limited, has been extended; and (b) in place of single purpose societies, emphasis is now being laid on multipurpose societies. These societies are being designated as "service co-operatives".

Nevertheless, a number of weaknesses have crept into the system. These are: (i) The co-operative societies do not command adequate resources. The savings by members have registered only small increase. Even from the point of view of the use of resources, the working of these societies is reportedly so inefficient that even the loans advanced by the RBI often go under-utilised. (ii) Similarly, farmers who are starved of credit, get very little succour from cooperatives. As a result, many farmers, in particular small farmers, continue to struggle to get out of the clutches of moneylenders. (iii) Because of its preoccupation with the provision of credit, the movement has not done much in non-credit activities. (iv) Besides, the movement is neither properly managed, nor does it find the right type of leadership. Evils of favouritism and nepotism are rampant, particularly in connection with the distribution of its resources among members. The management of these institutions often passes into the hands of big landlords who use them for their private gains. (v) The principle of self-reliance, which is basic to the movement, is not promoted effectively. For a considerable part of their finances, these institutions depend upon outside sources. Their own resources, viz., share capital and deposits, do not show much increase over time. (vi) The financial working of the credit societies remains weak and incompetent with large overdues, in some years rising to as much as 45 per cent of the loans. The reduced availability of loanable funds affected loan disbursements and the image of the societies was tarnished. (vii) Weaker sections of the population such as Scheduled Castes and Scheduled Tribes continue to suffer from the grave incompetence and inadequacies of co-operatives.

Land Development Banks (LDBs): Long-term Credit

For extending long and medium-term credit to agriculture, a specialised institution in the form of land development banks was established in the country by as early as 1929. Now there are 19 state (or central) land development banks in India. The SLDBs give loans to their members for productive investment.

The working of the LDBs suffers from several defects common to the co-operative movement in India. Large overdues, inadequate and incompetent staff for doing project appraisal, monitoring and evaluation, corruption and excessive dependence on outside sources of funds are some of the major weaknesses (Gupta, 2001).

Regional Rural Banks (RRBs): Rural Credit

Regional Rural Banks (RRBs) sponsored by major banks were set up in backward areas in India since 1975. The main objective of RRBs is to provide credit and other facilities particularly to small and marginal farmers, agricultural labourers, artisans and small entrepreneurs so as to develop agriculture, trade, commerce, industry and other productive activities in the rural areas. The capital of a RRB is owned by the Government of India (50%), the state government (15%) and the (state-owned) commercial bank which agrees to sponsor it (35%). There are now 196 RRBs spread over 23 states with 14,500 branches. As at the end of June 1996, RRBs had raised aggregate deposits worth Rs. 14,200 crore and had advanced Rs. 7,500 crore by way of short-term crop loans, term loans for agricultural activities, and loans for rural artisans, village and cottage industries, retail traders and the self-employed and consumers.

The Narasimham Committee which examined the financial system of the country evaluated the working of RRBs and pointed out that RRBs have only low earning capacity, that their wage and salary scales have been rising and that the sponsoring banks themselves are also running their own rural branches in the very area of operations of the RRBs. This situation has given rise to certain anomalies and to avoidable expenditure on controls and administration of RRBs.

Nationalisation of Banks

The nationalisation of fourteen major banks in 1969, which comprised ninety per cent of the total banking assets in the country, was a bold step towards expanding rural credit. The overriding objective of nationalisation was the taking of banking to the 'masses'. The government envisaged that 40 per cent of the total credit of the nationalised banks/commercial banks should be channelised to priority sectors (of which 18 per cent was for agriculture and ten per cent for weaker sections), groups or regions to support activities that were either considered to be socially beneficial or inherently risky and borrower groups that were likely to be marginalised in the credit markets, at lower rates of interest. This was an important step in the direction of asserting the developmental role of banks.

These measures had a strong impact on rural economy. The vast branch expansion of nationalised banks helped the people in remotest areas to have access to financial services. The number of branches, which had been only 8,262 at the time of nationalisation, steadily year after year, rose to 65,621 in 2000. The population per bank office declined from 65,000 in 1969 to 15,000 in 2000. The growth and extension of rural credit displaced village moneylenders to a significant extent (Bell, 1990) and led to modest increases in aggregate crop output, sharp increases in the use of fertilizers and in investments in physical capital like tractors, pump sets and animal stocks. A substantial positive effect is seen in non-farm employment and output also (Binswanger and Khandker, 1992).

On the other hand, these measures distorted the capital market structure. In general, three kinds of government interventions in financial markets that constituted financial repression may be seen, viz., high reserve requirements, interest rate controls and directed credit programmes. Mckinnon (1971) argued that these repressions had constrained the size of the financial system in these countries with adverse consequences for investment and economic growth. As the reserve requirements were high in public sector banks in India, profitability was low since the 1970s (Varghese, 1983). A good part of the financial surplus generated by the banks went to the government in the form of subsidised funds (SLR/CRR requirements) and special interest tax. The interest rates held below market levels led to a variety of undesirable results like inefficiency in investment and fragmented market. They endangered the financial viability of institutional lenders (von Piscke, 1981; Gonzalez-Vega, 1985). The directed credit programmes, which had the provision of cheap and subsidised credit were often diverted from poor people, the real target group. Since the subsidies were valuable, politically powerful groups, usually not poor, managed to grab a share (Morduch, 2000).

Although the banking system has experienced phenomenal growth in terms of geographical spread, deposit mobilisation and disbursal of credit in rural areas after nationalisation, bank credit remains by and large, inaccessible to the poor. The poor both in rural and urban areas do not have the necessary capabilities to approach and negotiate with formal financial institutions. The drive of very poor people to help themselves through self-employment is ignored by the formal financial sector. Because the very poor have not traditionally been recognised as creditworthy or able to save, they are not perceived by the conventional agencies as bankable clientele for credit.

Further, the rural credit system entrapped by the twin problems of high transaction cost and poor repayment performance, reduces the profitability of rural branches of nationalised banks. The incompetence of management of individual banks also increased the non-viability of the rural credit delivery system (Analyst, 1993). The creditworthiness criteria adopted by institutional credit are alienating small farmers from borrowing as lending is closely linked to the landholding status of the borrower. The formal credit institutions neglected consumption needs of the poor and emphasised only on production credit. People continue, therefore, to depend on exploitative moneylenders, rotating savings and credit associations like chit funds. Paying exorbitant rates of interest to moneylenders, the poor remain poor, passing this burden, and often the debt too, on to future generations.

The spread of the system has been uneven across regions and wealth groups. The proportion of the poor obtaining credit from the banking system has been lower than their share in the total population. This was because of several reasons which include complicated procedures, distant location, cultural gap between officials and the poor, short banking hours, political interference, unscientific lending policies and absence of provision for consumption credit. Moreover, there is widespread belief that the poor are unbankable. There are also internal problems such as absence of linkages of credit with marketing and investment credit having no provision for working capital. Inadequate staff and managerial deficiencies within the banking system have also been causing problems (Rajasekhar, 1994).

The political environment is another problem which affects repayment of loans in India. Several state governments have enacted laws for writing-off all loans in default, of particular categories of borrowers. The Governments of Maharashtra (1978), Tamil Nadu (1979) and Andhra Pradesh (1987) are cases in point. The Union Government declared an amnesty in October 1989 on all overdue agricultural debts, with an outstanding balance of up to Rs. 10,000 [the Agricultural and Rural Debt Relief Scheme (ARDRS)]; a total amount of Rs. 13,000 crore was thus written-off. The combined effect of these past actions is eroding the credibility of threats from creditors to take punitive action in respect of small agricultural overdues (Mosley, 1996b).

The financial sector reforms begun in 1992 were intended to liberalise the financial sector. But the reforms have been systematically moving away from the social objectives of the banking sector by abolishing concessional interest rates, insisting on collateral security even for small borrowers and making large stipulated minimum balance compulsory for granting loans to small savers from the system (Mujumdar, 1995). In consequence, the number of small borrowal accounts has declined and it has resulted in misallocation of funds, especially diversion to investment (in government securities and A class securities) from credit to the small borrower, expansion of foreign banks new generation private banks serves only the elite in urban areas (Joshi, 1999). In short, the formal financial sector in India is shifting its focus from "mass banking" to "super-class banking".

Development Programmes of Government of India

Apart from these institutional arrangements, the Government of India have been launching a number of development programmes to improve the living conditions of the poor people.

The Community Development Movement started in 1952 and the National Extension Service started in 1953 were the foremost and the most forward-looking attempts in development process involving the rural community. In order to reduce the disparities between the affluent and the weaker sections, the Small and Marginal Farmers Development Agency (SFDA) was formed in 1968-69. It was the first innovative step towards a defined target group in India.

In addition, several programmes were launched by the Government of India for alleviating poverty. The important anti-poverty programmes may be broadly classified into programmes for: (i) self-employment and income generation to the poor (e.g. MFAL, SFDA, IRDP, DWCRA, etc.), (ii) programmes for wage-employment to the poor (e.g. RLEGP, EAS, FWP, PMRY, JRY, etc.), (iii) special area development programmes (e.g. DPAP, CAD, DDP, HADP, TADP, etc.), (iv) programmes imparting technology and skill formation (e.g. IADP, HYP, TRYSEM, SITRA, etc.), and (iv) programmes pertaining to land/institutional reforms (e.g. MWS, GKY, 20-Point Programme, etc.) (Table 4.1).

However, IRDP and DWCRA were the two programmes which directly reached the poor. An appraisal of these two programmes is given below:

Integrated Rural Development Programme (IRDP)

In 1977, Integrated Rural Development Programme (IRDP) was launched as a comprehensive programme covering all sectors of the rural economy: agriculture and allied activities, village and cottage industries and tertiary sector activities. It is the largest ever anti-poverty programme in India, launched during the Sixth Plan, uses the banking channel to direct assistance (by way of a combination of credit and subsidy) to households

Table: 4.1: Major Anti-Poverty Programmes of Government of India

Categories	*Programmes*
Programmes Providing Self-employment and Income Generation to the Poor	Marginal Farmers and Agricultural Labourers (MFAL) Small and Marginal Farmers Development Agency (SFDA) Integrated Rural Development Programme (IRDP) Development of Women and Children in Rural Areas (DWCRA)
Programmes Providing Wage-Employment to the Poor	Rural Landless Employment Guarantee Programme (RLEGP) Employment Assurance Scheme (EAS) Food for Work Programme (FWP) Prime Minister's Rozgar Yojana (PMRY) Jawahar Rozgar Yojana (JRY)
Special Area Development Programmes	Drought Prone Areas Programme (DPAP) Command Area Development (CAD) Desert Development Programme (DDP) Hill Area Development Programme (HADP) Tribal Area Development Programme (TADP)
Programmes Imparting Technology and Skill Formation	Intensive Agricultural Development Programme (IADP) Training Rural Youth for Self-Employment (TRYSEM)
Programmes Pertaining to Land/Institutional Reforms	Million Wells Scheme (MWS) Ganga Kalyan Yojana (GKY) 20-Point Programme

below the official poverty line. Thus the target group of the programme consists of small and marginal farmers, landless agricultural labourers, rural artisans, socially and economically deprived sections like SC/ST, women and the physically handicapped. The programme gave financial assistance to enhance production and employment opportunities. IRDP provided capital assets such as livestock and irrigation equipment to the rural poor and the landless through a mixture of government subsidy and loans from the banking system (in the ratio of 1:2). By March 1997, about 50 million poor families were covered with a total investment of Rs. 286 billion in the form of bank loans of Rs. 176 billion and a capital subsidy of Rs. 110 billion.

Drawbacks

Being a general government programme channelised through the state machinery, leakage of funds to the non-targeted non-poor was reportedly substantial. The real poor have found it difficult to gain access to the programme. The programme was not designed to meet the demand for small credit desired by the poor (i.e., accessible small amounts for consumption and working capital purpose) but was essentially supply driven (i.e., amount larger than absorption capacity for activities with which the poor were not familiar or which were not viable). Several evaluations of the IRDP show that the projects undertaken under the programme suffer from numerous defects especially sub-critical investment levels, unviable projects, lack of technical and institutional capabilities in designing and executing projects, utilising local resources and expertise, illiterate and unskilled beneficiaries with no experience in managing an enterprise, indifferent delivery of credit by banks (high transaction cost, complex procedure, corruption, one time credit and poor recovery), overcrowding of lending in certain projects such as dairy, poor targeting and selection of the non-poor; absence of linkage between different components of the IRDP, rising indebtedness, and the scale of operations of IRDP outstripping the capacity of government and banks to absorb.

Development of Women and Children in Rural Areas (DWCRA)

Development of Women and Children in Rural Areas (DWCRA) was an important sub-component of IRDP for providing self-employment opportunities to poor women on group basis. It aimed at starting income generating activities. Under DWCRA, a group of women is granted assistance to take up viable economic activities with Rs. 15,000 as a one-time grant to be used as a revolving fund. Each group consists of ten to fifteen women, which may take up economic activities suitable to their skills, aptitude and local conditions. The approach emphasises on activities of social welfare, health, nutrition, employment and education.

DWCRA was launched in the IRDP, at first as a pilot project, in fifty districts. In the Seventh Plan, it was extended to more districts. At the end of the Seventh Plan period it was in operation in 161 districts. In the Seventh Plan about 28,000 groups were formed against the target of 35,000, with a membership of 4.6 lakh women.

Drawbacks

In principle, this scheme is a sound one; but in practice, its impact has been inadequate. This is due to lack of cohesion among women groups formed under DWCRA and their inability to identify activities that could generate sustained incomes. Lack of training and skill formation and inability to find raw materials for the production process are other problems. Inadequate flow of finance to continue the income generating activities also constrained improvement of a lot of women (Damayanthi, 1999).

From the above account, it is clear that the Government of India launched a number of programmes and policies to alleviate poverty in the country through extending credit. But the institutions which were meant to cater to the needs of the rural poor and agriculturists failed to fulfil their objectives for various reasons. Most of them became unprofitable and unviable. The programmes which were launched (especially IRDP) also failed to reach the needy poor and the subsidies were cornered by the rich. The poor were driven away from approaching formal financial institutions. They continue to depend on usurious moneylenders and informal forms of credit.

In this context, a paradigm shift appears necessary for reaching the poor. International experience shows that lending through self help groups with members having similar risk characteristics, is successful. Small and homogeneous groups involved in savings and credit activities are expected to take care of these risks through peer monitoring. The credit fund, if it comes from an outside source, is disbursed to individual members according to agreed criteria and the group undertakes joint liability for debts of each member. Thus, joint liability provides incentives or compels the group to undertake the burden of selection, monitoring and enforcement that would otherwise fall on the lender (Rajasekhar, 1997).

Microfinance in India: An Overview

It was on this background, that the idea of microfinance emerged in India. In a vast country like India with multi-class societies and with heterogeneity in terms of religion, caste, language, agro-economic climate and social systems, a single model or approach may not be suitable for all regions. Freedom to adopt models best suited to the local conditions is essential to enhance financial services in these regions. As a result, numerous microfinance institutions/programmes of various types and structures emerged also in India, as was the case in other countries.

NGOs such as Self Employed Women's Association (SEWA) and Mysore Resettlement Development Agency (MYRADA) were the pioneers in the field. Later many more came into the field. NABARD also launched a programme for linking formal financial institutions with the informal groups. Government of India initiated programmes like Rashtriya Mahila Kosh (RMK), Swarna Jayanthi Shahari Swarozgar Yojana (SJSSY), and Swarnajayanti Grama Swarozgar Yojana (SGSY) to reach the poor.

Microfinance and NGOs

In India, a major step towards enlisting the support of NGOs for rural development was taken while formulating the Seventh Five Year Plan. It was stated in the plan document that serious efforts would be made to involve voluntary agencies in developmental programmes. During this plan period (1985-1990) it gave a substantial role to NGOs, particularly in the areas of rural development, basic needs and poverty alleviation. Today, NGOs operate over a wide range of activities, including government's anti-poverty programmes, training of rural youth, promotion of safe drinking water, rural housing, promotion of Science and Technology, wasteland development, health care and family welfare, education and welfare of women, children, S.C. and S.T.

In India there are 15,000 registered NGOs and many more non-registered informal groups. These organisations have touched the lives of an estimated number of 15 million persons. According to an international estimate, 100 million persons have been helped worldwide by NGOs of one sort or other. NGOs follow different methods to reach the poor. Those who follow the 'grassroot' or the 'barefoots' approach have attracted a good deal of admiration (Dunkley, 1993).

NGOs contribute significantly to improving the quality, sustainability and effectiveness of social programmes by:

(i) Developing and experimenting with innovative approaches;
(ii) Promoting popular participation and community ownership;
(iii) Encouraging programme uptake;
(iv) Extending benefits to those segments of the population otherwise difficult to reach (e.g. Tribals).

Microfinance helps the NGOs all over the world in alleviation of urban and rural poverty through promoting microenterprises as a solution to the problems of unemployment and underemployment among the poor. NGOs undertake the responsibility of forming self help groups, give training to members, and monitor business performance and promptness in repayment.

In India also, NGOs use this methodology for financing the poor. MYRADA in Karnataka and SEWA in Gujarat are the forerunners in the field in India. SEWA has promoted a co-operative bank exclusively for women and is engaged in financing income generating activities of women. Friends of Women's World Banking (FWWB) Ahmedabad, an affiliate of Women's World Banking, New York, co-ordinates with NGOs in giving financial assistance to women groups. The Working Women's Forum (WWF) Chennai has organised women co-operative societies for pursuing income generating activities and has facilitated empowerment of women. Attempts have also been made to replicate Bangladesh Grameen Bank model by SHARE in Andhra Pradesh and RDO in Manipur (Agarwal *et al.*, 1997).

Typology of NGOs in India

The institutions which engage in microfinance services in India follow three types of approaches, namely:

(i) The Grameen Bank approach;
(ii) The co-operative societies (which are members of a co-operative bank) approach;
(iii) The SHG Programme approach.

The Grameen Bank Approach

Some NGOs follow the model developed by the Grameen Bank of Bangladesh. They undertake individual lending but all the borrowers are members of groups within which peer pressure is the key factor in ensuring repayment. Each borrower's creditworthiness is determined by the overall creditworthiness of the group. Savings are a compulsory component of the loan repayment schedule but they do not determine the magnitude or timing of the loan.

The Grameen Bank Approach has been applied in various parts of the world, with replications in developing countries such as Malaysia, the Philippines, Indonesia, Sri Lanka, India, Vietnam, Bhutan, Guinea, Kenya, Malawi, Zambia, Mali and Burkina Faso in Africa, Chile, Bolivia and Peru in South America, Nepal and Pakistan. It has also been adopted in

Canada, France and the U.S., where it is being used to help people become income generators. Society for Helping and Awakening Rural Poor through Education (SHARE) in Andhra Pradesh and Nirdhan in West Bengal are examples of this model in India.

The Co-operative Societies (which are Members of a Co-operative Bank) Approach

In the case of co-operative banks, all borrowers are members of the organisation either directly or indirectly, being members of primary co-operatives or associations which themselves are members of the bank. Credit worthiness and loan security are a function of co-operative membership within which peer pressure is assumed to be a key factor. The magnitude of savings and the timing of loans are unrelated though a special effort is made to mobilise savings from members. There are only a handful of co-operative credit societies in India devoted specifically for providing financial services to the poor.

The SHG Programme Approach

The operations of SHGs are based on the principle of revolving of the members' own savings. External financial assistance augments the resources available to the group-operated revolving fund. Savings thus precede borrowing by the members. In many SHG programmes, the volume of individual borrowing is determined either by the volume of member savings or the savings of the group as a whole. The vast majority of MFIs in India have SHG-based programmes (Dunkley, 1993).

However, there are two distinct models, which are emerging in the SHG-led microcredit movement in India: an organic model and an affiliation frame model. An 'organic model' is based on bottom-up approaches. Mutually Aided Cooperative Societies (MACS) in Andhra Pradesh is an example of this model. The 'affiliation frame', falls in the category of super-imposed structural arrangements. The bank linkage programme of NABARD is one such example (Mohanan, 2002).

NGOs in India: An Appraisal

In Bangladesh and Pakistan, NGOs have developed national networks. But in India, NGOs continue to work in very limited areas; say a few villages, a block, or a district. Moreover, the distribution of effective NGOs is very uneven across the country. While the state of Gujarat has one NGO per 29,184 persons, Kerala has one NGO for 41,532 persons. On the other hand, the corresponding number for more backward states is much larger: one NGO per 119,016 persons in Madhya Pradesh and 102,313 persons in Rajasthan (Misra, 2002).

While many NGOs enjoy strong community ties and are credible and competent, there are several NGOs which are inexperienced, inefficient or stronger in rhetoric than in action. NGOs often lack organisational and financial skills, and need significant inputs with regard to capacity building. A number of international NGOs are now working closely with national NGOs to strengthen the latter financially and through networking support.

NABARD and Microfinance

National Bank for Agriculture and Rural Development (NABARD) is the apex financial body in India for rural development and agriculture through refinancing. With the formal credit system failing to effectively reach the poorest of the poor, various alternatives were being explored by NABARD to find a solution. The concept of self help group as one of the alternatives caught the attention of NABARD during the 1980s. To gather a definite feedback on the SHG-Bank linkage, an Action Research Project on "Savings and Credit Management of SHGs" sponsored by MYRADA was funded by NABARD in 1986-87. The project results provided useful insights into aspects like dynamics of group organisation, saving potential, approach to use of financial resources, prioritisation of needs and repayment performance.

SHG Linkage

An innovative scheme in rural delivery system launched by NABARD is the linking of SHGs of the poor with banks and bulk lending through NGOs. NABARD considers SHGs a pre-microenterprise stage for a majority of the rural population. The linkage project envisages active involvement of NGOs who play a crucial role in formation, nurturing, stabilising and guiding the SHGs into cohesive and dynamic groups inculcating the habits of thrifts and credit management and ultimately establishing linkage with the banks (see Appendix VI).

The pilot project of linking the SHGs was introduced in the year 1992. Besides 100 per cent refinance support to the banks, NABARD provides policy guidance, technical and promotional support mainly for capacity building of NGOs and SHGs, the exposure training to banks/NGOs having potential and in promoting SHGs. External funding like bank credit is infused into the groups only after proper evaluation of the functioning and ascertaining their maturity. After six months of initial membership, the group members are considered for linkage of formal credit for income generating activities.

Under the SHG-bank linkage programme, three linkage models have broadly emerged. Under the first model, banks directly link SHGs without the intervention of the NGOs. In the second model, banks provide credit to SHGs and NGOs act as Self Help Promoting Institutions (SHPIs). Under the third model, NGOs act both as SHPIs and financial intermediaries for channelising credit from banks to SHGs.

NABARD provides refinance support to banks under the linkage project. As per operational guidelines of NABARD, banks sanction savings-linked loans to SHGs (varying from a saving to loan ratio of 1:1 to 1:4). The present interest rate structure stipulated by NABARD at different levels under the SHG-Bank Linkage Programme is as shown on next page.

(i)	NABARD to Banks (Refinance)	: 6.5%
(ii)	Banks to SHG	: 12.0%
(iii)	Banks to NGOs/Voluntary Agencies	: 10.5%
(iv)	NGO/Voluntary Agencies to SHGs	: 12.0%
(v)	SHG to members	: As decided by the SHG

Progress of Linkage Programme in India

The progress of the linkage programme in India is encouraging. The cumulative number of SHGs linked with commercial banks, RRBs and co-operative banks up to March 2007 is 2,924,973, of which 686,408 SHGs are provided with loans during 2006-07. The linkage programme covered 587 districts in India. The total number of households covered is nearly 40.95 million. The coverage of women under the SHG linkage programme was 90 per cent (Table 4.2).

Table 4.2: Progress of SHG Linkage Programme in India

Cumulative No. of SHGs provided with bank loan up to 31 March 2007	2,924,973
No. of new SHGs provided with bank loan during 2006-07	686,408
Percentage of women groups	90
No. of participating banks	498
No. of districts covered	587
Bank Loan Rs. in billion	180.41
No. of poor households assisted (in million)	40.95

Source: NABARD annual report, 2007.

About 498 various banks participate in this programme all over the country. Through these bank branches loans worth Rs. 180.41 billion were disbursed to the SHGs as of March 2007. Thus the average loan amount disbursed to SHG comes to approximately Rs. 44,342. Thus the linkage programme helped the poor to move nearer to formal financial institutions to some extent.

The quick studies conducted by NABARD in a few states to assess the impact of the linkage project have brought out encouraging and positive features like increase in loan volume of the SHGs, definite shift in the loaning pattern of the members from non-income generating activities to production activities and significant reduction in the transaction costs for both the banks and the borrowers. Repayment levels of the loans under this project are almost 100 per cent.

At the same time, there are some disparities in the spread of this programme in the country. The southern states had a lion's share (of 52%). The states in central region had a total of eleven per cent and eastern region had seventeen per cent of the linked groups. The western region had a share of ten per cent. The northern region and north eastern region performed very poorly with only six per cent and four per cent respectively.

As microfinance has emerged as an effective tool for alleviating poverty, the Central Government directed NABARD and Small Industries Development Bank of India (SIDBI) to cover 50,000 SHGs to develop microenterprises. To give a further boost to this programme a Micro Finance Development Fund was created in NABARD with a start up contribution of Rs. 100 crore from RBI, NABARD, banks and other financial agencies. This fund would provide start up funds to microfinance institutions and infrastructure support for training and systems management and data building. Special emphasis would be placed on promotion of microenterprises in rural areas set up by vulnerable sections including women, SC, ST and OBC. Successive Union budgets have laid emphasis on microfinance.

Government Programmes and Microfinance

Government of India had initiated IRDP and DWCRA for reaching the poor with credit facilities. Later, it was found that these programmes failed to reach the needy due to various reasons. Therefore, the government launched some other programmes—RMK, SJSRY and SGSY—to enhance the living conditions of the poor through self-employment activities.

Rashtriya Mahila Kosh (RMK)

The National Credit Fund for Women (Rashtriya Mahila Kosh) was set up on 30th March 1993 with a corpus fund of Rs. 31 crore with the major objective of meeting the credit needs of poor women, particularly in the informal sector. Its main objectives were the following:

(i) To facilitate credit to poor women for generation of their employment and to promote and support experiments in the voluntary sector using innovative methodologies;
(ii) To sensitise the existing government delivery mechanisms and increase the visibility of poor women as vital and viable clients for benefiting from credit;
(iii) To promote networking of grassroots level organisations for experience-sharing and development of skills in social organisation and entrepreneurship amongst women.

RMK provides short-term loans (repayable in fifteen months) up to Rs. 4,000 per borrower and medium term loans (repayable in two to five years) up to Rs. 6,000. The rate of interest on these borrowings is eight per cent to the NGO or other financing institution, which may lend either to poor women directly or through women's self help groups. In case, loans are channelised through SHGs, the SHGs may charge up to 18.75 per cent on the members (Misra, 2002).

The RMK extended benefits to 549,641 women through 1,244 NGOs (Table 4.3). Besides extending microfinance, RMK has adopted a scheme to support the formation and stabilisation of women's SHGs. Under this scheme RMK has given an interest-free loan of Rupees one lakh for formation and stabilisation of 55,434 SHGs in India. The loan is convertible into grant on fulfilment of certain conditions. As on 2006-07, an amount of Rs. 18,714.84 lakh was sanctioned to SHGs out of which Rs. 14,987.72 lakh were disbursed.

Table 4.3: Year-wise achievement of Rashtriya Mahila Kosh

Year	*Loan Sanc-tioned*	*Loan Disbursed*	*No. of NGOs/No. of Others*	*No. of SHGs*	*No. of Women benefi-ciaries*
1993-1994	439.33	140.82	24	3707	37066
1994-1995	512.45	29.53	28	2506	25059
1995-1996	861.66	563.83	48	3750	37502
1996-1997	1700.55	916.76	70	9106	91064
1997-1998	1271.40	1395.39	85	5962	59621
1998-1999	1484.62	1141.50	133	5198	51982
1999-2000	1958.75	1384.64	324	5809	58089
2000-2001	2118.50	1675.80	151	4656	46559
2001-2002	739.11	633.76	154	1618	16183
2002-2003	1600.23	1058.37	89	4430	44290
2003-2004	2505.60	1446.07	69	3637	36371
2004-2005	1549.74	1886.87	40	2232	22321
2005-2006	1930.90	2068.42	82	2730	27305
2006-2007	42.00	234.15	09	93	930
Total	**18714.84**	**14987.72**	**1244**	**55434**	**549641**

Source: RMK website.

Swarna Jayanti Shahari Rozgar Yojana (SJSRY)

The Swarna Jayanti Shahari Rozgar Yojana (SJSRY) which subsumed the earlier three urban poverty programmes, viz., Nehru Rozgar Yojana (NRY), Urban Basic Services for the Poor (UBSP) and Prime Minister's Integrated Urban Poverty Alleviation Programme (PMIUPAP) came into operation from December 1997. It seeks to provide employment to the urban unemployed or under-employed people below the poverty line and educated up to tenth standard, through encouraging the setting up of self-employment ventures or provision of wage employment. The scheme gives special impetus to empower and uplift poor women and launches a special programme called Development of Women and Children in Urban Areas (DWCUA) under which groups of urban poor women setting up self-employment ventures are eligible for subsidy up to

50 per cent of the project cost. An allocation of Rs. 181 crore has been made in 1999-2000 (Budget Estimate).

The SJSRY rests on a foundation of community empowerment. It operates as a single window mechanism of community-based organisations that support all poverty alleviation programmes, social sector schemes and environmental improvement schemes in urban centres. This programme relies on the traditional method of top-down implementation, but it relies more on creating and promoting community based structures, organisation of women to provide institutionalised mechanism for local development and participation of communities as active stakeholders.

SJSRY has two components such as the Urban Self Employment Programme (USEP) and the Urban Wage Employment Programme (UWEP) which give assistance to individuals. The Urban Self Employment Programme consists of assistance to individual urban poor, assistance to groups of urban poor women under DWCAU and training of beneficiaries/potential beneficiaries by the concerned department of the state government.

Swarnajayanti Gram Swarozgar Yojana (SGSY)

The self-employment programmes of IRDP, Training of Rural Youth for Self Employment (TRYSEM), Development of Women and Children in Rural areas (DWCRA), Ganga Kalyan Yojana (GKY) and Million Wells Scheme (MWS) have all been merged into a single self-employment programme called the Swarnajayanti Gram Swarozgar Yojana (SGSY). The major objectives of the programme are: (a) focused approach to poverty alleviation, (b) capitalising advantages of group-lending and (c) overcoming problems associated with the multiplicity of programmes.

The scheme seeks to focus on the formation of self help groups. It is a holistic programme of microenterprises covering all aspects of self-employment, viz., organisation of the rural poor into self help groups and their capacity building, planning of activity clusters, infrastructure build up, technology, credit and marketing. It lays emphasis on activity clusters based on the resources and the occupational skills of the people and availability of markets. The activities would be taken up in suitable clusters to enable extension of appropriate facilities. The major share of SGSY assistance will be in activity clusters.

It integrates various agencies—District Rural Development Agency (DRDA), banks, line departments, Panchayat Raj Institutions (PRIs), NGOs and other semi-government organisations. Selection of key activities will be with the approval of the Panchayat Samitis at the block level and the District Rural Development Agency (DRDA) or Zila Parishad (ZP) at the district level. The *grama sabha* will authenticate the list of families below the poverty line identified in the Below Poverty Line (BPL) census. Identification of individual Swarozgaris (self-employed persons) will be made through a participatory process. The objective of SGSY is to bring the existing poor families above the poverty line by providing them income generating assets through a mix of bank credit and government subsidy and to ensure that an assisted family has a monthly net income of at least Rs. 2,000. Subsidy under SGSY is uniform at 30 per cent of the project cost subject to a maximum of Rs. 7,500. In respect of SC and ST, it is 50 per cent subject to a maximum of Rs. 10,000. For SHGs, the subsidy is 50 per cent subject to a ceiling of Rs. 1.25 lakh. SGSY is funded by the centre and states in the ratio of 75:25.

At least half of the groups at the block level are to be exclusively women's groups. It aims at establishing a large number of microenterprises in the rural areas. A significant aspect of SGSY is that every family assisted under this programme will be brought above the poverty line in three years and thus aims at creating substantial additional incomes for the rural poor. It is proposed to cover 30 per cent of the rural poor in each block within a period of five years. The programme has been designed to provide proper support and encouragement to tap the inherent talents and capabilities of the rural poor. It targets at reaching at least 50 per cent women and three per cent disabled.

Table 4.4: SHGs under SGSY, Indian States (as in November 2000)

State	*SHGs formed*	*Persons Taking up economic activities*	*Percentage of disadvantaged*				*Credit disbursed (lakhs)*	*Subsidy Disbursed (lakhs)*
			SC	*ST*	*Women*	*Handicapped*		
Andhra Pradesh	197,617	2,171	37.31	9.25	64.71	2.71	3,295.23	1,881.55
Assam	4,895	189	14.42	29.40	47.79	0.59	215.23	96.02
Bihar	7,788	2,193	29.27	1.10	28.35	0.26	5,526.55	2,868.83
Chandigarh	11,528	1,624	8.43	49.89	38.72	0.08	328.36	149.36
Gujarat	3,439	303	15.96	34.45	32.08	1.33	1,785.47	1,028.00
Haryana	482	3	24.57	0	28.88	0.40	772.57	231.30
Himachal Pradesh	1,635	543	37.28	12.34	51.42	0.52	1,082.54	344.55
Jharkhand	3,920	808	20.60	38.25	35.77	1.23	2,210.68	1,223.50
Karnataka	4,103	961	32.52	8.05	63.07	1.12	804.04	480.33
Kerala	11,703	267	29.90	1.60	57.37	0.44	1,494.94	733.90
Madhya Pradesh	24,682	351	22.94	29.28	25.23	0.56	3,097.50	1,319.41
Maharashtra	12,411	505	21.97	12.79	33.22	0.40	4,316.90	1,607.39
Orissa	14,712	364	25.14	20.75	24.87	0.33	2,739.63	1,555.31
Punjab	649	35	60.22	0	32.43	0.51	918.96	394.57
Rajasthan	1,139	7	24.55	16.93	36.22	0.53	4,821.75	1,359.72
Tamil Nadu	34,190	2,053	48.38	0.84	83.60	0.45	3,541.76	2,341.51
Uttar Pradesh	28,888	42	47.26	1.04	27.34	0.69	2,000.04	984.28
Uttaranchal	2,004	0	40.58	14.49	5.80	0	16.73	5.73
West Bengal	5,158	569	35.69	7.71	77.46	0.08	250.34	130.32
All-India	**371,003**	**13,208**	**29.42**	**13.93**	**44.5**	**0.73**	**29,858.77**	**19,080.86**

Source: Mohiuddin *et al.*, 2001.

As on November 2000, 371,003 self help groups had come into existence under SGSY programme. Of these groups, 13,208 have taken up some economic activities. Nearly 45 per cent of them are women groups, 29.42 per cent are SC groups, 13.93 per cent are ST groups and 0.73 per cent groups are handicapped. Through these groups Rs. 29,858.77 lakh was disbursed. Of this Rs. 19,080.86 lakh was subsidy (Table 4.4). Among the states, Andhra Pradesh formed the highest number of SHGs (197,617) which accounted for 53 per cent of the total groups formed in the country. On the other hand, Haryana has the least number of groups, 482 (0.13%).

Criticisms

Although these programmes are laudable, they are not free from criticism. The new programmes such as SJSRY and SGSY have been saddled with the burden of subsidies. Subsidies are provided under the premise that the poor are not credit worthy and therefore, their needs must be catered to by a system of subsidy-driven programmes and charity-driven implementation agencies. Unfortunately, while programmes such as the SGSY have the full weight of the government behind them, MFI/Ps have to battle a highly restrictive legal framework and an unhelpful, even unfriendly, political environment. Yet, if support for poverty reduction programmes is really the means by which politicians wish to prove their empathy with the people there is another way: enable the spread and growth of a network of professional institutions that are dedicated to serving the financial needs of the poor. But, programmes such as the SGSY hold only short-term satisfaction for the government in proving the poverty focus of its programmes. In the long-term it carries the risk not only of failure but also of corrupting the more sustainable microfinance system emerging in the country (Sinha, 2000).

The inadequacy of formal financial institutions in India and of other institutional arrangements and of development programmes led to the unprecedented growth of microfinance activities in India. NGOs were in the forefront in popularising the idea of microfinance in India. SEWA, MYRADA and WWF did a commendable work. The NABARD accepted the idea and launched a project to link the SHGs formed by the various NGOs and other organisations with the commercial and other banks in the country. The Government of India is also trying to reach the poor through various programmes of microfinance such as SGSY and SJSRY. Yet, there remains a wide gap between the reached and the unreached poor in the country. There exists also a need for evaluation of these programmes and organisations at the national level in order to get a complete picture of the performance of these institutions.

5

The Kerala Model and Relevance of Microfinance

Kerala is a small state in the southern part of India. But it has gained international acclaim due to its development experience during the second half of the twentieth century. The basic characteristic of Kerala's experience is that it has gained high levels of social development despite low levels of per capita income. In Kerala, 94.2 per cent of the males and 87.9 per cent of females are literate. The corresponding figures for all-India are 75.9 per cent and 54.2 per cent for men and women respectively. The sex ratio in Kerala (1058/1000 males in 2001) is higher than that of most countries in South Asia. The infant mortality rate is also one among the lowest in the country with 17 per 1000 live births. The female life expectancy of 74.4 years is the highest among all the Indian states. The male life expectancy is also high, but five years lesser than women's (68.8 years). One of the peculiarities of Kerala's development experience is that there is not much gender difference in social development compared to other states in India. It can be argued that the Kerala model owes its genesis to Kerala women.

In spite of these achievements in the social sector, women in Kerala face a variety of problems such as educational discrimination, gender discrimination in the labour market, wage discrimination, deprivation, lack of health care, violence and sexual atrocities and lack of public space. Many of the problems of women have gone unattended and neglected by social reform movements and organisations in Kerala. Section one of this chapter gives an account of women's position in Kerala economy, their strengths and limitations.

In section two, the institutional arrangements which took place in Kerala and their limitations are dealt with. In Kerala, prior to attainment of independence, formal financial institutions had been set up. In 1914 itself, the Travancore state introduced the cooperative movement. Commercial banks had started functioning in the rural and semi-urban areas of Kerala from the first quarter of twentieth century. This was because of the commercial character of the state's economy. In terms of per capita deposits and average population per branch, Kerala fares well compared to other states in the country. But in the case of credit-deposit ratio, Kerala stands far behind. This has a direct impact on the poor sections of the population in the state.

It was against this background that the idea of microfinance came up. Microfinance is now considered as a solution to many problems faced by the women in Kerala, especially emancipation from low economic and social status. Many microfinance institutions and programmes (MFI/Ps) have been launched in Kerala by different agencies. Besides, the state government has been keen in forming self help groups among poor women for imparting the benefits of microfinance to them. A programme known as 'Kudumbashree' has come up under government auspices. The People's Plan Campaign (PPC) initiated during the Ninth Five Year Plan period saw women self help groups as micro level organisations for developing political participation and empowerment of women. The relevance and emergence of various programmes and institutions in the field of microfinance in Kerala are discussed in section three.

Women and Kerala Model of Development

The 'Kerala Model of Development' has its roots in the history. The Maharani of Travancore declared thus in 1817: 'the state shall defray the entire cost of the education of its people in order that there may be no backwardness in the spread of enlightenment among them, that by the diffusion of education they become better subjects and public servants.' Later in 1865, the Maharaja of Travancore made the following statement at the opening of the Trivandrum civil hospital, 'I take this opportunity earnestly to impress this fact on the minds of all my native subjects and to urge them to seek for themselves, for their children, for their friends and their servants the great protection of vaccination. They will see the strength of my conviction in the fact that there is no member in my family who has not had this protection conferred at an early age.' These two pronouncements show that the rulers of pre-independent Kerala, at least in the parts ruled over by native princes, had made valuable contributions in the field of social development.

During the post-independence period also, various governments, in the face of mounting demand of the public, promoted liberally the social development process of the state. Kerala has stood ahead of the rest of the country in social sector development for the past several decades. Even though it is an advanced state from the demographic and the social development point of view, Kerala remains one of the poorest states in the country, in terms of economic development with low per capita income ($ 420), wide income disparities, and high incidence of unemployment, especially among the educated.

It may be argued that the Kerala model is indebted to Kerala women and that, in turn, it has helped women in Kerala. The matrilineal family tradition and female education surely helped the state's social development. Women in Kerala enjoy high life expectancy, high literacy, and low maternal mortality when compared to their counterparts in other Indian states. These are the results of the indiscriminate treatment given to women in terms of health and education. But with the unsustainability of the Kerala model of development looming large, the recurrence of economic crises has adversely affected the life of women in the state in different ways. Consequently, their social and cultural life is also facing challenges.

Education

In terms of literacy, Kerala women fare well. This is evident from Fig. 5.1. The literacy level of women in Kerala was higher than the all-Indian average even before the attainment of independence. The 2001 census shows that the literacy level of females in Kerala is as high as 87.90 per cent. The corresponding figure for India is only 54.20 per cent.

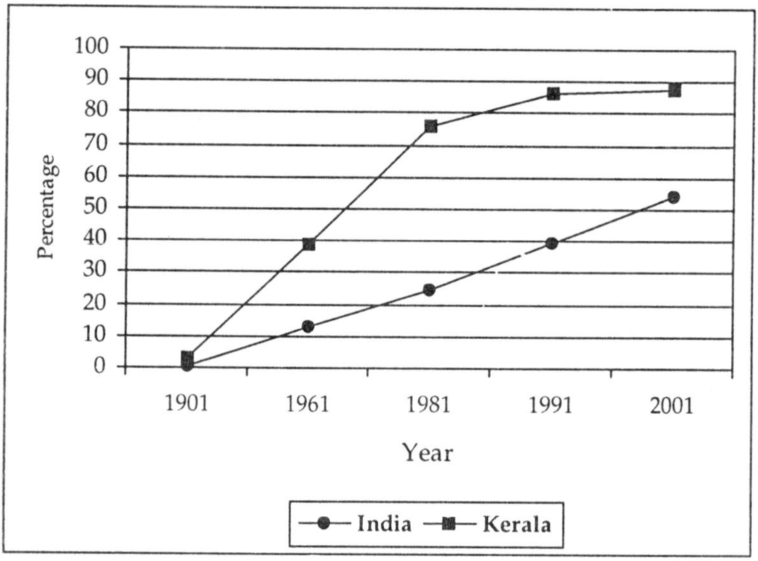

Fig. 5.1: Trend in Female Literacy

In the field of higher education also, women in Kerala are in the forefront. They form more than 50 per cent of the total number of students enrolled at the tertiary level. Of all the college students in Kerala in 1994, 54 per cent in the pre-degree course, 60 per cent in the degree course and 64 per cent in the postgraduate course were women. Out of the India's total female population in 1991, only 3.9 per cent is in Kerala. But the share of Kerala's women in higher education is 6.3 per cent of all-India. On the other hand, the share of females in technical education is very low.

Unemployment

Kerala shows a paradox in the matter of unemployment. Unemployment in Kerala is the highest in India. The unemployment rates in Kerala are several times the national rate. The rate of unemployment among females is still higher. While the unemployment rate of men in rural Kerala is 83 per thousand persons as against the Indian figure of 21, for women the corresponding figures are 309 and 31 per cent (Table 5.1). The same trend can be observed in the case of urban areas also.

Table 5.1: Usual Status unemployment rates during 2004-05 per 1000 persons

	Rural			*Urban*		
	Male	*Female*	*Persons*	*Male*	*Female*	*Persons*
Kerala	83	309	158	90	429	199
All India	21	31	25	44	91	53

Source: Government of Kerala, 2007.

A significant and peculiar feature of Kerala's unemployment is that women outnumber men who seek employment through employment exchanges. Women job-seekers in the year 2000 numbered 23.13 lakh compared to 18.72 lakh men. In other words, 54.5 per cent of the unemployed persons registered in the employment exchange of Kerala are women.

At the same time, non-availability of workers is felt in some sectors such as plantations and construction. In-migration of labourers from neighbouring states is also taking place. Likewise out-migration of female labour from Kerala to other states for low wage employment in prawn peeling and similar activities is also considerable. A large number of women also emigrate seeking jobs like nurses, teachers and housemaids.

Work Participation

In all the economies of the world, with economic development, work participation among women is found to increase. Paradoxically in Kerala with economic growth female work participation rates are found to remain low and declining. From 19.7 per cent in 1961, it decreased to 16.61 per cent in 1981 and to 15.85 per cent in 1991. The 2001 census shows the rate has stagnated at the 1991 level. The spread of higher education among women and the prevailing low birth rates should normally be expected to raise women's work participation rate.

Table 5.2 shows the employment in the public and private sectors in Kerala from 1997 to 2005. While 7.3 lakh men were engaged in employment, the corresponding figure for women was only 4.48 lakhs. The data show a general decline in employment status among men and women in the state, but the more affected are the women.

Table 5.2: Employment in the public and private sectors in Kerala

Year	*Women*	*Men*	*Total*	*Index*
1997	448156	730060	1178216	100
1998	464019	755566	1219585	103.51
1999	477864	754400	1232264	104.59
2000	487257	764275	1251532	106.22
2001	484159	749946	1234105	104.74
2002	473604	746700	1220304	103.57
2003	464218	704615	1168833	99.2
2004	453310	692561	1145871	97.26
2005	430345	671693	1102038	93.53

Source: Government of Kerala, 2007.

The primary sector which is the mainstay of employment of women has been losing its importance in Kerala economy. Decline in cottage industries, fall in the area of paddy cultivation and mechanisation of agricultural operations have reduced women's work opportunities. Activities like rice husking, plaiting of coconut leaves, basket making and mat weaving which were done exclusively by women have decreased drastically. Women have lost jobs in various other traditional activities as well due to modernisation, e.g., services of washerwomen, physicians and midwives, nurses (women used to give maternity and child care), of the traditional type.

Table 5.3: Changes in the Employment Structure of Women in Kerala

Industrial activity	*Employment structure*			*Female-male ratio*		
	1961	*1981*	*1991*	*1961*	*1981*	*1991*
Total workers	100	100	100	427	321	296
Cultivators	16.25	4.95	5.56	302	101	116
Agricultural labourers	27.42	43.55	36.09	893	599	477
Other primary sector	5.27	6.73	6.96	223	188	184
Primary sector: subtotal	**48.94**	**55.33**	**48.61**			
Cottage industry	17.82	7.65	5.93	1590	1014	1110
Non-household industry	8.11	12.47	14.78	347	330	411
Construction workers	0.18	0.85	0.94	44	74	57
Secondary sector: subtotal	**26.11**	**20.97**	**21.65**			
Trade	1.41	3.22	4.54	80	76	91
Transport and communication	0.45	1.60	1.50	52	84	61
Other services	23.09	18.98	23.65	376	525	553
Tertiary sector: subtotal	**24.95**	**23.80**	**29.69**			

Source: Census of India, 1991.

The proportion of women agricultural labourers decreased during the period from 1981 to 1991 due mainly to decline in the area of paddy cultivation. The areas under foodcrops are increasingly shifted to other crops especially cash crops like rubber. In paddy cultivation, women did the jobs like planting, weeding and harvesting. But in rubber cultivation, most jobs go to men. Modernisation and mechanisation of traditional industries also reduce employment opportunities for women. The decreasing proportions of women's participation in primary sector jobs and jobs in cottage industries are reflected clearly in the sex ratio shown in Table 5.3. As most of the women are unskilled and untrained, they are not able to take up the jobs in modernised industrial units. One example is coir industry. It was a woman-intensive sector; but it is now increasingly moving towards mechanisation. In 1961, cottage industry accounted for about 18 per cent of the total employment of women; the proportion declined to less than eight per cent in 1981 and further to nearly six per cent in 1991.

In the registered factories sector of Kerala, women are employed, but mostly in conventional types of low-paid jobs. For instance, three-fourths of the total workers in food-processing industries such as cashew, coffee and fruit processing are women. Also 50 to 75 per cent of women are engaged in embroidery, garment-making and matchbox manufacturing. Likewise, in the fish processing units 40 to 50 per cent are women. All these industries consist of small units, employing women at low levels of wages. In more modern industries such as oil mills, textile mills, powerlooms and tea factories, the proportion of women in the workforce is less than one-fifth.

Most of the jobs done by Kerala women are of the informal, unskilled and unorganised type. Such jobs require neither training nor expertise. In the employment sector, it is usually the low-paid jobs that are set apart for women. Now, women are offered higher order jobs also. Most women workers in the tertiary sector are found in stores as sales-girls, in food-processing units and petrol pumps. In these places, wages are very low—even lower than the prescribed minimum wages—with poor working conditions.

Table 5.4: Wage Differentials between Women and Men in the Unorganised Sector (In Rupees)

Year	*Construction sector*		*Agriculture sector*	
	Male	Female	Male	Female
1980-81	12.30	9.62	11.13	7.91
1985-86	25.31	19.08	26.08	15.10
1990-91	37.34	29.23	35.77	21.11
1995-96	76.59	62.80	77.17	51.17
1996-97	88.19	73.80	92.18	60.52

Source: Economics and Statistics Department, Government of Kerala (various issues).

Employment rights are not safeguarded in many sectors especially in the unorganised sector. In the unorganised sector, casualisation of labour, taking workers on contracts and quotations to work teams, are on the increase. This development also affects the womenfolk badly. Labour laws are not observed for the well-being of women. Denial of maternity leave, non-preference of married women for work, lack of crèche facilities for child care, denial or inadequate provision of sanitation facilities and long hours of work are some of the problems faced by the working women in the sector.

Apart from the exploitation of female labour in terms of poor working conditions and denial of basic rights, there is ample evidence of a gender bias in wage rates as well; wage differential between women and men is quite large in many occupations. Table 5.4 shows a wide wage differential in the sectors viz., construction and agriculture in which large numbers of female workers are concentrated. During 1996-97, in construction sector, while males were able to fetch on an average Rs. 88.19, females earned only Rs. 73.80. The differential in the agricultural sector is even wider. During 1996-97, the average wage rates were Rs. 92.18 and Rs. 60.52 for males and females respectively.

Poverty

Land reforms, collective bargaining, social welfare schemes, and universal education have ameliorated the intensity of poverty in Kerala to a certain extent. The available evidence shows that the absolute number of the poor in Kerala is steadily declining in recent years. The successive rounds of National Sample Survey found out that the head count index of poverty is decreasing. In rural areas it was 66.88 in 1957 as against 31.07 in 1994. In urban areas the corresponding figures are 52.60 and 23.07 respectively. At constant prices, the mean consumption expenditure per month increased from Rs. 47.27 in 1957 for rural areas to 73.44 in 1994, for urban areas the increase was from Rs. 60.59 and Rs. 89.32. This is due to steady improvement in the distribution of foodgrains all over the state through an effective public distribution system.

However, indications are that the number of female-headed households below the poverty line has been increasing. About 35 per cent of the families below the poverty line in Kerala are female-headed. Girl children in poor families are discriminated against boys in terms of education and health. Further, for making a livelihood, poor women are often forced to work in low-paid and stressful jobs in the absence of alternatives.

Health

Kerala performed well in terms of health indicators such as low mortality rates, high life expectancy and favourable sex ratio. While the expectation of life at birth among females in India was 23.2 years in 1911, the corresponding figure for Kerala was 27.4 years. The gap between all-India figures and figures for Kerala has been progressively widening over the decades, which is shown in Fig. 5.2.

Increase in life expectancy has led to a steady rise in the proportion of the population of the aged. Kerala leads all other Indian states in respect of the proportion of women above the age of 60. Moreover, even the distribution of elderly women among the three age groups—60-64 years, 65-69 years and 70-

plus, is strikingly different in Kerala from that of all-India. The population of elderly women in Kerala, which was 0.1 million in 1961, is expected to increase to 0.6 million in 2011.

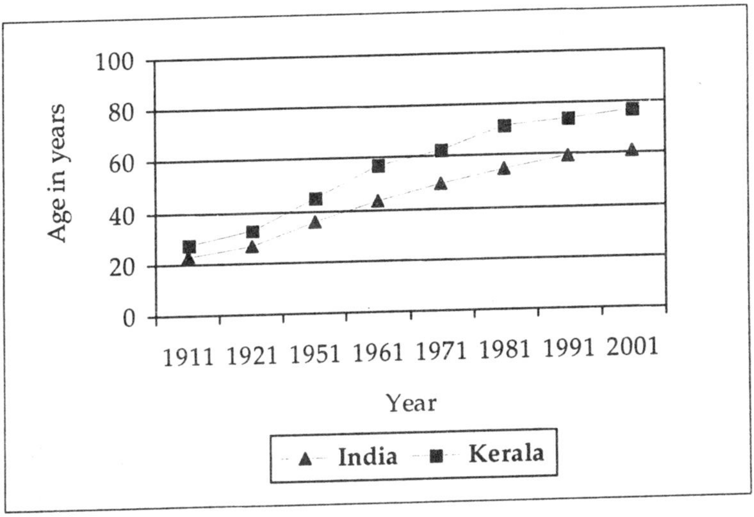

Fig. 5.2: Female Life Expectancy

There exist a few security measures in Kerala to rescue the aged from familial isolation. The proportion of widows in the aged population is higher than that of widowers due to the higher expectation of life of women and the age difference between spouses. The age of wife is usually lower than that of husband, on the average, by more than five years. The heavy female concentration among the very old, mostly widows, is emerging as a grave social problem for Kerala; while only one per cent of the male population is widowed, female widows come to about nine per cent—double the national average. While only 19 per cent of 70 plus men are widowers, widows in this age group are over 80 per cent; since most of them do not have any independent means of support, they depend totally on their children or relatives for a living. The sudden drop of the women's work participation rate once women reach the age of 60 years is alarmingly large, aggravating their dependency even further (Menon, 1998).

Sex ratio is not only high in Kerala, but also it has been increasing over the decades (Table 5.5). According to the 2001 census, it was 1,058. This shows that the women in Kerala get better care in health services than their counterparts in the rest of India, where the ratio has remained at much less than 1000 throughout the twentieth century.

Table 5.5: Females per Thousand Males in Kerala

Year	*Sex ratio*
1961	1021
1971	1016
1981	1032
1991	1040
2001	1058

Source: Census India 2001.

Though the life expectancy is higher for women, it cannot be considered as an indicator of their good health status. Morbidity among women is increasing over the years. Health problems are seen to be quite high among low-income groups and the marginalised sections of the society such as fishermen folk, scheduled castes and scheduled tribes. Among these sections, poverty, escalating cost for health services, ignorance of immunisation, and neglect in maintaining health are the reasons for deterioration of health status. These factors lead to an increase in overall morbidity of women which is higher than that of men in Kerala (Table 5.6). The total incidence of disease is 155.80 for females and 137.50 for males. Diseases, like hypertension, cancer, goitre and bone and joint disease, are higher among women. Diseases of old age, psychological disorder and stress are very high among Kerala women.

It was found that inadequate food intake also contributed to the high morbidity levels of the poor women in Kerala. A study (Ukkuru *et al.*, 1994) was conducted among 250 women belonging to the rural areas of Thiruvananthapuram district who had taken up stone-breaking as their major activity, for assessing their nutritional profile. The intake of roots and tuber and fish was found adequate in their diet. But the consumption of cereals was 65 per cent of the suggested levels while that of pulses was only twenty-two per cent. Owing to inadequate nutritional standards and high work burden, eighty-two per cent women suffered from anaemia, ten per cent from vitamin A deficiency and nine per cent from vitamin B deficiency.

Table 5.6: Intensity of Illness among Females and Males (per 1000): 2000

Illness	*Females*	*Males*
Leprosy	0.37	0.50
Tuberculosis	4.05	8.60
Filaria	0.78	0.74
Bronchitis asthma	16.80	16.30
Hypertension	14.60	8.90
Heart disease	4.40	5.60
Cancer	1.00	0.81
Peptic ulcer	4.40	9.90
Diseases of uterus	9.10	—
Urinary diseases	4.80	4.70
Bone and joint disease	22.50	13.90
Goitre	3.20	0.99
Diabetes	2.90	3.90
Others	66.40	61.90
Total	**155.80**	**137.50**

Source: Health and Development in Rural Kerala, KSSP, 2000.

Crimes and Sexual Violence

Gender based violence is a clear manifestation of women's inequality. Sexual violence in the work place is also on the increase. Violence against women in Kerala is widespread and it is ever increasing. Irrespective of their marital status, women fall prey to domestic violence across all socio-economic groups (Panda, 2001).

According to a study undertaken by National Crime Records Bureau between 1997 and 1999 in seven cities of India including Thiruvananthapuram, among women between 15 and 49 years of age, the rate of prevalence of psychological violence was high in Thiruvananthapuram. In case of molestation (37.91 in Kerala while 30.56 in India) and domestic violence (37.95 in Kerala and 35.45 in India), Kerala stood ahead of the national average.

Table 5.7: Atrocities Committed Against Women in Kerala

Offences	*Year*					
	1992	*1995*	*2000*	*2003*	*2004*	*2005*
Rape	227	266	552	394	480	478
Molestation	5523	810	1695	1947	2260	2339
Kidnapping and abduction	86	110	89	102	142	175
Eve Teasing	1	14	69	68	133	129
Dowry death	12	21	25	33	31	21
Cruelty by Husband or Relatives	290	787	2418	2930	3222	3283
Others	939	1305	2773	1754	1413	1662
Total	**2078**	**3313**	**7621**	**7228**	**7681**	**8087**

Source: Government of Kerala, 2005 and 2007.

Sexual offences like rape, molestation, cruelty by husband or relatives are fairly high in Kerala. The rates have been increasing in recent years (Table 5.7). The total number of cases reported during 1992 was 2,078 and that in 2005 is 8,087 registering an increase in 289 per cent in the span of 14 years. During the same period, rape increased by 110.6 per cent, molestation increased by 347 per cent, kidnapping and abduction increased by 103.5 per cent, eve-teasing increased by 128 per cent and dowry death by 75 per cent. The highest increase is shown in the case of cruelty by husband or relatives during the period 1992 to 2005 (1032%).

Public Space

The proportion of women occupying high places in the public sphere is low. It is noted that in Kerala legislature, the proportion of women legislators never went beyond eight per cent. Not many women occupy high positions in institutions such as Universities (as Vice Chancellors, Registrars or Controllers of Examinations), Corporations, Boards and Commissions. Nor are women seen in large numbers in the cooperative sector and sports-clubs. In organisations such as trade unions and political parties, the women are not in majority. Even in the case of office bearers, their number is not much. Only in local self-government do we see women in some large measure, thanks to the 33 per cent reservation criterion specified in the Panchayati Raj Act.

Kerala has a history of several social uprisings and organisational efforts to fight against the evils of the society. But they had neglected the importance of empowerment of women.

Credit Institutions in Kerala

Formal financial institutions such as cooperative banks and commercial banks had appeared in Kerala even during the colonial era. In this section, a brief account of these institutions and their limitations is given.

Co-operative System in Kerala

The British government introduced the co-operative system in India on the lines of co-operative and land mortgage institutions in Germany. The Travancore state took the initiative for introducing the co-operative movement in 1914. Co-operative societies were formed in Travancore under the Travancore Cooperative Societies Regulation. In 1933, there were 715 communal societies in Travancore. These societies were called '*Paraspara Sahaya Sanghams*' (Societies for Mutual Benefit). At the time of reorganisation of states in 1956, there were 3,987 societies functioning all over Kerala. Of these 53 per cent were Primary Agriculture Credit Societies. Co-operative banks enjoy the patronage of the state government; they are engaged both in mobilising deposits and in lending (Venkiteswaran, 1984). The state of Kerala occupies a prominent position among the states of India in the organisation and promotion of co-operative credit movement.

Through the system, both short-term and long-term loans are advanced.

Commercial Banks in Kerala

Most of the commercial banks in India had restricted their operations almost entirely to urban and metropolitan centres till nationalisation of banks in 1969. But in Kerala, commercial banks had started functioning in the rural and the semi-urban areas of the state even before nationalisation. The commercial character of the state's agrarian sector encouraged banks to go into rural areas. Even as early as the 1950s, the banking sector in Kerala had been giving due importance to agriculture and allied activities. The increase in the number of marginal and small landholders due to large-scale sub-division of landholdings consequent on legislations redefining property right raised the demand for agricultural credit. The other factors which favoured the development of banking activities in Kerala were the large-scale reclamation of land, commercialisation of agriculture and the sporadic development of agro-processing and trading activities backed by sound transport facilities.

The expansion of bank credit to agriculture was also due to increase in area under non-foodcrops, and implementation of the Kerala Chit Fund Act passed on August 25, 1975, which led to the reduction of *kuris* and thereby to an increase in the need for institutional credit (Sunanda, 1994). Through comprehensive branch expansion programmes, introduction of the lead bank scheme and the service area approach, the banking infrastructure became well developed both in the urban and the rural areas in Kerala.

In the state, nationalised banks, private sector banks, regional rural banks, co-operative banks and foreign banks operate side by side (Table 5.8). In the case of total number of bank branches, Kerala stands ninth in India. The population served per branch in Kerala was 35,000 in 1969 and 9,000 in 2006. In terms of total deposits and per capita deposits Kerala has fared well.

Table 5.8: Bank-wise performance 2005-06, Kerala

(Rs. crores)

Type of Banks	*Total Deposit*	*Total Advance*	*C.D. Ratio*
State Bank group	25506.07	16399.11	64.29
Nationalised Banks	24377.87	16212.24	66.50
Regional Rural Banks	2100.54	2295.89	109.30
Private Sector Banks	25246.27	16772.38	66.00
Foreign Banks	446.31	238.90	53.53
Co-operative Banks	2838.22	3395.58	119.64
Total	**80515.28**	**55,343.10**	**68.70**

Source: SLBC—Kerala, 2006.

Although the banking indicators show a bright picture, the Credit-Deposit (CD) ratio is lower in Kerala than in many other Indian states. Among the various groups of banks in Kerala, the highest CD ratio was recorded by the co-operative Banks (119.64) and regional rural banks (109.30). The CD ratio at all-India level in respect of public sector banks was 69.92 in June 2006 while in Kerala the corresponding figure was 66.21.

The CD ratio of Kerala which had been 65.8 in 1969 declined to 43.01 in 2000. It has shown some revival since 2003 and stood at 67.1 in 2006 (Table 5.9). As in December 2007, CD ratio was 72.08. In 1999, out of aggregate credit disbursement of Rs. 299,274 crore by all banks at the all-India level, the share of Kerala was Rs. 8,570 crore, amounting to 2.86 per cent only. Bank deposits in Kerala increased at an average annual rate of 18 per cent over the period from 1988 to 1999 whereas advance registered an average annual growth rate of 14 per cent during the period.

In spite of the widespread coverage of bank branches in all parts of Kerala, the poor had not been able to avail themselves of the benefits of the banking system to any considerable extent. The cost of credit remains high and beyond the reach of the poor. The banks insist on collateral security for sanctioning loans. Owing to the prevailing practice in the public sector banks, the poor seldom approach them. Simultaneously, informal financial institutions are mushrooming because of their simple procedures of granting loans; but the interest rates charged by these institutions are usurious. Despite this, the poor depend on them and get ruined in the process. It is in this context that microfinance which charges only reasonable rates of interest and grants, loans with the minimum of procedural formalities, becomes important and relevant.

Table 5.9: Credit-Deposit Ratio of Public Sector Banks in Kerala

Year	*Credit-Deposit Ratio*
1969	65.80
1996	44.10
1997	44.41
1998	45.71
1999	44.28
2000	43.01
2001	43.56
2002	44.94
2003	46.62
2004	50.82
2005	59.50
2006	67.10

Source: Government of Kerala, 2007.

Microfinance has the following characteristics: easy availability, quick decision, transparency, timeliness and absence of collateral security. Under microfinance, even bank loans were sanctioned without collateral security or third party guarantee. However, involvement of all the members of the borrowing group such as a SHG has helped to ensure prompt loan repayment. Thus microfinance is an efficient and equitable alternative to bank credit for the poor people in Kerala.

Emergence of Microfinance in Kerala

The idea of microfinance had germinated long before the advent of the modern MFI/Ps. Many church-based development institutions in Kerala had promoted credit unions early in the twentieth century. A credit union organised the poor into large groups of 150 to 200 members and pooled their small savings for common benefit. The basic objective has been to help the poor meet their emergent needs and come out of the clutches of moneylenders. These credit unions lacked, however, the participatory decision making practice found in SHGs. Microfinance institutions/programmes of the modern type emerged in Kerala in the late 1980s and the early 1990s. Some of such institutions/programmes are given hereunder:

Community Development Society, Alappuzha

In 1991, the centrally sponsored Urban Basic Services for the Poor (UBSP) and the Community Based Nutrition Programme (CBNP) of UNICEF converged to target the poor women of Alappuzha town. For that, a community-based administration system called Community Development Society (CDS) was set up for enabling women from poor families to plan, implement and monitor schemes for their own benefits. The Community Development Society (CDS) has a three-tier federated structure. At the ward level, women from high-risk families form an Area Development Society (ADS) and all the ADSs of the town form a CDS. Both ADS and CDS have elected governing bodies.

Its basic unit is the Neighbourhood Group (NHG) comprising women from 25 to 40 families with high risk. The authorities at first conducted a survey with the help of a poverty index (see Appendix V). The index consisted of nine risk factors. Out of the nine components, a family having four or more risk factors was identified as poor. Thus 10,304 families were identified as poor on the basis of the poverty index.

A NHG has an elected five-member neighbourhood committee comprising: (i) a community health volunteer; (ii) a community infrastructure volunteer; (iii) a community income generation volunteer; (iv) a secretary; and (v) a president. The NHG conducts surveys of felt needs of each member family and of the NHG. The NHG committee also ascertains the sources of resources.

Each NHG meets once in a week/fortnight. The members of the group are encouraged to cultivate the habit of thrift. Small savings of the members are collected on a regular basis and deposited in banks which could be further augmented by outside loan/grant/subsidy etc. The CDS, by working as a thrift society, is an informal banking system operating in the doorsteps, and carries one per cent interest per month. With the emergence of CDS, the influence of indigenous moneylenders has greatly decreased. Members get loans at any time in the year without undergoing vexation procedures (Suresh, 1998).

There are 350 Neighbourhood Groups (NHGs) and 24 ADSs under Alappuzha CDS covering 10,304 poor families; they had made thrift of Rs. 23 lakh in about 18 months by an average monthly thrift of Rs. 10 per family. CDS had generated 4,000 jobs with an average loan amount of Rs. 3,000 by 1996. Their savings amounted to Rs. 37 lakh.

The CDS model of empowering women through self-management and economic activities was first extended to Malappuram district and then to other urban localities in Kerala. At present, CDS activities in the state are coordinated by a state government programme called 'Kudumbashree'.

Kudumbashree

Kudumbashree is a woman-based participatory poverty eradication programme launched on 1st April 1998 by the State Government with the financial support of NABARD and the Central Government. Thus, it is a partnership of four major agents—Central Government, State Government, local bodies and NABARD. The programme envisages a total investment of Rs. 858.80 crore. The main objective of the programme is to eradicate absolute poverty from the state within a decade by involving the poor actively in planning, managing and monitoring of programmes for their development. It is exclusively focussed on women, women in family and women in community. It is an organisation of women from below the poverty line. The core activity of this is to empower women through microfinance, microenterprise and convergent community action (Chathukulam, 2002).

The major components of the project are: (a) generation of employment to poor women and men, (b) provision of housing for the poor, low cost sanitation and community water supply, (c) establishment of literacy centres, (d) conduct of training programmes for skill upgradation and setting up of urban public health centres. The project also envisages establishing 'Informal Bank of the Poor' at local body level under three-tier system, to act as the sub-system of the formal banking sector (Government of Kerala, 2001).

The strategy of self help group approach is followed. The NHGs are organised together at the ward level into Area Development Societies and federated as panchayat/ municipality level Community Development Societies which in turn are registered as charitable societies. There are 986 Area Development Societies (ADSs) and 59 Community Development Societies (CDSs). Kudumbashree has organized Community Based Organization (CBO) of the poor in all the 53 municipalities and five corporations in the State. The CBOs in the urban areas act also as Thrift and Credit Societies and facilitate savings and credit to the poor.

As per current statistics, there are 167,406 NHGs formed in rural areas and 13,111 NHGs in urban areas in Kerala. In addition, 2,452 NHGs were formed in nine tribal districts. Thus, the grand total of NHGs functioning in Kerala under Kudumbashree is now 182,969 (Table 5.10). Through these NHGs, more than 36 lakh families were already covered. The total thrift of these families was about Rs. 885 crore and the total loan outstanding amounted to Rs. 2,255 crore.

Table 5.10: Status of NHGs Formed under Kudumbashree as in June, 2007

Area	*No. of NHG formed*	*No. of Families Covered*	*Amount of Thrift*	*Amount of Loan*
Urban (58 Urban Local Bodies)	13111	370351	502570591	573894814
Rural Total (999 Grama Panchayats)	167406	3230378	8264512137	21813874437
Tribal (9 Districts)	2452	39543	82478950	168203361
Total	**182969**	**3640272**	**8849561678**	**22555972612**

Source: Reports of Kudumbashree, 2007.

The project now acts as a conduit of Central Government poverty alleviation programmes. Thus in the state, Kudumbashree became the authority to implement the Swarna Jayanti Swarozgar Yojana (SJSRY) programme launched by the Central Government. The physical achievements of SJSRY in Kerala are discussed in the Table 5.11. Kudumbashree is giving more importance to the development of individual enterprises as well as group enterprises and is imparting training to the persons.

Table 5.11: Physical achievements of SJSRY in Kerala

Year	*Individual enterprises developed*	*Group enterprises developed*	*Persons trained*	*Mandays created under wage employment*
2002-03	803	181	1829	1000
2003-04	432	176	—	2000
2004-05	1615	139	4736	164000
2005-06	2055	179	4496	67000
2006-07	1334	172	3239	32111
Total	**6329**	**847**	**14300**	**118511**

Source: Government of Kerala, 2007.

Under the SJSRY, so far Kudumbashree has developed 20,477 microenterprises. Of which 1,696 units are group enterprises (each group with minimum 10 women) organised under DWCUA and 18,781 are individual enterprises initiated under USEP (Government of Kerala, 2007).

Local Governments and Microfinance

In Kerala, the People's Plan Programme initiated in 1996 gave impetus to the development process of the economy. The programme envisages devolvement of adequate resources to lower levels and provision for functional and financial autonomy at the levels of decision making. The programme also gives importance to women's development. The Women Component Plan (WCP) factor which is ten per cent of the total plan fund has also spawned village-level collectives in the form of neighbourhood and self help groups. In the past, most such groups were essentially savings and microcredit units, initiated and nurtured in general by NGOs.

However, in the wake of the People's Plan Campaign (PPC), both existing groups and newly formed ones were registered by panchayats in order to become eligible for WCP funds and presumably, to encourage their active participation in the decentralisation process. Thus the SHGs in the panchayats do not restrict themselves to savings and credit and income generation activities alone; they also use the forum to discuss a wide range of issues relating to women's lives and rights. The experience of panchayats such as Ulloor, Thiruvallam, Madikkai, Aralam, Koduman and Vazhoor are notable ones (Seema *et al.*, 2000). Many of the women in these panchayats have started some self-employment activities.

Another important outcome of the focus on women's needs through the WCP is the increased participation of women in *grama sabhas*, the essential foundation of decentralised governance, which has reportedly risen from 26 per cent in the initial stages to 60 per cent more recently. Women also constitute two-thirds of the beneficiaries under individual beneficiary-oriented programmes. The existence of active women's collectives as an integral part of the development process at the village level, has, no doubt, contributed to the programme (Joseph, 2000).

NGOs in the Field of Microfinance

Several NGOs are now engaged in the field of microfinance throughout the state. Many of them have done commendable work. They perform a wide range of activities such as credit unions, farmers' clubs and SHGs.

Madappally Service Cooperative Bank Limited, a Primary Agricultural Credit Society (PACS) started a farmers' club in 1991. The bank also organised women self help groups to empower poor women and to liberate them from the clutches of moneylenders. Another NGO *Shreyas* is the official organisation of the diocese of Bathery. Its operational area is spread over 13 civil districts of Kerala, Karnataka and Tamil Nadu and 115 tribal colonies of Wayanad. The organisation has formed more than 115 self help groups covering 10,000 tribals in Wayanad district alone. It has 147 registered women's organisations having 17,000 women as members. Another 18,000 farmers were registered under 100 farmers' clubs and 80 credit unions also exist with 20,000 members.

Pazhakulam Social Service Society (PASSS) established in 1975 is a unique case of success of entrepreneurial endeavour on cooperative basis. PASSS formed 200 farmers' clubs with a total membership of 20,000 small/marginal farmers. A farm club consists of 30 to 3,000 members and an executive committee of the club is elected from the members to implement the activities of PASSS at the local level. The area of operation spreads from Pazhakulam village to about six districts of the state and the volume of service has increased every year. Apart from farmers' clubs, credit unions were also promoted by PASSS. There were 100 credit unions under PASSS with a total membership of 6,000 (Suresh, 1998).

Another NGO, *Bharat Sevak Samaj* (BSS) has organised self help groups of women in three districts of Thiruvananthapuram, Kottayam and Kasargode. It has organised 21,099 SHGs in Thiruvananthapuram, 9,024 in Kottayam and 2,415 in Kasargode. The voluntary organisation in Thiruvananthapuram, 'Dale View', conducts microcredit programme among women. It also imparts training programmes for microenterprises, awareness generation for women empowerment, gender development, etc. Rural Agency for Social and Technological Advancement (RASTA), an NGO in Wayanad promotes savings and conducts a credit management programme for income and employment generation of women. At present, the organisation has 400 women self help groups.

NABARD in Kerala

The combined efforts of Community Development Societies, Kudumbashree, Panchayats and NGOs have helped in forming

SHGs all over Kerala. Most of them are able to link with the commercial banks, cooperative banks and regional rural banks in the state.

Table 5.12 shows that about 1.21 lakh SHGs have been linked in the state so far under the SHG-Bank Linkage programme. SHGs had linked up with various banks in the state. Of the total SHGs, in 105,564, women are members.

Table 5.12: Progress of SHG Linkage Programme in Kerala as in 2006

Mode of Linkage	*No. of SHGs Financed*		
	Total	*Of which*	
		Under govt. sponsored	*Women SHGs*
Financing SHG directly by banks	56,907	16,892	47,393
Financing SHGs directly with the facilitation of NGOs	27,782	4,480	24,113
Financing SHGs through the medium of NGOs	36,240	NA	34,058
Total No. of SHGs linked	**120,929**		**105,564**

Source: SLBC—Kerala, 2007.

In short, the unprecedented growth of microfinance in Kerala due mainly to the initiatives and actions taken by the agencies in the field of microfinance. This would certainly help to improve the overall status of women in Kerala because the self help groups formed under microfinance train women in income generation, sensitisation and democratic processes. The available evidence suggests that microfinance has already made tremendous success in many parts of the state.

6

Study Area and Microfinance Organisation

Microsavings and microcredit are the major characteristics of microfinance. Microfinance helps the poor to mobilise and pool their meagre savings and to use them as a major source to cushion their economic shocks. Likewise, microcredit enhances economic choices and opportunities of the poor. Microfinance institutions also supply credit to the poor for meeting their various needs. Microcredit is given to the poor for production and even for consumption.

With a view to assess the performance of microfinance institutions in Kerala, a field survey was conducted in one of the microfinance organisations in a panchayat in the outskirts of Thiruvananthapuram city. The microfinance organisation selected is the *Samatha Vanitha Swayam Sahaya Sangham* (SVSSS) in the Ulloor panchayat.

Study Area: Ulloor Panchayat

Ulloor panchayat is a special grade panchayat in Thiruvananthapuram district. It has an area of 16.67 sq. km. The panchayat comes under the jurisdiction of Vattiyoorkavu rural block and consists of two revenue villages, namely Ulloor and Cheruvikkal. The panchayat is divided into fifteen wards. The broad details of the panchayat are furnished in Table 6.1.

Though the panchayat is located in the outskirts of Thiruvananthapuram city, Ulloor has the characteristics of an urban fringe. Some of the wards lying close to the city are densely populated (Nalanchira, Parottukonam, Bappuji Nagar,

Prasanth Nagar, Kochulloor) (see Appendix VIII). The wards, which lie further away from the city limits are less densely populated and show a tendency of economically worse off.

Table 6.1: Basic Information of Ulloor Panchayat

Area	16.67 sq. km.
Total Population	47,005 (1991 census)
Grade	Special
Block	Vattiyoorkavu Rural Block
Revenue Villages	Ulloor, Cheruvikkal
Total Number of Houses	9,856
Total Number of Families	10,013

Source: Ulloor Panchayat, 1997.

It is observed that in the course of expansion of the city of Thiruvananthapuram, the richer sections of the population have managed to settle down in and around Thiruvananthapuram Corporation. In fact, such new settlements have grown in the form of housing colonies (named as 'Nagars' or 'Lanes'). In these settlements, the rich people had bought housing plots and constructed posh buildings near the main roads. Most of the earlier settlers of these areas had sold off their plots for higher prices and moved to hinterlands. Yet, a few are staying on in tiny plots acquired or inherited for reasons of proximity to places of work.

The Ulloor panchayat consisted in the past mainly of farmlands and its population was purely agricultural, comprising cultivators and agricultural workers. But as urbanisation crept into this area, the traditional agricultural activities declined and people engaged in these activities increasingly moved to other occupations like construction, transport and trade (see case one in appendix to this chapter). The number of auto rickshaw drivers, petty traders and automobile mechanics increased steeply.

Traditional workers such as washermen and barbers lost their occupations due to socio-economic changes that brought in trades and profession (see case two in appendix to this chapter). Most of these people who lost out in the bargain are from lower castes (either SC or OBC). A few of the poor sections who lost their work and were up-rooted from their homesteads have encroached upon commons (*porombokes*) for constructing hutments (see case three in appendix to this chapter). In-migration from other parts of the state has increased the population density of the area and the demand for housing. The number of families living in rented houses has increased considerably in recent decades. Most of them are poor and are engaged in low-paid jobs (see case four in appendix to this chapter).

For the purpose of the present study, 323 women from 34 SHGs functioning in the Ulloor panchayat under SVSSS have been selected. In the following sections, the characteristics of the members and SHGs are explained.

Demographic Characteristics of Members

Age Composition

The majority of the women in the organisation belonged to the middle age group. More than four-fifths of the members were in the age group of 21 to 50 years (Fig. 6.1). Since the majority of women in the middle age group are unemployed, it is they who have the urgency and the time to engage themselves in some kind of productive activity.

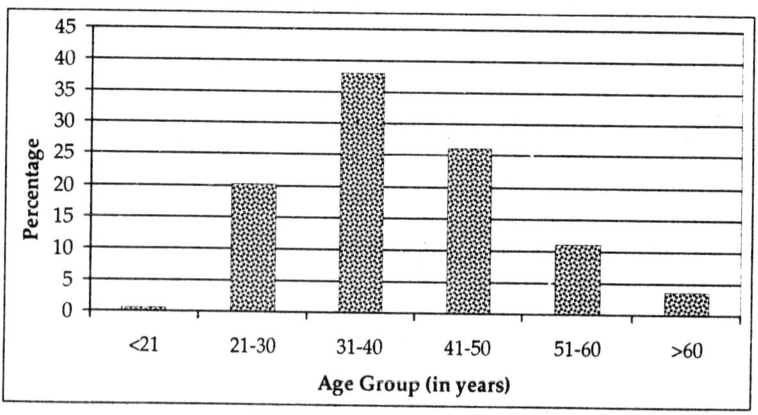

Fig. 6.1: Distribution of Beneficieries by Age

The representation of the elderly is low in the MFO (about 15% above 51 years). In the cases of elderly women members, they take loans in their names, only for usage by their children (see case five in appendix to this chapter). As the old women may not need money for own use, they help their kith and kin. Some old women help their children in times of needs. They feel that savings with the SHG may help them in future (see case six in appendix to this chapter). In some groups, it was observed that old women were purposively excluded. This was because younger women felt the presence of elderly women unnecessary and a handicap. Obviously, there was a wide generation gap between them and the old people.

Marital Status

The majority of the beneficiaries (80.2%) are married. Unmarried women form 4.9 per cent. Women from female-headed households also take part (Table 6.2). Widows, separated and divorced women who bear the entire burden of looking after their families have found the self help group as a source of sure support. They felt that the women in their group were able to understand their difficulties and they expected that the group would be a great support to them in future (case eight in appendix to this chapter). Many of them who had initiated some income generating activities found that the group became a great support for each of them during times of financial difficulty.

Table 6.2: Distribution of Beneficiaries on the Basis of Marital Status

Marital Status	*Frequency*	*Percentage*
Married	259	80.2
Unmarried	16	4.9
Widowed	27	8.4
Separated/Divorced	21	6.5
Total	323	100

Educational Level

More than three-fifths women in the organisation had education of the high school level or more. Graduates formed only about two per cent and persons with higher secondary come to thirteen per cent. The percentages of women having lower primary education (13.6%) and upper primary education (20.1%) were comparatively low. Illiterates accounted for about five per cent (Fig. 6.2).

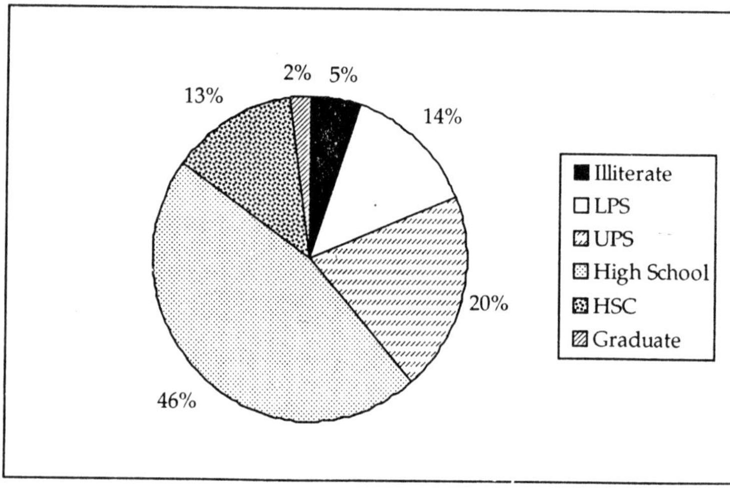

Fig. 6.2: Distribution of Beneficiaries by Education

Women with technical qualification or training were less in number. Nearly three-fourth did not have any kind of technical training. Some of the untrained women had some skills in conventional vocations such as tailoring, typewriting, nursery teaching, *anganwadi* teaching and ITI trades. This fact points to the potential need for imparting training to women for enabling them to take up income generating activities.

Community Composition

Seventeen per cent of the members belonged to Scheduled Castes and 55 per cent to other backward communities. Only about 28 per cent came from forward communities. The vast majority of them (92%) were Hindus and the rest eight per cent Christians.

Alcoholism

The presence of alcoholics seems to be a major problem in many of the sample households. Problems like indebtedness, economic and social insecurity, deprivation of other material and social facilities aggravate the menace. About eleven per cent of the households in the sample had alcoholism as a major problem.

Income and Assets

Income

Researchers usually face the problem of under-reporting of income by their respondents. From the income data which may contain a certain degree of under-reporting, it was found that about one-eighth of the women members had an annual income of less than Rs. 10,000.

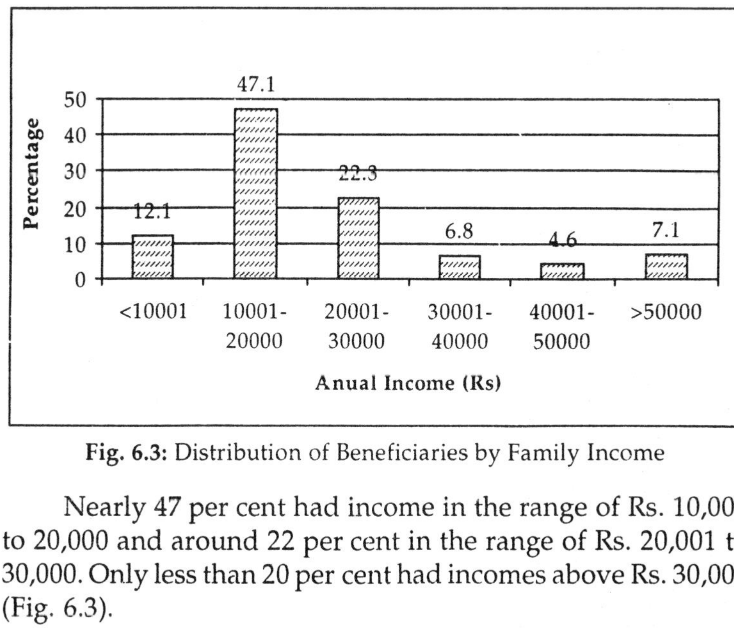

Fig. 6.3: Distribution of Beneficiaries by Family Income

Nearly 47 per cent had income in the range of Rs. 10,000 to 20,000 and around 22 per cent in the range of Rs. 20,001 to 30,000. Only less than 20 per cent had incomes above Rs. 30,000 (Fig. 6.3).

Ownership of Land

Land is a valuable asset in Kerala. Allotment of plots of ten cents each in rural areas and five cents each in municipal area to poor landless households as part of the Agrarian Reforms implemented in Kerala during the end of the 1960s has improved the standards of living of thousands of families in the state. Yet in the sample, it was found that nearly 28 per cent of the households were absolutely landless.

Table 6.3: Total Land Owned by the Beneficiaries

(% in Parenthesis)

Land Area	*Land in Homestead*	*Cultivable Land*	*Non-Cultivable Land*
No land	89 (27.6)	304 (94.1)	284 (87.9)
1-3 cents	56 (17.3)	1 (0.3)	5 (1.5)
3.5-6 cents	90 (27.9)	2 (0.6)	11 (3.4)
6.5-10 cents	45 (13.9)	4 (1.2)	11 (3.4)
10.5-15 cents	17 (5.3)	—	6 (1.9)
15.5-25 cents	15 (4.6)	7 (2.2)	3 (0.9)
25.5-50 cents	8 (2.5)	3 (0.9)	3 (0.9)
>51 cents	3 (0.9)	2 (0.6)	—
Total	323 (100.0)	323 (100.0)	323 (100.0)

The disaggregated data on the ownership of land (homestead, cultivable and non-cultivable) show that homestead is an important asset as far as poor people are concerned. But 27.6 per cent of the beneficiaries had no homestead land. Nearly three-fifths of the beneficiaries had landholding below ten cents. The poor holding land had plots of one to six cents in extent. In consequence, they find it difficult to have space for starting any enterprise, to grow vegetables, or rear cattle, poultry, etc. There were households with large size land, but their proportion was quite small. The area of agricultural land is also very low among the beneficiaries. Only 19 persons (5.9%) had agricultural land and 39 persons (12.1%) possessed non-cultivable land (Table 6.3).

Ownership of House

The standard of living of a person is reflected in the housing condition of his/her household. The majority of beneficiaries had their own houses (70%). While 9.3 per cent of the beneficiaries lived in rented houses, another 20.7 per cent lived with their relatives, or in their ancestral houses or in common lands (*porombokes*).

Most of the beneficiaries who did not possess houses expressed the view that their priority was to build new houses. To have a house of their own is a dream for most of the poor people. The rising costs of building materials and labour deny the opportunity for them to build a house. Many of the beneficiaries who joined the groups said that they would be able to build a house using the loans from the organisation. On the other hand, using microcredit, many people have already improved their housing conditions by tiling roofs, adding toilets, digging wells, taking electricity connection, etc.

Basic facilities like toilets are not available to about six per cent of the sample households. It was observed that sanitation facilities were low in residential areas of low-income groups such as the *lakshamveedu* colony and that people live in common lands in ramshackle structures. Kerala is the state in which electrification is claimed to be total in village areas. But here a small percentage of people (nine per cent) still do not have electricity connection to their houses.

Ownership of Livestock

Livestock is a major type of income generating asset for people in many parts of the developing countries. Eight per cent of the beneficiaries own cows, 1.9 per cent own goats and another 2.2 per cent own chicks (Table 6.4). However, the majority of the households (87.6%) do not own any type of livestock for want of land required for rearing cattle; poultry is very less for most of the households.

Table 6.4: Type of Livestock Owned

Type of Livestock	*Frequency*	*Percentage*
No livestock	283	87.6
Cow	27	8.4
Goat	6	1.9
Fowl	7	2.2
Total	323	100

Financial Position of the Members

Savings with Formal Financial Institutions

The proportion of beneficiaries having family savings kept in financial institutions is low. Only four per cent of the sample households had savings in formal financial institutions such as banks and cooperatives. A larger proportion (26.9%) has savings in the form of Life Insurance Corporation of India (LIC) policies (Table 6.5). But the majority of the beneficiaries (69%) do not have institutional savings of any type at all.

Table 6.5: Family Savings of Beneficiaries other than MFO

Savings at	*Frequency*	*Percentage*
Banks	10	3.1
Co-operatives	3	0.9
LIC	87	26.9
No savings	223	69
Total	323	100

The reason for the presence of LIC policies is that LIC has agents who come and collect the monthly/quarterly/half yearly/yearly premium from the people. The people find it convenient to keep the savings with LIC. This experience suggests that poor people need the financial services of institutions for collecting and keeping their savings. Otherwise they would lack the incentive and the wherewithal for approaching formal financial institutions. When an arrangement comes to them they readily accept it and attempt to make use of it. This seems to be in fact the major factor underlying the success of microfinance institutions.

Problem of Indebtedness

Indebtedness was the major problem observed among the members in the study area. A good percentage of people (64.1%) have outside loan liabilities. Most of the loans were taken from moneylenders, especially those who come from Tamil Nadu (they are known as *'annachi'*, meaning elder brother; for details see case nine in the appendix of this chapter). Apart from borrowing from *annachis*, they pledge their gold ornaments in times of difficulties with local moneylenders and informal money lending institutions (usually not with the institutions such as private banks or commercial banks).

Their indebtedness to institutional financial agencies is quite small. However, they are in deep debt to private moneylenders. The average amount of outstanding loans per borrower is found to be less than Rs. 50,000. The poor people find it extremely difficult to repay. Most of them fall deeper into indebtedness, over time, when they borrow for expenses like daughter's marriage, medical treatment and house construction. After becoming members of self help groups, women find that their degree of dependence on outside (non-institutional) loans has drastically come down. They feel that self help group helps them to avail loans from institutional sources at moderate rates of interests when an exigency arises. The members are also very much interested in taking additional loans from their self help groups. The majority of the people resorted to new loans for repayment of existing loans. On the other hand, there exist also cases in which the existence of other loans makes them unable to take new loans.

Samatha Vanitha Swayam Sahaya Sangham (SVSSS)

The *Samatha Vanitha Swayam Sahaya Sangham* (SVSSS—Samatha Women Self help group) was formed in 1997 at the Ulloor panchayat in Thiruvananthapuram district. The broad objective of the organisation was to ensure sustainable livelihood for women belonging to low-income groups. The organisation, therefore, formed self help groups (SHGs) in various parts of the panchayat. Each self help group consists of 20 to 25 women from low-income groups from the neighbourhood.

Table 6.6: Performance of SVSSS in the Ulloor Panchayat

Status of SVSSS	*1999*	*2001*
Number of SHGs formed	100	163
Number of members	2,200	3,522
Assets of SHGs (in Rs.)	1 crore	1.5 crore

Source: Compiled from reports of SVSSS.

During 1999 there were 100 SHGs formed all over the panchayat. By 2001, the number of the self help groups had risen to 163. Enrolment in SHGs increased from 2,200 women in 1999 to 3,522 women in 2001. The total assets (own savings and bank loans) of the organisation during 1999 were to the tune of Rupees one crore. By 2001, the organisation had Rupees one crore as own savings and Rs. 50 lakh as bank loan. Thus, the total fund of the MFO amounted to Rs. 1.5 crore in 2001 (Table 6.6).

Organisational Set Up

SHGs are usually organised at a locality in a panchayat ward. Typically, volunteers of the *Kerala Shastra Sahitya Parishad* (KSSP), the panchayat (ward) member or village extension officer takes the initiative for forming SHGs. In rare cases, members in the microfinance organisation have helped the formation of groups in other neighbouring localities. Each group is registered under the Charitable Societies Act. This helps them to avail of benefits from block panchayat and commercial banks. The SHGs have evolved their own byelaws and norms for management of their savings and loan operations and for taking up of productive activities usually with the guidance of volunteers of the KSSP. Each group has a secretary and a president. The president is the person who convenes the weekly meetings. The secretary has to organise the members, collect microsavings, distribute loans on members' directions, keep records and prepare minutes of the weekly meetings.

Functions of Self Help Groups

Microsavings of Self Help Groups

Savings form the asset of the SHGs. The amount of own savings helps them to recycle the amount and offer it as security for availing loans from the banks to which they are linked. It also helps to increase the economic capability of poor women. Each member in the SHGs under study has saved Rs. 20 to 25 per week. The total savings of the studied groups ranged from Rs. 14,200 to Rs. 89,295. While for about 15 per cent of the groups, the average savings were less than Rs. 25,000, about 30 per cent had savings of more than Rs. 65,000 (Fig. 6.4). The total amount of the savings for 34 groups was more than Rs. 17 lakh.

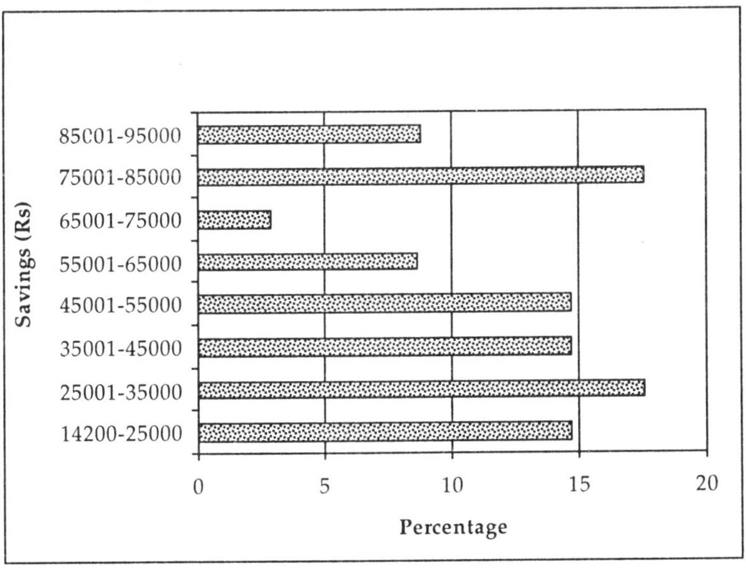

Fig. 6.4: Savings of Self Help Groups

The members receive interest on their savings. In *Samatha*, each self help group shares its annual profit once in a year, in proportion to the savings of the members. A vast majority of them have already received their share. Interest-sharing serves as an incentive to save regularly.

Microcredit from SHGs to Members

The SHGs give microcredit to members from the microsavings (own fund). In addition to that, the SHGs distribute funds borrowed from banks. In SVSSS, sanction and distribution of loans are made by the SHGs themselves. Each SHG has set its own criteria for sanctioning loans. The widely accepted criterion for sanctioning loans is 'first come first serve'. The secretary accepts loan applications from members. The applications would contain details of the purpose of the proposed loans and the amounts required. The SHG secretary registers the applications seriatim. When the SHG finds that it has adequate funds in the kitty for meeting the needs of the first applicant, the secretary issues a cheque for the loan amount to her with the consent of all the other members. In normal cases, a member is able to borrow again only after the loan is repaid and all the other applicant members are given loans. Members discuss the purposes for which loans are required by the members and the urgency for granting them in the weekly meetings of SHGs. If any of the members is in urgent need of loan for purposes such as medical expenses, the SHG gives preference to that member.

Until 31 March, 2001, the self help groups surveyed had granted 573 loans, the total amount lent being Rs. 2,173,900. The average loan amount would be around Rs. 3,800. More than 30 per cent of the members had taken only one loan each; more than 35 per cent had taken two loans each. About one-sixth of the loanees had taken three loans each. There were members who had taken even four or more loans each, and their proportion came to around six per cent.

Purpose of Microcredit

Microcredit is given for purposes such as consumption, social functions, festivities and production activities. However, in SVSSS, 166 loans out of 573 were solely utilised for repayment of loans raised earlier from indigenous moneylenders and by pledging their gold ornaments and jewellery, at very high rates of interest. The amount utilised for this purpose represented nearly 30 per cent (Rs. 660,100) of the total loan amount (Table 6.7).

Education was the second most important purpose for which loans were utilised. Till March 2001, 114 loans (19.89%) with a sum of Rs. 306,800 were lent for educational purposes. Usually, money is needed for meeting expenses of education such as tuition fees, admission fees, travel expenses, school uniforms, books and stationery. Now-a-days, private tuitions also have become an expensive educational requirement.

Table 6.7: Distribution of Microcredit and Purposes for which they are Utilised

Purpose of Loan	*Number of Loans Availed by Members*	*Total Amount Availed (Rs.)*
Repayment of other loans	166 (28.9)	660,100 (30.37)
Trade, business, agriculture and self-employment	72 (12.56)	275,500 (12.67)
Hospital and death expenses	21 (3.67)	59,000 (2.71)
Buying land and house	**9 (1.57)**	**45,500 (2.10)**
Consumption	63 (10.99)	172,000 (7.91)
House maintenance and construction	99 (17.28)	477,000 (21.94)
Education	114 (19.89)	306,800 (14.11)
Buying cow, auto rickshaw and lorry	16 (2.79)	88000 (4.05)
Marriage expenses	13 (2.26)	90,000 (4.14)
Total	**573 (100)**	**2,173,900 (100)**

The proportion of loans spent on housing is quite high. Besides maintenance and repairs of houses, expenditure is incurred on existing houses for renovation, electrification and sanitation. The members of SHGs in our sample are found to have utilised a significant proportion (17.28% of the total loans but 21.94% of the total amount), of their loans on housing and related items.

Loan amounts were used on other items like medical treatment, funeral expenses and marriages. For household consumption, more than one-tenth of the loans were expended. The poor are highly vulnerable to economic shocks arising from deaths, diseases, marriages, childbirth and other social obligations. They are, therefore, interested to find sources of quick credit on easy and affordable terms. In our sample, the beneficiaries have utilised their loans to a significant extent on marriages of their own, of their children and of their immediate relatives.

Investment in income generating activities accounted for only one-eighth of the total loan amount. In short, income generating activities by the members have remained one of the neglected areas in their prioritisation of requirements. Utilisation of loans for non-income generating items creates problems for loan repayment.

Mode of Repayment of Loans

Quantum of repayment and repayment schedule vary from one SHG to the other. The self help group itself decides the amount payable in each instalment. The total repayment period ranges from five to forty months depending upon the loan amount and the decisions taken by the SHGs concerned. Repayment schedule is fixed on monthly basis by most of the groups. However, the members are free to repay either on weekly or on monthly basis. The rate of interest is fixed for all groups at twenty-four per cent per annum. The interest rate is very low compared to the rates charged by other lenders (except commercial banks, cooperative banks and cooperative societies). Again, interest is calculated only on outstanding balances in the loan accounts.

Loan Recovery

The groups take care to ensure that the money lent comes back. The borrowing members have to sign a loan document on a stamp paper of Rs. 50, for all loans exceeding Rs. 3,000. This enables the groups to take legal action against defaulting members. However, it was observed that, none of the SHGs in the sample had undertaken any legal action against its members for loan recovery. On the other hand, SHGs use peer pressure to ensure loan repayment. Since most of the members in a group happen to be from the same neighbourhood, it is easy to exercise peer pressure. All the members of a group go to the house of the defaulter regularly and try to get the loan repaid. If the savings of a loanee are found sufficient to cover the loan amount, then with the consent of all the members, some groups credit the savings amount in the loan account and close it.

SHG-Bank Linkage

In SVSSS, as soon as a SHG is formed, it starts an account with a neighbouring nationalised or cooperative bank. All the groups are linked with Syndicate Bank, Kesavadasapuram and Sreekariyam branches and Ulloor Service Cooperative Bank, Pongumoodu. Bank accounts of SHGs are maintained in the joint account of the president and the secretary.

All the SHGs keep their savings with these banks. The banks lent loans in proportion to the total savings of the groups. Of the total self help groups, 29 groups have already availed loans from banks. The total amount was Rs. 8.65 lakh. If the first loan is repaid without default, the banks would give second loan. Thus ten groups have availed second loan also. The total amount of second loan was Rs. 7.26 lakh. It is to be noted that the average amount given as second loan is considerably higher than that of the first loan. Thus the liquidity of the groups has increased to a considerable extent.

APPENDIX

Case One: Lalitha of Cheruvattikonam I self help group is 55 years old. She is an unmarried woman who studied up to third standard. She lives with her nephew in her ancestral house which is thatched one.

***Occupational mobility*:** Lalitha was an agricultural worker in her younger age. When the agricultural lands were used for other purposes, she started selling tapioca. Later it was difficult for her to carry headload of tapioca. Due to non-availability of the product, she switched to cattle rearing.

Present day livelihood: Now she owns two cows. She bought one cow with her own savings and the other with the SHG loan. By way of cattle she earned Rs. 900 per month. But at the time of dry seasons it was very difficult for her to survive. To add her problems the cost for fodder is increasing.

Problems of repayment of microcredit: Lalitha has a SHG loan of Rs. 3,000. She feels that it is not easy for her to repay the monthly instalment of Rs. 150 with her meagre income. So she is reluctant to take additional loans from the SHG any more. She has fears about her old age. There is no pension or other social security. So she is promptly remitting the weekly savings with the SHG in the hope that it will help her in future.

Case Two: Radha is 43 years old washerwoman. She belongs to Navajyothi group. She has two sons—both are working as manual labourers. Her family lives on the banks of a canal. She and her husband were engaged in the job of washing of clothes for a number of years. But when the job became unremunerative and difficult to make a living out of it, her husband started going for construction works. But she is still doing the work. She gets the laundry from the neighbourhood and washes for them. She says that after all the expenses she is able to earn only a meagre amount. That itself is highly fluctuating over the months. The major problem she cites is that in many houses, nowadays washing machines are there. So services of people like her are not demanded by the people.

Case Three: Chandrika is 40 years old widow. She belongs to Punoorkonam self help group. She has got education upto third standard. She belongs to other backward caste. Her husband committed suicide three months before the researcher visited her. Her son is in jail. She is all alone. She does not own land. So she lives in a common (*poromboke*) land for some years. For fear of eviction, she is not able to build a pucca house in that place. So her house is made of coconut leaves. As there are no male members in her house to help her, for making a living she is working as a housemaid in a house.

Case Four: Vimala belongs to Mannankonam self help group. She is 30 years old and has four children—two sons and two daughters. All of them are below four years. Her husband is a manual labourer. She belongs to Nedumangad Taluk of Thiruvananthapuram district. They do not have any land For making a living they have migrated to this place. They live in a room of a mud walled thatched house. For that small place, they have to pay a rent of Rs. 400 per month. Her husband was an alcoholic. Hence for making a living she works as a housemaid. From that she gets Rs. 600 per month. But it is not sufficient to look after her large family. She says that she feeds her children with the leftover from the house she works. She wanted to go to more houses for making a little more money. But as she is a mother of small children she is not able to go away from home for a long time.

Case Five: Swarnamma is 65 years old. She is a member of Cheruvattikonam I self help group. She is a widow and she lives with her daughter. She gets an old age pension of Rs. 300 per month. From the pension, she saved Rs. 2,075 with the SHG.

Acting as dummies for relatives: Swarnamma had taken a loan of Rs. 2,000. When asked for what purpose the loan was taken, she said that she had taken that loan for the education of her daughter's child and it was the daughter who was repaying her loan. There is no need of loan for her. If she avails a loan, it would not be possible for her to repay the same.

Case Six: Shyamala is a 55 year old Scheduled Caste woman. She is a widow. She studied up to sixth standard. Her children are married and settled. For making a living for herself, she has been taking up the job of fish vending for the last 15 years and earning an average of Rs. 1,500 per month.

Savings is useful while microcredit is insufficient: She has got savings of Rs. 1,800 with the SHG and she is promptly remitting it. She feels that the money will help her in future. But she has not taken any loan from the SHG. While asked why she did not avail any loan, she replied that the SHG loans would come once in a while and have to be repaid on weekly or monthly basis. But she needs daily credit in order to conduct her business. So she is still depending on moneylenders for credit on daily interest basis.

Case Seven: Lalitha is a member of Surabhi self help group. She is a 40 year old widow. She lost her husband ten years ago. She belongs to Scheduled Caste. She studied up to eighth standard. She has two sons; both are studying in high school. She is working as a housemaid. She has only three cents of land. It is situated in a remote area without any approach road. In that land she has a house built up of mud walls. She has savings of Rs. 1,175.

Increased participation in grama sabha and getting benefits from it: She is not participating in any of the business or social organisations in the panchayat. But she regularly attends *grama sabhas* of the panchayat. As a result, she got grant from panchayat for tiling her house from panchayat. For improving her house she is in need of money. She hopes that the membership in the SHG will help her in the future.

Case Eight: Padmakumari of Cheruvikkal self help group is a new entrant. She is 41 years old. Her husband was a construction worker. He suddenly died of pneumonia. She has a 12 year old daughter. She is studying in eighth standard. She felt that she was left all alone in the world after her husband's death. She has got training in tailoring. But she is not able to make a living out of it because there are skilled tailors in the locality. Her basic problem is that of insecurity. Because her daughter is a young girl, she took a loan of Rs. 20,000 from bank mortgaging her house for construction of wall around her house. As she has no means, now she is unable to repay the loan. She feels that the women in the group would understand her difficulties and would be with her when necessity arises.

Case Nine: Most of the women in the self help group were sharing their experiences with *'annachi'* (meaning elder brother), the local moneylenders. The *annachi* lends small amounts (say Rs. 500 or Rs. 1,000) to women (occasionally also to men). He charges high rates of interest on the loan (as per respondents' accounts which come up to even Rupees ten for Rupees Hundred per month). If they want Rs. 1,000, the moneylender would give Rs. 900 only. The borrower has to pay Rs. 20 per day. If the women have not defaulted loan repayment to *annachi*, he readily lends still more amounts (even up to Rs. 25,000). The women who borrow the money are supposed to repay on a weekly or daily basis. The *annachi* provides a card to each borrower for entry of repayments. If a woman defaults, he manages to get back the money, by any means, fair or foul. We found that the *annachi* is a regular visitor to poor and lower middle class households. These classes of people are usually in need of loans in small amounts for a variety of purposes such as medical care, children's education and consumption purposes.

7

Microfinance, Capacity Building and Empowerment

Microfinance is primarily an informal institution which performs financial functions. But it has several linkages with formal financial institutions like banks and other political institutions say local bodies, State Government and Central Government. Thus it acts as a sub-system of these institutions and takes part in activities of eradicating poverty as well as of capacity building processes of women who take part in it. Thus, microfinance plays an instrumental role in enhancing the capacities of poor women.

Microfinance also acts as a means to enhance the economic capacity of the poor women. It is considered as the first step for microenterprises. Now-a-days, microfinance is used by a number of governmental agencies, non-governmental organisations and voluntary organisations to reach the poor people and ameliorate their poverty. These agencies help people organise themselves to improve their capability through training, monitoring and guidance for initiating and operating gainful microenterprises.

The microfinance organisation under study, *Samatha Vanitha Swayam Sahaya Sangham* (SVSSS) has also been trying to enhance the resource base of the community through microfinance by helping the poor women in the locality by mobilising their savings, giving credit on convenient basis and initiating income generating activities by them. In the first part of this chapter, we discuss how the MFO helped women in low-income group in Ulloor panchayat to increase their democratic capacity building. In the second part, it deals with the analysis on the extent of enhancement of economic capacity of the members achieved through this microfinance organisation, SVSSS.

PART-I

Capacity building at the Institutional Level: People's Plan Campaign

Although the Panchayat Raj Institutions (PRIs) were constituted with elected members in the 1970s itself, the idea of decentralised planning did not become a reality till the mid-1990s due to the strategy of centralised planning followed in the country during the past five decades. Following the 73rd and the 74th constitutional amendments which provided certain uniform guidelines on the structure and functioning of the PRIs, the Government of Kerala launched the 'People's Campaign for Decentralised Planning' on August 17, 1996. This campaign is unique in the sense that local bodies (i.e., the panchayats, municipalities and corporations) were given substantial powers and resources to make them active agents of social change. As a first step in this direction, 35 to 40 per cent of the state's ninth plan outlay was devolved to projects and programmes drawn up by the local bodies. The campaign envisaged a development strategy through enlisting the involvement of people right from the stage of identifying local developmental problems and project formulation to the stage of implementation and evaluation of programmes.

People's Plan Campaign (PPC) and Women

As part of People's Campaign, the following gender-sensitive measures were initiated:

(a) Guidelines were issued to encourage participation of women in each stage of the planning process;
(b) Local bodies were given instructions to elect one-third of the resource persons for People's Campaign from among women activists;

(c) During the discussions in the *grama sabha*, a separate subject group on women's development was made mandatory. A structured questionnaire on gender problems was provided to facilitate the discussions;

(d) In the Development Report, guidelines were given to have a separate chapter on women and development, which should include a historical review of the status of women and their problems, both economic and social;

(e) A separate task force was to be constituted to prepare projects for women development based on the recommendations of the Development Report;

(f) Every plan document should have a separate chapter on women development (Manjula, 2000).

Democratic Capacity Building through Self Help Groups

The PPC laid the foundation for a massive and unprecedented effort for building capacity for decentralised planning, formulation and implementation of the state plan. This initiative helped in the formation of a series of institutional innovations including ward committees (*grama sabhas*), beneficiary committees, neighbourhood groups (*ayalkoottams*) and self help groups (*swayam sahaya sanghams*). In many of the panchayats in Kerala below the structure of *ayalkootams*, women self help groups were formed to enable them to participate in the economic and political processes.

Ulloor panchayat is a unique case of such an experiment. The panchayat did succeed in popularising the idea of self help groups among women as part of the campaign.

State of Women Organisations in Ulloor Panchayat

The panchayat has a few women's organisations (like *mahilasamajams* and *vanithasanghams*) run by organisations such as Nair Service Society (NSS), *Sree Narayana Dharma Paripalana Sangham* (SNDP) and government. But they did not reach the women in an effective way. Nor were women from the lower strata (both economic and social) taking part in these organisations. In consequence, women remained, by and large, unaware of opportunities for their social and economic well-being.

Participation of Members in Social and Business Organisations

It was observed that participation of the beneficiaries of SVSSS in social and business organisations is very low (19.2%). The vast majority of members (80.8%) are not participating in any of these organisations. It is further noticed that participation of the poor is lower than that of the non-poor. About one-fourth of the non-poor is participating in organisations, while hardly 15 per cent of the poor do so (Table 7.1).

Table 7.1: Participation in Social or Business Organisation: Poor and the Non-Poor

Level of Participation	*Non-Poor*	*Poor*	*Total*
Yes	38 (24.1)	24 (14.5)	62 (19.2)
No	120 (75.9)	141 (85.5)	261 (80.8)
Total	158 (48.9)	165 (51.1)	323 (100)

Involvement in other business and social organisations helps the members to participate in SHGs more effectively (see case one in Appendix to this chapter). Women participate, in general, in various political, cultural and social organisations. Some take part in political parties and trade unions. Among them are also members of *Kerala Shasthra Sahithya Parishad* (KSSP), Parent Teacher Association (PTA) and Residents' Association. Many of them are participating in NSS and SNDP. It instils confidence in women and attracts them to MFO. Unfortunately, the majority of women did not have any earlier exposure to such organisations.

Participation in Grama Sabhas

As a result of the People's Plan Campaign, *grama sabhas* have become the fora for discussing people's problems and development needs. However, it was only after joining SHGs that most of the women in the study area came to know about *grama sabhas*. In fact, the SHGs motivated many of the beneficiaries to take part in *grama sabhas*. In the group meetings of the SHGs, the members used to discuss their needs and problems which included drinking water, toilet, public hygiene and housing. Identification of problems and formulation of ideas for their solution have helped them to take part in the planning process effectively and meaningfully. Thus women from financially and educationally backward classes were empowered to take part in development process and discourse concerning gender-sensitive planning.

Table 7.2: Level of Participation in Grama Sabhas

Participation in Grama Sabhas	*Non-Poor*	*Poor*	*Total*
Yes	75 (47.5)	86 (52.1)	161 (49.8)
No	83 (52.5)	79 (47.9)	162 (50.2)
Total	158 (48.9)	165 (51.1)	323 (100)

Table 7.2 shows that nearly one-half of the beneficiaries take part in *Grama Sabha* of the Ulloor panchayat. Many of them have received benefits such as cow, poultry, sewing machine, construction, renovation or maintenance of houses, toilet and well through *Grama Sabhas* (see case two, three and five in Appendix to this chapter). This must be the reason why participation of the poor in *Grama Sabhas* was higher than that of the non-poor. It was also observed that the SHGs of SVSSS in Ulloor could effectively enhance the democratic capacities of poor women by making them participate in *Grama Sabhas.*

Enhancement of Economic Capacity through Microfinance Organisation

Microsavings and microcredit are the major parts of microfinance. Microfinance helps the poor to mobilise and pool their meagre savings and to use them as a major source to cushion economic shocks. Likewise, microcredit enhances economic choices and opportunities of the poor. Microfinance institutions also supply credit to the poor for meeting their various needs. Microcredit is given to the poor for production and even for consumption.

The major objective of microfinance is to ensure sustainable livelihood for poor women. Microcredit is given for starting a new business or for strengthening an existing business. In other words, microfinance is the first step for microenterprise. The enterprise may be either individual or group-based. The success of any income generating activity can be measured by the profit gained from the activity and the improvement in the economic condition of the beneficiaries. While the economic participation of the poor women increases, they are empowered in social and political grounds also.

For analysing women's empowerment Mayoux (1998) has developed a framework (see Appendix IX). In the framework, the power or the capacity for change for individual women includes the following:

(a) Access to income;
(b) Access to productive assets and household property;
(c) Control over loan use;
(d) Control over income from loan and other household productive activities;
(e) Control over productive assets and household property;
(f) Freedom from the burden of domestic work including childcare.

This section deals with the role played by the microfinance organisation, SVSSS, to initiate, organise, manage and enhance microenterprises and other income generating activities by the SHGs under them.

Position of Microenterprise in the MFO

Of the 323 women studied, only 63 (20%) were engaged in income generating activities. The activities may be broadly classified into four: (a) trading and commercial establishments; (b) animal husbandry units; (c) production and processing; and (d) service enterprises.

The activities formed by the members in the groups are mostly conventional in nature (Table 7.3). Some enterprising women were found, however to have been engaged in non-conventional enterprises. One woman manufactured *ayurvedic* medicines and treated her patients. She started her business very recently. She is not a qualified medical practioner, but she inherited the skills from her father who was a physician. She is planning to expand her business by registering her unit as a small-scale industrial unit and to avail loan from financial institutions like banks.

Table 7.3: Type of Income Generating Activities of Women in Organisation

Trading and commercial establishments	Vegetable trade, fish trade, fuelwood trade, rice trade, snack trade, lemon trade, papad trade, readymade garment sale, shops such as tea shop, provision store, stationery shop, etc.
Animal husbandry units	Rearing of cows and goats.
Production and processing	Soap-making, pickle-making, toy-making, bag-making, copra-making, curry powder-making, stone breaking, etc.
Service enterprises	Tailoring, catering, hiring out chair and other articles, *ayurveda* medical service

Women started trade and small business units rather than production and manufacturing units. The proportion of women engaged in trading and related activities was as high as 57 per cent (Table 7.4). The majority of them are engaged in trading items such as fish and vegetables which have ready demand throughout the year. Tea shops, grocery shops, petty shops, fuelwood shops and provision stores are usually attached to their houses so that they could manage the business effectively. Some feel that inter-member competition is becoming a major problem as new shops are coming up in the neighbourhood.

Only 14 per cent of them are engaged in cattle rearing. But the rising cost of fodder and the limited area at their disposal for rearing cattle were the constraints for most of them.

The dry periods of cattle also give them an additional burden (see case one in Appendix to chapter 6).

Table 7.4: Number of Members Engaged in Each Activity

Type of activities	*Number of members*	*Percentage*
Trade and commercial establishments	36	57.1
Animal husbandry units	9	14.3
Production and processing	9	14.3
Service enterprises	9	14.3
Total	**63**	**100**

Another fourteen per cent are engaged in production and processing of food items. Production or manufacturing entails problems of marketing. Marketing is a serious problem for units engaged in soap-making, pickle-making and copra-making. The profit margin in these activities is low and the activities are tedious since entrepreneurs themselves have to procure raw materials, arrange finance and do the marketing. The absence of adequate demand and increase in cost of raw materials are the other serious problems. Activities like bag-making, curry-powder-making, papad-making and toy-making are done according to orders received. In these areas of activities, absence of adequate orders and increase in the cost of raw materials are seen as the major problems. About fourteen per cent of the enterprising women were engaged in rendering services to customers such as tailoring, catering, hiring out chair and other articles and dispensing *ayurveda* medicines.

Level of Education

Figure 7.1 shows that the education status of women entrepreneurs in the MFO is highly unequal. About eight per cent of them are illiterate. They mainly do jobs like cattle rearing and small business. More than one-fifth of them have lower primary education; an equal proportion has education of upper primary level. More than one-third have higher secondary level; the proportion of graduates among them is as low as three per cent.

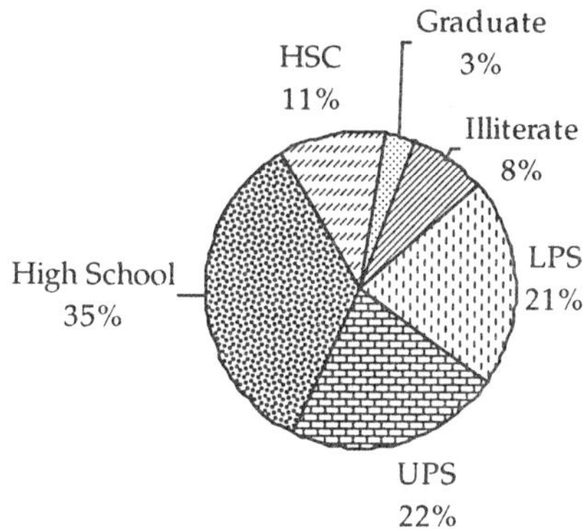

Fig. 7.1: Distribution of Enterpreneurs by Education

Education, by itself, does not seem to have acted as a help or a hindrance for starting income generating activities. Motivation, self-confidence and entrepreneurial capacity seem to be the decisive factors (see case four in Appendix to this chapter).

Age of the Enterprises

Thirty-two women (50%) started their activities after joining the groups. This shows that the microfinance organisation helped them to gain confidence to start economic activities (see case five in Appendix to this chapter). The other 50 per cent of the enterprises had been started even before the functioning of the MFO in the panchayat (Table 7.5).

Table 7.5: Duration of Enterprises Started by Women

Year	*Number of members*	*Percentage*
<1year	16	25
1.2 to 3 years	16	25
3.2 to 10 years	18	30
11 to 20 years	9	14
>21 years	4	6
Total	**63**	**100**

Control over Productive Assets

Nature of Business Premises

The majority of the enterprises (54%) were run in their own premises and land. All the dairy units, 33.3 per cent of the trade and business establishments, 66.7 per cent of the production and processing activities and 77.8 per cent of the service units were run in the own premises and land of the entrepreneurs. 14.3 per cent of the premises are on lease.

Only 22.2 per cent of the business establishments and 11.1 per cent of the service units are housed in rented premises. This shows that the entrepreneurs are not much interested in taking premises on rental basis due to the fact that they would lose a good part of their income and that their scale of activity is very low. While 4.8 per cent were using authorised sites like market places for trading purposes, another 7.9 per cent used unauthorised sites. These persons were in constant fear of getting evicted. About one-fifth of the women traders had no assured localities for marketing their wares. These women walked all the way carrying their wares on their heads or in hand-bags to and from their market areas. Only one woman among them owned an auto rickshaw, which she used for vending fish.

Home-based Business

In India, most of the enterprises run by women are home-based and form an extended home activity. In our sample also the majority (57.1%) of the enterprises are located in homes. It helped them to look after the household chores and manage their enterprises simultaneously (see case six in Appendix to this chapter). Most of the production, processing and service units were home-based; see Table 7.6. However, more than 60 per cent of the trading units were located in places outside home.

Table 7.6: Home-based Business Units

Location at Home	*Trade and Commercial Establishments*	*Animal Husbandry Units*	*Production and Processing*	*Service Enterprises*	*Total*
Yes	13 (36.1)	9 (100)	6 (66.7)	8 (88.9)	36 (57.1)
No	23 (63.9)	—	3 (33.3)	1 (11.1)	27 (42.9)
Total	36 (100)	9 (100)	9 (100)	9 (100)	63 (100)

Nature of Ownership

About three-fourth of the entrepreneurs organised, ran and managed their enterprises, all on their own. More than 50 per cent of the trading establishments, more than 77 per cent of the dairy units, two-thirds of the production units and nearly nine-tenths of the service units were exclusively run by women (Table 7.7).

Table 7.7: Ownership Structure of the Enterprises

Ownership Pattern	*Trade and Commercial Establishments*	*Animal Husbandry Units*	*Production and Processing*	*Service enterprises*	*Total*
Sole proprietorship	26 (72.2)	7 (77.8)	6 (66.7)	8 (88.9)	47 (74.6)
Family partnership	9 (25.0)	2 (22.2)	—	1 (11.1)	12 (19.0)
Non-family partnership	1 (2.8)	—	3 (33.3)	—	4 (6.4)
Total	**36(100)**	**9(100)**	**9(100)**	**9(100)**	**63(100)**

Family partnerships and non-family partnerships accounted for 19 per cent of the total number of business units. Non-family partnerships did business in association with neighbours and other members of self help groups. One-third of the production and processing units were run by self help groups. This shows that the majority of the women have control over the productive assets. This helps them to have personal income and independence (see case five and seven in Appendix to this chapter).

Access to Income

Other Income Generating Activities

The survey showed that 93 per cent of the entrepreneurs have no income generating activity other than the microenterprise (Table 7.8). This indicates that they are solely dependent on their activities. It was also observed that 15 per cent of the women engaged in entrepreneurial activities were from female-headed households (one-half of them widows and the other one-half separated). They were forced to take some kind of income generating activities for sustaining their families. Another 15 per cent of the women belonged to the households having alcoholics as their heads (either father or husband, but mostly husband). Of the total entrepreneurs, this section seemed more vibrant and keen to sustain their enterprises on a sound basis (see case five and eight in Appendix to this chapter).

Table 7.8: Other Income Generating Activities besides the Enterprise

Income Generating Activities	*Number of Members*	*Percentage*
None	59	93
Other service enterprise	3	5
Wage employment	1	2
Total	**63**	**100**

Source of Start up Fund

The enterprises started by women used various sources of funds as seed money for setting up their units, the amounts varying from one another depending on the nature and scale of activity. Nearly 30 per cent of them availed loans from the self help groups to which they belonged, while about one-fifth managed to get loans from financial institutions and other sources (Figure 7.2). On the other hand, loans from moneylenders were the source in about one-fourth of the cases. Household or personal savings provided the initial funds in the case of more than one-fifth. Gifts from parents, friends and relatives were available only for two per cent.

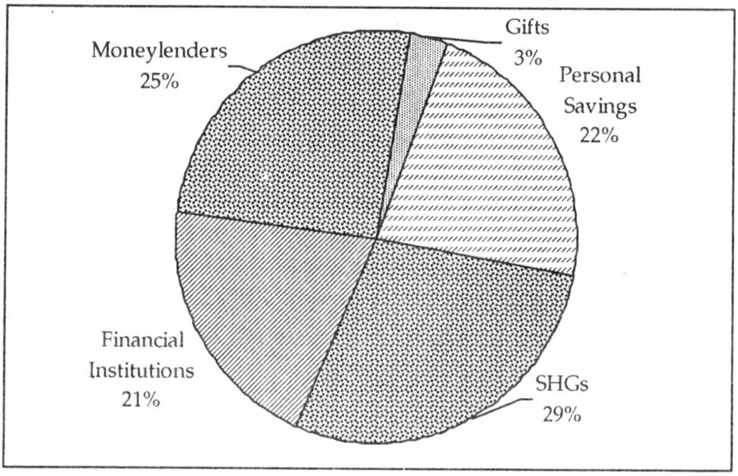

Fig. 7.2: Sources of Start up Fund of Enterprises

It was observed that only 19.5 per cent of the trading units, 22.2 per cent of the dairy units, 66.7 per cent of the production units and 33.3 per cent of the service units had been started exclusively using SHG loans. The major observation which can be made in this context is that the amounts that SHGs were able to offer were not sufficient for establishing viable enterprises. Loans from moneylenders had to be resorted to in a large number of cases (see case eight in Appendix to this chapter). These types of loans were availed mainly by fish and vegetable traders. The former needed cash on a daily basis for purchase of their merchandise. Such loans are not available from any formal financial and microfinance institutions. However, the entrepreneurs agreed that the small loans from SHGs had helped them to develop their business and were available when necessity arose. Some of them increased their stocks and improved the scale of their services using SHG loans. Another section of the members said that they used SHG loans for developing their children's enterprises.

Cash Flow

The average income that women entrepreneurs were able to earn per month was not much. Nearly two-fifth of them earned less than Rs. 500 per month. An equal proportion earned incomes between Rs. 501 and Rs. 1,000. The proportion which earned more than Rs. 1,000 a month comes to less than one-fourth. The maximum amount these microentrepreneurs could earn was Rs. 3,000 per month. The majority also experienced wide fluctuations in income from month to month depending upon the volatility of market conditions.

Work Burden

Women are the managers of their houses. They look after their children, manage household affairs and do all household chores. Women entrepreneurs have to bear double burden. More than two-fifths of them worked for two to five hours a day for their enterprises (Table 7.9). Another 46 per cent spent six to ten hours a day. There were around 11 per cent who spent more than eleven hours. There was a solitary case of a woman who reported that she was working for seventeen hours a day for her enterprise.

The majority of the women, nearly seventy per cent, engaged in trade and business activity, worked for more than six hours a day. Most of the women who are engaged in vegetable and fish trade wake up early in the morning, go to market and buy the things for sale (see case four in the Appendix to this chapter). Nearly three-fifths of them worked for six to ten hours daily. Those who are engaged in other income generating activities work less than ten hours a day. All this is in addition to the usual work burden at home. This excessive burden takes its toll from these women—in terms of ill-health and inability to work continuously. Surprisingly, there were a few among them who took up odd jobs such as housemaid over their businesses and household chores (see case seven in Appendix to this chapter).

Table 7.9: Average Hours of Work in a Day

Hours	*Trade and Commercial Establish-ments*	*Animal Husbandry Units*	*Production and Processing*	*Service Enterprises*	*Total*
2-5	11 (30.6)	6 (66.7)	5(55.5)	4 (44.4)	26 (41.3)
6-10	17 (47.4)	3 (33.3)	4(44.4)	5 (55.5)	29 (46.1)
11-15	7 (19.5)	—	—	—	7 (11.2)
16 and above	1 (2.8)	—	—	—	1 (1.6)
Total	**36 (100)**	**9 (100)**	**9(100)**	**9 (100)**	**63 (100)**

In the present time, a redoubled interest is in evidence in raising the economic status of poor families by giving microfinance to the women. Microfinance enables them to start microenterprises and thereby to enhance their families' economic status. In this situation, the additional burden that falls upon women goes unnoticed. In most cases, there may not be any sharing of responsibilities with the other members of the family, especially husband. This is a major reason why women take up low profile activities, which are manageable and less time consuming.

Shortcomings

A large number of income generating activities have been undertaken by SHG members in the Ulloor panchayat. However, the MFO has not taken any steps to coordinate the activities at the local or the panchayat level. Such an effort would have helped in solving the problems of marketing and increasing productivity of these activities. Many linkages could have been made among the activities within the organisation. For example, coconut oil manufactured by one unit could have been used for producing soap in another unit; bakery items could have been bought and sold by tea shops, provision stores, etc.

The urban character of the Ulloor panchayat is another problem. The availability of consumer goods in the affinity prompts them to purchase goods rather than produce. It is found that consumerism is sweeping in almost all the households of the panchayat irrespective of whether poor and non-poor. Hence, the motivation to produce things for consumption and for sale is very low among these families.

Another feature is that 80 per cent of the members are not engaged in any enterprises. The main reason is that most of them are unskilled and they lack technical qualifications or experience. The MFO has failed to give training or organise entrepreneurial development programmes for the members. The MFO also failed to upgrade the skills and technical know how of its members. This is considered to be the main reason for the reluctance on the part of the majority of the members to take up any kind of income generating activities.

Poor women lack in general, human capital such as skills and education. Therefore, it is difficult for them to initiate and manage an enterprise. The agency which provides microfinance is expected to give some inputs to them in terms of institutional support and linkages and provide them training and information regarding the starting and management of microenterprises. Ideally speaking, these items of assistance should be given in a package along with microcredit. Then only the said objectives of microfinance could be achieved.

PART-II

SVSSS Federation: Network of SHGs

Networking may be defined as a chain of people or institutions working together to achieve common goals. The merits of a network are the following:

(a) Bargaining power increases;
(b) Skills, information and resources are increased by sharing among member (individuals or institutions);
(c) Reduces time, money and cost of activities;
(d) Enlarges group knowledge and activity;
(e) Increases confidence and participation;
(f) Creates a shared pool of skills and resources;

(g) Keeps group leadership accountable and workload is shared;

(h) Impacts government policy.

The *Samatha* SHGs have been federated at the panchayat level. The federation was set up after two years of its functioning. It is the coordinating body of the organisation. All the presidents and the secretaries of the 163 groups are the members of the federation. The federation meets once in a month. The federation elects a President, a Vice President, a Secretary, two Joint Secretaries and a Treasurer from among the members. There is also an executive board. It consists of fifteen ward convenors and three co-ordinators (volunteers of KSSP). It is the co-ordinators who are organising and monitoring the functioning of SHGs.

The major aims of this federation are to provide a place for its members to interact with the members of other groups, share experiences of various groups, frame new systems, initiate new ventures, settle disputes inside the groups as well as among the groups, interact with its members, create awareness, circulate important announcements, impart new ideas to the groups, develop effective leadership, ask for consultation, share the problems regarding sanctioning of bank loans, monitor the functions of the existing groups, form new groups and cultivate discipline among the group members.

Each member of the groups has to contribute Rupees three per month to the federation. Of this, Rupee one is earmarked for giving assistance to unforeseen exigencies like accidents and death of the members, Rupee one for medical help (welfare fund), 50 paise for a newsletter and 50 paise for the expenses incurred for holding meetings of the federation, holding annual meetings and conducting extra curricular activities for women members and their children. This fund is collected at the federation meeting. When a member of any SHG dies, the heirs get Rs. 1,000. And for accidents the federation gives Rs. 500 to the member concerned from the federation fund. Already it has distributed Rs. 35,000 (Rs. 14,000 for deaths and Rs. 21,000 as medical help) as part of welfare measures.

In addition to these welfare measures, the federation arranges training programmes and awareness programmes for its members. Several batches underwent training on soap-making, catering, etc. On the first Saturday of every month a group of doctors from Thiruvananthapuram Medical College conducts classes for health care for the members. This helps to improve the health consciousness of the members. Another venture initiated by the federation is setting up of a provision store for distributing provisions at a low rate to its members as well as others. For making it a reality, the federation collected Rs. 1,000 from each self help group. The members in the groups themselves are currently running the store. This creates employment in packing, selling, etc. Thus the federation acts as a supporting system for its members in addition to the SHGs.

Linkages with Other Institutions

Linking with other institutions—democratic and financial—helps the women in different ways. In this section, it deals with how the Microfinance Organisation, SVSSS acts as a sub-system to the other institutions.

Linkage with the Panchayat

The Ulloor panchayat is assisting the women in the SHGs to improve their social and economic status in several ways. So the linkage with the panchayat has proved to be helpful to women in poor families. As the panchayat comes under the special grade category, its annual plan fund comes to about Rupees eight lakh to Rupees nine lakh. The People's Plan Campaign gave guidelines for each and every panchayat to set apart 10 per cent of the total plan fund for the Women Component Plan (WCP). Hence the allocation for the women in the panchayat is around Rs. 80,000. The panchayat is supposed to allocate the fund under WCP for projects that help women to obtain direct benefits, to organise themselves or to get direct income from such organisation.

Accordingly, Ulloor panchayat committee extended financial assistance to more than 30 SHGs of Samatha for setting up of income generating activities which included four tailoring units consisting of forty sewing machines, two catering units, two book-binding units, two soap-making units, three pillow-making units and fifteen bakery units. Besides, the panchayat provided revolving fund assistance to the SHGs as seed capital. This helped the women to take part in the planning process. In the panchayat, it was observed that women participation in development seminars and *Grama Sabhas* was very high.

SHG—Bank Linkage

After six months of formation of SHGs, if the groups show their viability, the banks lend money. The money is lent in such a way that at first the loan is sanctioned on a 1:1 basis of the group savings. After repaying the loan, the bank increases the ratio to 1:2 to 1:3. The banks lend at an interest rate of 12 per cent per annum. The group in turn lends the money at 24 per cent to the members. Thus the group earns a margin of 12 per cent on the loans. This income is given back to the members as interest on their savings. In case, a member defaults repayment, the group is liable to make it. Hence, the chance for default is low.

In SVSSS, all the groups are linked with banks. The majority of the groups have already availed loans from banks. The banks give loans on an assessment of the overall performance as well as the total savings of the groups. The repayment record of all the groups is found to be very encouraging. The self help groups under SVSSS have already taken bank loans to the tune of Rs. 50 lakh.

From the discussions with group members, we found that they are enthusiastic in getting bank loans. Most of them had bitter experiences; their requests for loans had been turned down by banks for want of collateral security and guarantee. Even the very few who had received some paltry amount by way of bank loans, had bitter experiences of the harassments they had to undergo. But it was very easy to get SHG loans with minimum formalities (see case one in Appendix to this chapter).

In SVSSS, as soon as a SHG is formed, it starts a bank account with a neighbouring bank. In order to develop banking habits among members, the organisation directs that the group savings are remitted every week by the member who holds the meeting. This practice would also ensure transparency. The secretary issues cheques from the member's own savings and for bank loans. It has to be withdrawn by the member herself. The functionary responsible for dealing with bank account differs from group to group. Only less than one-half of the groups follow the direction of the umbrella organisation; in the case of the others, it is the secretary or president who remits the amount in the bank. However, a large number of women improved their banking habits after becoming members of the MFO.

Many of the members reported that they had great reluctance to go to a bank or any government offices, or engage in self-employment activities prior to their joining the groups because of low education and fear (see case nine in the Appendix to this chapter). But after joining the group, they got the courage and confidence to go to banks and do all the formalities with the banks. Thus the advent of the self help groups certainly improves the banking habits of many of the members in the group.

In short, the *Samatha* SHGs have helped women to come out of their homes. No other organisation—religious or communal or social—could reach the women of the poor and lower middle classes in such a big way. The organisation has already covered 15 per cent of the total female population of the panchayat.

The basic approach of the microfinance organisation is to address the economic problems first, and then pursue their social problems. The self help groups addressed the economic problems of the poor women by providing access to credit, technical advice and training. To some extent, the organisation was able to expand the resource base through improvement of socio-economic status of women in the family and community. It also helped to increase the level of awareness and confidence among women by giving them training in microsavings, banking habits and starting microenterprises. Thus self help groups are striving for a change in the status of women.

Now-a-days microfinance is viewed as a panacea for many ills of women. It is true that the SHGs could become agents for change, but only over a long period of time. Change on a sustainable basis would come about only by enhancement of the level of public awareness, active participation in group discussions, broadening of the sphere of activities, and appropriate training.

APPENDIX

Case One: Indira is 48 years old. Her husband is an auto rickshaw driver. She has two children, a son and a daughter. She had her own savings of Rs. 5,215 and got Rs. 36,500 as loans (of this Rs. 1,500 is the SHG fund and the remaining Rs. 35,000 comes from the fund provided by bank).

Participation in other organisations helps to participate in the SHGs efficiently: She was an active member of *Kerala Shastra Sahitya Parishad* (KSSP) before becoming the member of the MFO. It was through the organisation she came to know about microfinance and she took the initiative to form the group. She also helped to organise other self help groups in her neighbourhood. She witnessed that her participation in KSSP helped a lot in organising and participating in SHG.

Difficulties faced by the poor in availing bank loans: Indira reminds the researcher of her experience of seeking for a loan for building her house with the same bank before becoming the member of the SHG. The bank authorities asked for a number of documents and they took several days for sanctioning the loan. But in the case of SHG loan, there were not much procedures and the bank sanctioned loan in a day's time. The group she belongs to is Shanti Nagar and the group got Rs. 125,000 as bank loan.

Case Two: Latha is an unmarried woman. She is 27 years old and belongs to S.C. She studied up to SSLC. She knows tailoring also. She lives with her parents in their own thatched house.

Participation in SHGs helps to participate in Grama Sabhas: She does not participate in any business and social organisation other than SHG. She is the secretary of the group she is participating and acting as the ward convenor (co-ordinator of the SHGs in a panchayat ward) she is representing. After joining the group she regularly goes to *Grama Sabhas*. She got a sewing machine from the panchayat and now she is making a living out of it.

Leading to voice against problems in the society: She shared her experience with the researcher. Her place of residence in a *lakshamveedu* colony, where people from low economic status live so closely. In the colony, the drunkards usually make nuisance to the people. This problem is discussed by the members of SHGs. They decided to stop it. One day, when a drunkard made noise, the members of the SHG asked him to stop making noise. The incident was noted by the other people in the colony. She says that without the SHG, she would not have the courage to do such things in her locality. In other words, only with the support of her fellow members she was able to do it.

Case Three: Lalitha is a member of Surabhi self help group. She is a 40 year old widow. She lost her husband ten years ago. She belongs to Scheduled Caste. She studied up to eighth standard. She has two sons; both are studying in high school. She is working as a housemaid. She has only three cents of land. It is situated in a remote area without any approach road. She put up a hut on the plot. She has savings of Rs. 1,175.

Increased participation in grama sabha and getting benefits from it: She is not participating in any of the business or social organisations in the panchayat. But she regularly attends *grama sabhas* of the panchayat. As a result, she got grant from panchayat for tiling her house. For improving her house she is in need of money. She hopes that the membership in the SHG will help her in the future.

Case Four: Sheela is 28 years old. She has two children—a son aged ten years and a daughter aged seven years. She studied up to tenth standard. She owns two cents of land. On the land, she has built a small house thatched with asbestos. She is the secretary of Edavacode SHG, one of the earliest formed SHGs in the panchayat. She has savings of Rs. 4,375 with the SHG. Her husband was a construction worker.

Starting of an enterprise with SHG loan: As the availability of work for her husband became irregular and difficulty arose, she started vending vegetables. The seed capital for starting the trade came from SHG loan of Rs. 2,000 in November 1998. After conducting the business, she feels that the profits are minimal and the repayment of loan is difficult. Hence, she thought of a different business. Her mother-in-law came to her help. She was vending fish on a small-scale for some years. She rendered necessary help and advice to her daughter-in-law. Sheela took the way of her mother-in-law and decided to sell fish in and around her locality availing another SHG loan of Rs. 6,000 in March 1999.

Facing problems with confidence: The decision caused an uproar in Sheela's family because she was a member of a backward community; none of the family members had taken up fish vending before. So, Sheela had to face a lot of difficulties from her family side as well as from her husband. Her husband used to beat her and asked her to stop the business. But Sheela was so bold and she continued her activity.

Expanding the enterprise with the help of husband: In due course of time, her husband accepted his wife's decision. After some time, availability of work for Sheela's husband became very limited and he used to stay back in house when her wife was out for work. This made him to think. He extended his support to the business. For that they decided to buy a pick-up auto rickshaw and sell fish in other places in addition to their locality. Sheela's husband liked the idea and he took a driving licence. For buying an auto rickshaw they borrowed Rs. 20,000 from a commercial bank and Rs. 25,000 from outside source. Now both of them sell fish in the outskirts of the city with the help of their pick-up auto rickshaw. They sell fish everyday. From the enterprise, they get a profit of Rs. 3,000 per month after repaying the bank loan.

Work burden: For going for business, Sheela wakes up at two o'clock in the morning and prepares food for her family. Then she and her husband start from home at four o'clock for Pangode, the wholesale fish market of Thiruvananthapuram district. After buying fish, they go to the city area at seven o'clock for selling it. They are in round for about three to four hours a day for selling fish. If the entire daily stock of fish is not sold out, they go to fish market for selling it. Thus Sheela works for seven hours on average for her enterprise daily. By afternoon they come home. Husband usually takes rest after the business hours. But Sheela may not be able to take rest as she has to take her children after their school by 3.30 p.m. She can take rest only during night for an early travel.

Case Five: Prabha, a 38 year old woman in Edavacode SHG is separated from her husband for seven years. She has three daughters aged 18, 12 and 10 respectively. She participated in *Grama Sabhas* and she got grant for a house and a toilet. With that she built a small house in two cents. She has a savings of Rs. 4,325 in SHG.

Microcredit as start up fund: She took a loan of Rs. 1,000 from the SHG and started trading clothes and garments in other places on instalment basis. Later she took two more loans (for Rs. 2,000 and Rs. 5,000) for expanding her business. She has taken a loan of Rs. 20,000 from a moneylender for house construction as the panchayat grant was insufficient. She wants to repay the loan and to expand her business. For that, she has applied for a loan of Rs. 10,000 from the SHG.

Case Six: Lalitha belongs to Nanma self help group. She is 35 years old. She has only primary school education. Her husband is a construction worker. She has a daughter and a son. She lives in a small house in three cents. She has a savings of Rs. 2,000 in SHG.

Home-based enterprise: Lalitha took a loan of Rs. 5,000 from SHG and started firewood trade in her household. She buys some trees from other places and she with the help of her husband keeps the firewood in a shed in the homestead. The customers come to her house and buy firewood. She does the odd jobs of breaking the logs and trading. As the location of business is in her household, she is able to manage her household chores and to attend her business without the help of any other person. She is promptly repaying the loan out of the receipts of the trade. She wants to increase her stock of firewood and to build a better shed to keep stock. So she is planning to apply for a larger loan from the SHG in the future.

Case Seven: Rema is a woman from a forward caste. She is 40 years old. She has got upper primary school education. She has four children—two sons and two daughters. The daughters who are younger are studying in college and school.

The sons are not going out for any work. Her husband is addicted to alcohol. She has savings of Rs. 4,225 and took four loans from the SHG. She bought a plot of two cents with her own savings and a loan (Rs. 5,000) from the SHG. From the panchayat, she got a grant for building a house. Thus she built a modest house. But it was not completed.

Work burden due to looking after a job as housemaid apart from enterprise: To earn a living she worked as a part-time housemaid in a nearby house. As the income was small, she started trading vegetables and dried fish in the local market. For buying the things for trade she gets up early in the morning to take the five o'clock bus which goes to the wholesale market. She returns to the locality by nine o'clock and carries on the business. On an average, she works for seven hours a day. In the morning she conducts the business and in the afternoon she is working as a housemaid. She takes a heavy burden. She says that her college-going elder daughter is helping her in doing her household chores.

Case Eight: Shyamala is a 55 year old Scheduled Caste woman. She is a widow. She studied up to sixth standard. Her children are married and settled. For making a living for herself, she has been taking up the job of fish vending for the last 15 years and earning an average of Rs. 1,500 per month.

Savings is useful while microcredit is insufficient: She has got savings of Rs. 1,800 with the SHG and she is promptly remitting it. She feels that the money will help her in future. But she has not taken any loan from the SHG. While asked why she did not avail any loan, she replied that the SHG loans would come once in a while and the loans have to be repaid on weekly or monthly basis. But she needs daily credit in order to conduct her business. So she is still depending on moneylenders for credit on daily interest basis.

Case Nine: Bindhu is 35 year old unemployed woman. Her husband is a mechanic in an automobile workshop, earning about Rs. 2,000 per month. She has two children—a son and a daughter aged 12 and 10 respectively. She has passed BA, but she lacks any kind of technical training. Later she joined as a member in Shanti Nagar self help group near Kariyam. This self help group is one of the earliest formed groups with the MFO.

Confidence to perform various activities: After becoming the member of SHG she had attended training programme for soap-making. She also gave classes for other women in some other parts of the state about the formation of self help groups and their benefits. She had Rs. 4,000 as own savings and borrowed Rs. 31,200 in three times. The purpose of first loan was education of her children, while the second and the third loans were used for redeeming gold ornaments pledged at informal financial institution. The third loan has a monthly instalment of Rs. 500 with a repayment period of forty months. She believes that without the help of self help group she may not be able to get the last loan. During the 2000-2002 period she became the secretary of the SVSSS federation. In order to improve her abilities further she is now attending computer classes. After becoming the member, she gained a lot of confidence. As a result, she now becomes an agent of Life Insurance Corporation.

8

Performance of Self Help Groups and Emerging Issues in Microfinance

In the microfinance system, self help groups are the basic units. The sustainability of the system largely depends upon the stability and performance of the Self Help Groups (SHGs). In the present study, 34 SHGs with SVSSS are analysed and the results are presented in the first part of this chapter.

Now-a-days, microfinance is considered a panacea for many ills of the society. A number of agencies, organisations and government take up the idea and popularise it. However, several issues are emerging as has been evident from the field enquiry which was conducted as a part of the present exercise.

Performance of Self Help Groups

Self help groups are small informal associations created for the purpose of enabling members to reap economic benefit out of mutual help, solidarity and joint responsibility. The benefits include basically obtaining savings and credit facilities and pursuing group enterprise activities. Studies reveal that certain elements become crucial for the successful functioning of SHGs.

Rating of Self Help Groups

The performance of the self help groups under study is assessed using twelve indicators. All the indicators are rated according to their importance for the functioning of the groups. The indicators and the rates are given in Appendix II.

It was found that the maximum score earned by any group in the sample was 28 points and the minimum 17 points. The SHGs came under three categories; those who performed well (scoring 25 to 28 points) and those who showed medium performance (21 to 24 points) and the performance of those SHGs was poor (20 points or less). Nine groups (27%) performed well; the majority (53%) came under the medium category; and seven groups (20%) which did not perform well came under the low category.

Comparison of Relative Performance of SHGs

An analysis was made to compare the performance within the different types of self help groups. All the indicators relating to the performance of SHGs were considered (Table 8.1).

Organisational Functions of SHGs

Attendance

Participation of the members in weekly meeting of SHGs is a major determining factor for the smooth and effective functioning of the groups. It was observed that only 14.7 per cent of the groups showed high level of attendance, i.e., in the class interval 80-100 per cent. About 85.3 per cent of the groups had attendance ranging from 60 to 80 per cent (Table 8.2). Low levels of attendance were seen among all the three categories. Only two groups among the high performers and three groups among the medium-performers had the highest level of attendance of above 80 per cent. All the groups in the low category showed low levels of attendance around 80 per cent.

However, it was observed that the levels of attendance in groups varied and the attendance tended to decline over a period of time. This may be due to the fact that the enthusiasm of the members was steadily on the decline. The members do not seem to have gained much group experiences. It is also observed that in some groups after their starting many people dropped out from the groups.

Table 8.1: Relative Performance of Self Help Groups

Variables	*Total*	*High*	*Medium*	*Low*
Attendance in meetings				
Mean	2.1471	2.2222	2.1667	2.0000
Standard Deviation	0.3595	0.4410	0.3835	0.0000
Regularity in savings				
Mean	2.4118	2.7778	2.3889	2.0000
Standard Deviation	0.6568	0.4410	0.6978	0.5774
Record keeping/book keeping etc.				
Mean	1.3235	1.6667	1.2778	1.0000
Standard Deviation	0.4749	0.5000	0.4609	0.0000
Operation of bank account/ dealings with the bank				
Mean	1.5294	2.0000	1.4444	1.1429
Standard Deviation	0.5066	0.0000	0.5113	0.3780
Percentage of members availing loan to total members				
Mean	2.9412	3.0000	3.0000	2.7143
Standard Deviation	0.2388	0.0000	0.0000	0.4880
Decision on loan taken during meeting				
Mean	3.0000	3.0000	3.0000	3.0000
Standard Deviation	0.0000	0.0000	0.0000	0.0000
Awareness about byelaws and whether they are written or oral				
Mean	2.0588	2.5556	1.4286	1.4286
Standard Deviation	0.7762	0.5270	0.5345	0.5345
Participation in discussion and group functioning				
Mean	1.0882	1.2222	1.0556	1.0000
Standard Deviation	0.3788	0.6667	0.2357	0.0000
Creation of emergency/ welfare fund				
Mean	0.5294	0.7778	0.5000	0.2857
Standard Deviation	0.5066	0.4410	0.5145	0.4880
Imposition of sanctions and enforcement of byelaws				
Mean	2.5000	2.7778	2.6667	1.7143
Standard Deviation	0.6629	0.4410	0.4851	0.7559
Participation in community needs				
Mean	1.3235	2.3333	1.0000	0.8571
Standard Deviation	1.3193	1.5811	1.0290	1.0690
Starting of income generating and other activities				
Mean	1.6176	2.8889	1.0556	1.4286
Standard Deviation	1.6880	1.2693	1.6618	1.5119

Table 8.2: Attendance in Group Meetings

Attendance	*Level of Performance*			*Total*
	High	*Medium*	*Low*	
80-100%	2 (22.2)	3 (16.7)	—	5 (14.7)
60-80%	7 (77.8)	15 (83.3)	7 (100)	29 (85.3)
Total	**9 (26.5)**	**18 (52.9)**	**7 (20.6)**	**34 (100)**

Record Keeping

Proper record keeping is very important for the efficient functioning of a group—to avoid replication of the same functions, to maintain trust among the members, to provide information about the attendance of members in group meetings, status of remittance of savings and of repayment of loans and on the financial situation of the group. Moreover, it is essential if groups want to have linkages with financial institutions such as banks. It also ensures transparency in the functioning of self help groups. In *Samatha*, membership register, attendance register, minutes book, weekly register, savings register, loan register, passbook and consolidated register are maintained.

Of the total self help groups, only 32.4 per cent groups kept all the required records and the registers. The vast majority of the groups (67.6%) kept only a few of the records systematically and neatly. While the majority of the high-performing groups (66.7%) kept all the records and registers, none of the low-performing groups kept the records in full. The majority of the medium-performer groups (72.2%) were also in the list which did not keep the entire list of records (Table 8.3).

Leadership and Incentives

Leadership of a self help group is a determining factor in the sustainability of the group. In the organisation, the more educated women in the groups are elected as secretaries who are capable of managing the accounts properly, commanding

Table 8.3: Maintenance of Records

State of Records	*Level of Performance*			*Total*
	High	*Medium*	*Low*	
All records maintained	6 (66.7)	5 (27.8)	—	11 (32.4)
Not all records maintained	3 (33.3)	13 (72.2)	7 (100)	23 (67.6)
Total	**9 (26.5)**	**18 (52.9)**	**7 (20.6)**	**34 (100)**

respect from the other group members and communicating with officials in banks and the panchayat. The organisation insists that leadership must change once in two years. But problems such as non-entry of new leadership due to over-dominance of old leadership and reluctance of other members to take up responsibilities were common in most of the groups.

Usually, the secretary of self help group keeps the registers and performs the functions on a voluntary and honorary basis. Laxity in the maintenance of records is often attributed to the pressure of work of the secretary. The secretary has to perform a number of functions (both organisational and financial). Absence of any incentive to perform these duties creates some degree of apathy on her part (see case one in the Appendix to this chapter). It is the duty of the secretary to continuously motivate the members and maintain their interest high in the activities of the SHGs, indeed a tiring job. So for the effective management of the groups it is desirable that the secretaries of SHGs are given reasonable monetary incentives.

In an organisation like SVSSS, which is exclusively owned and managed by poor women, they must pay for the services of the workers; only if they pay, the workers will be responsive to their needs and also accountable to members of groups who are their pay masters (Ratnam, 2002).

Duration of Weekly Meetings

Weekly meetings are one of the major functions of self help groups all over the world. In *Samatha,* groups meet on

Saturday and Sunday afternoons. But there are groups that meet on weekdays also. Meetings on weekends help women to come together, after attending their household chores, to discuss various issues—personal, political, social and cultural matters. The members remit their weekly savings to the secretary of the group at the meeting. Also decisions are taken on matters relating to sanctioning and repayment of loans and calculation of interest rates.

For performing all these functions, a group has, on an average, to meet for more than one hour. The majority of the groups (88.2%) meet for one to two hours a week, while 11.8 per cent groups (i.e., four groups) take less than one hour for meeting (Table 8.4). Interestingly, meetings of all the highly performing groups last for more than one hour. The majority of medium and low-performing groups also hold meetings of more than one hour.

Table 8. 4: Duration of Weekly Meetings

Duration	*Level of Performance*			*Total*
	High	*Medium*	*Low*	
< One hour	—	2 (11.1)	2 (28.6)	4 (11.8)
One to two hours	9 (100)	16 (88.9)	5 (71.4)	30 (88.2)
Total	**9 (26.5)**	**18 (52.9)**	**7 (20.6)**	**34 (100)**

Many members in the group felt that the time they spent for group meetings gave them exposure to the world of friends and fellows for sharing experiences and gaining insights. Housewives from lower middle class families have a lot of time to spare and invariably attend the meeting. On the other hand, a member working as a housemaid finds it difficult to attend the meeting. She therefore sends her daughter to the meeting as her proxy. For the poor, work for survival becomes the top priority (see case two in the Appendix to this chapter). This may be one of the reasons why poor women to keep away from these kinds of organisations.

Participation in Activities of SHGs

Participation in Discussions

The weekly meetings of the SHGs give opportunity to the women to speak openly. From the observations and the reports of the weekly meetings, we find, however, that most of the members in the group are only silent spectators in the meeting. Usually at group meetings, the leaders (president and secretary) take most of the time and two or three members dominate the proceedings.

In majority of the groups, participation of members in discussions is found to be low. Interestingly, the discussions are found to become lively and participation by members quite active when disbursement of loans is discussed. In most of the SHGs, it is felt from their functioning that overemphasis is given for financial aspects, rather than addressing gender issues and empowerment of women in general.

Creation of Emergency or Welfare Fund

The idea of microinsurance and welfare measures is included in the ambit of microfinance in recent times. As the majority of the members are poor, they often face financial stringencies. SEWA in Gujarat, the forerunner of microfinance in India, put forth the idea of microinsurance by collecting small amounts from members. In SVSSS also the majority of the groups (52.9%) have created funds for exigencies like medical treatment, funerals and welfare measures (Table 8.5). This fund is usually kept in a separate account.

The method of creating the fund varies from group to group but the usual method is to make periodic collections on a monthly basis. Sometimes, fines recovered from members are also deposited in the emergency fund. The majority of the high-performing groups (seven groups) have already created

Table 8.5: Creation of Emergency or Welfare Fund

Created Emergency/ Welfare Fund	*Level of Performance*			*Total*
	High	*Medium*	*Low*	
Yes	7 (77.8)	9 (50)	2 (28.6)	18 (52.9)
No	2 (22.2)	9 (50)	5 (71.4)	16 (47.1)
Total	**9 (26.5)**	**18 (52.9)**	**7 (20.6)**	**34 (100)**

the fund; on the other hand, the majority of the groups whose performance is rated low (five groups) have not done so. These groups have found it difficult to contribute to such a fund as they are already burdened with savings obligations and loan repayment responsibilities.

Enforcement of Rules

SVSSS has instructed the groups to exercise some control over the members to maintain discipline among them. A fine is imposed for late coming to (Rupees two) and for absence (Rupees five) at group meetings. For default in payment of loans, some groups charge double interest. These rules are evolved for the effective functioning of the groups. Unless care is taken to convince the members about the advantages of observing the rules, they may hesitate to cooperate. All the SHGs strictly follow all the rules during the initial stages of their formation; with the lapse of time, the spirit of implementing the rules is progressively lost.

The success story of Grameen Bank and of MYRADA reveal that they follow rules strictly and impose penalties for any deviation from rules. In SVSSS, while nearly three-fifths of the total groups strictly implement the rules, about one-third do not implement them always (Table 8.6). Around one-tenth of the groups have not observed rules and have not imposed sanctions on members. All the groups that do not impose the sanctions come under the low-performing category. But the majority—more than three-fourth—in the highly performing category strictly enforce rules (see case three in the Appendix to this chapter). In general, the groups which strictly enforce rules and impose sanctions have greater control over the members while in the case of others, the structure is loose and the performance poor.

Table 8.6: Imposition of Sanctions and Enforcement of Byelaws

Imposition of Sanctions and Enforcements of Laws	*Level of Performance*			*Total*
	High	*Medium*	*Low*	
Strictly enforced	7 (77.8)	12 (66.7)	1 (14.3)	20 (58.8)
Sometimes	2 (22.2)	6 (33.3)	3 (42.9)	11 (32.4)
Not at all	—	—	3 (42.9)	3 (8.8)
Total	9 (26.5)	18 (52.9)	7 (20.6)	34 (100)

Participation in Community Needs

Women self help groups in various parts of the world have taken up serious community issues (e.g. anti-liquor campaign in Orissa) and have fought for their resolution. In Ulloor panchayat the SHGs have not taken up such serious community issues.

The groups maintain intimate personal bonds with their members by participating in the functions and ceremonies of their members such as marriages, funerals and house-warming. The majority of the groups (94.1%) said that they collectively participated in community functions and *Grama Sabha* meetings.

Participation of members in *Grama Sabhas* has increased considerably after their becoming the members of SHGs. The panchayat also provides revolving fund assistance and assistance to start enterprises to these groups as a part of the Women Component Plan (WCP) of People's Plan Campaign. Revolving fund assistance and the assistance for starting the income generating activities are also received by SHGs from block panchayat and zilla panchayat

Other Activities Taken up by Self Help Groups

Besides dealing with loans and savings, SHGs take up other activities—financial, economic and cultural. Nearly one-eighth of the groups are engaged in financial activity. Conduct of *chitti* (rotating credit) is the major financial activity done by these groups among the members. One group conducts *chitti* with the non-members. This activity fetches additional income for the group. Only one group has conducted some kind of cultural activity, namely newspaper reading during weekly meetings (see case four in the Appendix to this chapter). Many groups celebrate their anniversaries also with clan.

The extra economic activities conducted by SHGs include trade (like rice and textile items), quarrying and manufacturing (e.g. soap-making, flour-making, squash and jam making and garment-making). Of the total 34 groups, 14 conduct some kind of economic activity. Some of the groups which have taken up economic activities, make good profits and perform well (e.g. bakery units and catering units) (Table 8.7).

Table 8.7: Other Activities Taken up by Groups

Activities	*Level of Performance*			*Total*
	High	*Medium*	*Low*	
No activity	1 (6.7)	11 (61.1)	3 (42.9)	15 (44.1)
Financial	—	3 (16.7)	1 (14.3)	4 (11.8)
Cultural	1 (11.1)	—	—	1 (2.9)
Economic and Financial	7 (77.7)	4 (22.2)	3 (42.9)	14 (41.2)
Total	9 (26.5)	18 (52.9)	7 (20.6)	34 (100)

On the other hand, many units like bakery, soap-making and flour-making, face the problems of marketing the products (case five in the Appendix to this chapter). There is no support system for this kind of enterprises either at the organisation level or at the panchayat level. The major drawback faced by these group enterprises is that most of them are not economically viable. Hence the profits earned by them are very low or even negative.

Another failure of this kind of group enterprises (e.g. provision store) is that not all the members actively participate in the activity (case six in the Appendix to this chapter). Two or three members take care of all the activities. But the profits are to be shared equally among the members. Such a situation creates ill-will among the members. Hence, most of the groups have been reluctant to take up any remunerative activity, while some others have expressed their readiness to take up additional responsibilities. However, some groups are content with their savings and credit functions alone.

In short, the self help groups which perform well have fared both in terms of organisational functions and proper participation in the activities of self help groups. But the medium and poor performers do not give much importance to the functions of the self help groups, which in turn affect the sustainability and existence of the groups.

Emerging Issues in Microfinance

One of the basic issues of the microfinance institutions/ programmes all over the world has been the inclusion of the non-poor in institutions exclusively meant for the poor. In addition to that various other problems like disparity in savings, mounting defaults, drops outs of members, multiplicity of promoting agencies, etc are cropping into the system.

The Outreach Issue

As one of the objectives of the study is to capture the involvement of the poor and non-poor in the organisation, a method of measurement of poverty is needed. For this purpose, the poverty index used was the one developed by Community Development Society (CDS) of Kerala for identifying poor families (see Appendix V). In the present study, it was found that out of the total 323 sample women studied, 158 (nearly 50%) were non-poor.

In most cases, the problem must have been due to inadequate targeting of the programmes and lack of safeguards against entry of well off groups in these programmes.

Problems of Poor in Microfinance

The members included in all SHGs are not homogeneous. Both the poorest and the not-so-poor are included in a group simultaneously. But the former would soon find themselves out of place in terms of culture, education, money, asset position and participation (see case seven in the Appendix to this chapter). On the other hand, the not-so-poor and the well off members are dominating the group because their absorption capacity as well as repayment capacity is comparatively higher than that of the poor members.

In microfinance, various activities are taking place. Of this, the important thing is to take part in group meetings and other activities. The poorest usually do not have much time to spare because they work hard for long hours, leaving very little time for respite. Thus even if such people are members of SHGs they may not be able to take part in this kind of organisation properly (see case two in Appendix to chapter six).

The poor are excluded from the system due to various reasons. Though it is a fact that microfinance is meant for the poor (and they need it also), some minimum terms and conditions are to be observed. Penalties and sanctions exert more pressures on the poor people. So within a short period, they are automatically (both voluntarily and involuntarily) excluded from the group. Some of them have begun to think of quitting the MFO due to their inability to observe the rules of MFO in respect of savings and repayment of loans as per schedule.

Non-Poor in Microfinance: A Discussion

The inclusion of middle and lower middle class women in microfinance organisations is due to several reasons. These women have better access to media and to cultural-political-religious activities going on around them. They get information and ideas from different sources. They have a lot of time to spare, as most of them remain unemployed. No wonder, they eagerly catch opportunities for activities that help them keep occupied and earn some economic returns (case eight in the Appendix to this chapter).

Many of the women whom we have identified for our sample as non-poor are not from highly well-to-do families (case nine in the Appendix to this chapter). They are just above or near the poverty line and devoid of financial facilities rendered by formal financial institutions. Through microcredit, they get cheap, quick and easy credit.

In microfinance, small loans are given, because the loans are suitable for the poor and it is easy for them to repay. The amounts are kept low to discourage the entry of the non-poor. As the microfinance organisation grows, the amount by the organisation would also increase. Such increase is called credit-deepening. When credit-deepening takes place, more non-poor are attracted to the organisation. Our sample organisation members were able to get loan amounts up to Rs. 25,000, which is not a small amount by any standard (see case eight in the Appendix to this chapter). This is another reason why the non-poor get included.

The poor would surmount poverty provided they get an opportunity to do so since poverty is not a permanent phenomenon. Hence, it is argued that persons who were poor at the time of becoming members of the MFO would graduate themselves to the category of non-poor in course of time. But it is very difficult to prove this contention because many members are still found to cluster around the poverty line.

The inclusion of the non-poor in the organisation does not mean that the poor are completely excluded from the system. But at the same time, the impact on the poor may be lopsided and delayed as the non-poor corner most of the benefits (see case seven in the Appendix to this chapter).

Disparity in Savings

Savings are the major component of microfinance. In SVSSS, members are asked to save Rs. 20 to 25 every week. Some beneficiaries in the organisation had savings of Rs. 5,000 which would not have been possible for them without the help of the MFO (see case ten in the Appendix to this chapter). However, there existed difference in the level of savings among the members.

Difference in the amounts of savings is noticed even at low levels but they become conspicuous at higher levels particularly for amounts higher than Rs. 3,000. While about 37 per cent of the non-poor saved more than Rs. 3,000, the corresponding proportion among the poor was less than 18 per cent (Fig. 8.1). The saving capacity of the poor is obviously much lower than that of the non-poor especially when the former has to bear the burden of repaying loans.

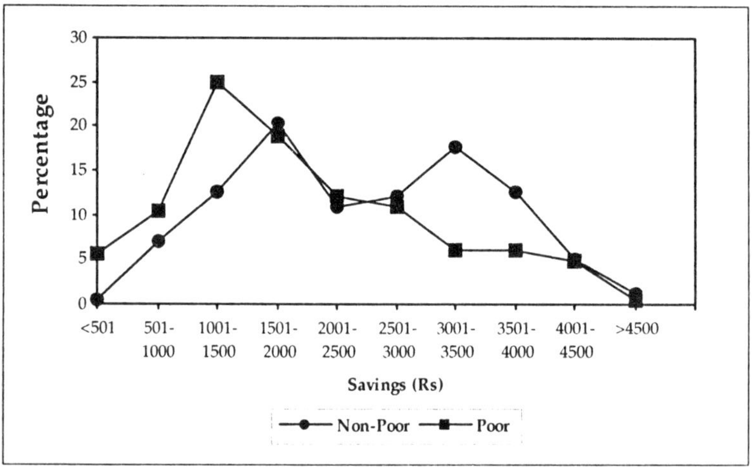

Fig. 8.1: Level of Savings of Beneficiaries

Problem of Default

The problem of mounting defaults has begun to emerge in the field of microfinance. Irregularity is found both in the case of remittance of savings and repayment of loans. When default occurs, recycling of funds gets interrupted. This would in turn affect the sustainability of the microfinance organisations.

Table 8.8: Distribution of Defaulters and Non-Defaulters among Beneficiaries by Poverty Status

Arrear	*Non-Poor*	*Poor*	*Total*
Defaulted	50 (31.6)	72 (43.6)	122 (37.8)
Not defaulted	108 (68.4)	93 (56.4)	201 (62.2)
Total	**158 (48.9)**	**165 (51.1)**	**323 (100)**

In SVSSS also arrears are mounting up. About 38 per cent of the beneficiaries made default in savings remittances and or loan repayments, at least once (Table 8.8). Most of the defaulters (53%) report irregular or extremely low-incomes as the major reason. The other reasons mentioned include lack of employment, ill-health and consumption needs (Table 8.9). The reasons are found to be mainly economic.

Table 8.9: Reasons for Default

Reasons	*Number of Members*	*Percentage*
Consumption	17	13.9
Ill health	12	9.8
Education of children, enterprises losses and house construction	3	2.5
Irregular income/low-income	65	53.2
Lack of employment	20	16.4
Repayment of other loans	6	4.9
Total	**122**	**100**

Since the poor avail larger loans, they find the burden of monthly repayment too heavy. Another reason noticed is that the funds borrowed by them are not always spent for remunerative activities. They find, therefore, repayment all the more difficult. Hence, recycling process is often affected and the sustenance of the groups becomes difficult.

Long Waiting Period for Loans

In microfinance, the loans are given in small amounts. But the poor expect to get it at the right time. The SHGs with *Samatha* give loans to its members on seniority basis. The secretary puts numbers on the application form seriatim. The application is considered according to the serial number. This helps the members to get loans in rotation. The waiting period for getting loan varies from group to group. As the procedure for applying for loan is simple (i.e., to make an application on a sheet of white paper), most of the members put up applications as soon as their previous loans are completely repaid. Usually the total number of members in a unit is in the range of 20 to 25. The NABARD directives point out that for efficient working of a SHG it is better to keep the number at 20 (optimum). Some of the groups have up to 30 members. The waiting period for getting loans would go longer with the increase in the number of members of a group (see case eleven in the Appendix to this chapter).

Dropping Out

The problem with several SHGs is that members leave them when some issues arise in the group. Many groups have lost their cohesion due to internal strife and personal rivalry. Some members left the groups for their failure to obtain loans on demand (see case twelve in the appendix to this chapter). In other cases, members leave the groups when they shift their residences subsequent to their marriages. In such cases, the groups have endeavoured to take new members who are not much experienced in taking part in MFO. This also creates some problems of cohesion and instability (see case thirteen in the Appendix to this chapter). Another problem is that these new members often happen to be women from not-so-poor strata of society.

Laxity of Non-financial Services and Improper Follow up

SVSSS has initiated entrepreneurial training (e.g. training in soap-making, garment-making, toy-making, etc.), technical assistance (in terms of advice regarding entrepreneurial activities), insurance provision (family medical insurance), voluntary saving and welfare provision, for the benefit of the members. But they have not reached the members in adequate measure. The problem of proper follow up from the animators was also seen as a major problem. This problem is found more prominent in groups which had taken up income generating activities. Many of these groups seem to have lost their motivation due to lack of training, technical assistance, etc. (see case one and five in the Appendix to this chapter).

Multiplicity of Promoting Agencies

Now in Thiruvananthapuram district, many other organisations and government programmes have also emerged to support SHGs of poor women. These 'promoting' agencies try to hijack the existing self help groups in the area. It is now noted that some of the members in *Samatha* are also joining groups promoted by other 'promoting' agencies. This creates problems for the existing groups as some of the members even make defaults and migrate to other groups putting the SHGs in jeopardy.

The above mentioned problems and issues are not exclusive to the MFO studied. They are observed in other microfinance organisations/programmes/institutions as well. While promoting new self help groups, these issues are to be given adequate attention.

APPENDIX

Case One: Kala is the secretary of Kovilvila SHG. She studied up to PDC. She got training in tailoring. Her husband is an auto driver. He drives auto rickshaw for another person in the neighbourhood. She has two sons. She has savings of Rs. 2,700. She has taken three loans amounting to Rs. 15,000. With this amount she has renovated her house.

No remuneration for responsibilities of group leader: Apart from acting as secretary to the SHG, Kala is acting as the ward convenor. She has to convene ward meetings and has to circulate the announcements of MFO to the SHGs in that ward. She complains that all the responsibilities have to be discharged on a voluntary basis. For a few days, there is no problem. But when it comes on a permanent basis, she would be unhappy. Naturally she demands for remuneration from the MFO. As she is a successful secretary the other members in the SHG do not allow her to leave the secretaryship. Even though election was conducted after two years, no other member wanted to take charge of the position because others felt that the secretary's responsibilities were too much.

Lack of proper training and motivation from the part of MFO: Kala wants to do some income generating activity. But she could not find a profitable enterprise so far. The MFO promises to give training on various trades. But due to lack of time and of insufficient funds, they are not able to impart the required training.

Case Two: Sasikala is a 35 year old woman. She has passed tenth standard. But she was not able to pursue her studies due to economic difficulties. She has three daughters aged eighteen, fourteen and thirteen respectively. They are studying in college and schools. Her husband is a carpenter. He is an alcoholic. So he would not give enough money for his family. In order to make a living, Sasikala has taken up a job of a cleaner in a private institution. Rest of her time, she works as a housemaid in a nearby house. Due to hard work, she earns Rs. 1,700 per month. But this money is not sufficient to bring up her children and for their education. After becoming the member of SHG she has taken a loan of Rs. 6,000 for their education. She feels that the financial assistance from SHGs helped her in a big way. But the problem she faces is that of time management.

Difficulties of poor women to take part in meetings and other activities due to lack of time: The weekly meeting of the SHG is convened while she is on her way for her work. So it is not easy for her to attend every weekly meeting. The group imposes fine for her absence. With the permission of other group members, she substituted her daughter for attendance. But when the daughter's college vacation is over, it is difficult for her to attend the meeting.

Case Three: Cheruvattikonam I is a high performing SHG. It has 20 members. The SHG has a savings of Rs. 55,000. The group has taken two bank loans amounting Rs. 60,000. All the members in the group are from homogeneous background. The major reason behind the success of this group is that it enforces all the rules and regulations strictly. It promptly collects fines for absence and late coming to the weekly meetings. It also charges double interest if there is a default in repayment. Although some of the members feel it is difficult, it contributes to the smooth functioning of the group.

Case Four: Mannanthala SHG has 20 members. Most of the members are from same economic background. The group has a total savings of Rs. 63,300. The group has not availed any loans from the bank; it could meet the credit needs of all the members of the SHG. The group has witnessed that if the funds are recycled properly, there is no need of external source of funds. This group has conducted a cultural activity, namely newspaper reading during weekly meetings. News items relating to women are given special attention in reading and they discuss important issues.

Case Five: The Paravoormele self help group is a high performer. The group has savings of Rs. 41,392. The group has taken up different activities in addition to the usual credit and savings. They conduct chitti with non-members also. They got financial assistance from the block panchayat and under SGSY scheme.

Problem of marketing of products from group enterprise: The SHG got a loan of Rs. 1.25 lakh with the assistance of which the group started a bakery unit. In the initial stage, *murukku*, *neyyappam*, etc. made by them were bought by the neighbouring shops. But when shopkeepers got the same items from other suppliers at lower prices, they stopped buying from the group. Thus the group finds difficult to repay the loan. Now the group is trying to sell their products in the locality. But the items the group supplies have very low demand.

Case Six: Surabhi is a self help group having many peculiarities. All the 18 members in the group belong to Scheduled Castes. Of the total members, four belong to female-headed households. Only one member in the group is self-employed. All the other members are unemployed.

Problem of non-cooperation of all the members in group enterprise: The Block Panchayat gave financial assistance of Rupees one lakh for starting an enterprise under Swarnajayanthi Grama Swarozgar Yojana (SGSY). Of this, 50 per cent is subsidy. The loan is taken for a group activity and it is registered with ten members in the group. The group thus started a provision store in the locality. For that they took a shop on lease. The secretary of the SHG took all the initiatives for the enterprise. But she complains that even though loans have been sanctioned to all other members in the group, she is not getting any support from other members. So she is fed up. She wants an arrangement for the functioning of the store. The group has not taken any arrangement for joint management. The members do not get any training or help from block panchayat or the MFO for financial management or other things. This aggravates the problem.

Case Seven: Shantha is 40 years old. She belongs to Kurunkulam Chenjeri self help group. She belongs to forward caste. She has a daughter who is nine years old. Her husband is a diseased person. Hence he is not able to go for work. She is the only earning member of the family. She rears three cows, of which only one cow is milch. But she has to give fodder for the three. Her father gave one of the cows years back. So she has not invested in the enterprise. She makes a living by selling the milk of her only milch cow to the neighbouring houses. It is very difficult for her to meet the expenses of the household with the meagre income from the cow, because the medical expenses for her husband are high. But she is not able to work as housemaid or so due to prestige. So she lives in a humble way. During the dry periods of the cow, she finds it very difficult to meet her daily expenses.

Disparity in case of loan allotment as the member is poor: She has saving of Rs. 2,385, while the other members saved more than Rs. 3,500 each with the SHG. When the researcher looked into the loan ledger, it was found that Shantha got only two loans during her membership in the group. On the other hand, all the members had availed three or four loans during the same period. The loan amount sanctioned to Shantha was also very low (Rs. 1,500 and Rs. 500). On an average, other members had availed more than Rs. 8,000 each from the SHG. While asked why it was so she said that it was because the group members were sceptical about her prompt repayment. The other members of the group hail from better off families. In this case the neighbours who know the financial position of the poor woman are purposely marginalising the woman in the group.

Case Eight: Padmaja is a 39 year old woman from forward caste. She has one son. Her husband is a vendor (document writer). She lives in a well furnished concrete house. She has 62 cents of land of her own. Even though she is unemployed, she hails from a well off family. She has savings with post office and bank. She belongs to Shanti Nagar SHG. Along with that she has savings of Rs. 5,000 in SHG. She has already taken three loans from the SHG (Rs 2,000, Rs. 4,400 and Rs. 25,000). The last loan she had taken for investing in her husband's business. The records show that she is prompt in remitting savings and in repaying loans. So she is a favourite member in the group. Apart from that, the group is formed among the relatives. So she is purposively included into the SHG in order to get adequate membership.

Case Nine: Sindhu is 30 years old. She belongs to Panavila self help group. She is married to a man who works in Gulf. He sends Rs. 2,000 per month for family maintenance. She studied up to Pre-degree, but she lacks technical training. She is a housewife. She has two children—one son and one daughter. She lives in her ancestral house. She has 25 cents of land. Though she started building a new house, it was not finished. She has a savings of Rs. 1,200 with the SHG. She has a savings bank account with the nearby bank. She has taken a loan of Rs. 5,000 from the SHG for completing the construction of her house. She testified that the SHG was a source of funds for her in times of necessity and she wanted to continue in the same.

Case Ten: Shyamala is an illiterate woman. She is 47 years old. Her husband is a sick old man. She lives in a small thatched house. After joining the SHG she came to know about the importance of *Grama Sabha* and attends it regularly. She got electricity connection as a part of it.

Savings is a boon to poor and small loans are useful for daily business: She has savings of Rs. 4,325. As she has no savings with any other institution, she was very proud of it and she showed her passbook to the researcher to prove her claim. She sells fish in her locality in a small-scale for the last 25 years. As her activity is in a small-scale, she takes small loans frequently from the SHG (Rs. 1,000-1,000-2,000-5,000-5,000). She says that the SHG helps her in times of contingencies and now she is not depending on moneylenders to buy fish on daily basis. Her problem is that she sells fish on wayside. She fears that in future she may be evicted. She also says that she is facing severe competition from those who sell fish in a large-scale.

Case Eleven: Cheruvikkal SHG is one of the earliest groups formed in the MFO. One day, one of the present members of the Cheruvikkal unit, Saradhamma happened to see that some women were going into a hall at Pongumoodu. She became curious and entered the hall for seeing what was going on there. She was surprised to see that it was a training camp for Samatha members. She was impressed with the idea of SHG and she shared the idea with some of her friends and relatives. They also felt that the idea was good and they joined together to make a SHG. The group became successful and a number of people in the locality joined it. Thus the number of members in the SHG has become 30. The problem which the secretary points out is that due to large number of members the rotation basis of sanctioning loans becomes difficult and she is holding loan applications for Rs. 2.5 lakh. But there are no funds for sanctioning loans.

Case Twelve: Nelluvila is a medium-performer. It has a membership of 25. The major issue of the meeting of Nelluvila group while researcher visited was the withdrawal of membership by one of the members—Padma. The reason was that her loan application for Rs. 10,000 was pending. The secretary presented the issue in the group. She also gave explanation to all her fellow members. On checking the account it was found that the balance in the account was only Rs. 7,920. The group had to repay the loan taken from the bank before 13th of every month. In addition to that one loan application requesting for Rs. 10,000 is pending. So Padma would get a loan only after sanctioning the other loan. All the members realise the situation and participate in the discussion. They are of the opinion that all the people have equal rights and are equal before the rules.

Case Thirteen: The self help group Navajyothi is situated in the end of a posh housing colony called Benedict Nagar. The housing colony has a number of residents who are well off. The members of this SHG live in the extreme end of this Nagar. Many original settlers of this place migrated to other places. But the majority of the members in this SHG are not able to go away because most of them have their own tiny plots and they work in different parts of the city for their livelihood. The striking feature of the colony is that these members are not the members of Residents' Association of the colony because they are poor. There are 15 members in the group. The members of this group are from low profile jobs. They are washerwomen, vegetable vendors, construction workers, housemaids, etc. When the researcher visited the group it was on the brink of break down. The secretary having high education hails from a well off family. Her husband was a Central Government employee. She keeps all the records and registers properly. But she is not interested to continue in the post. But no other member was ready to take up the post. So she has asked the co-ordinator to dissolve the group. Lack of homogeneity is the major problem of this group.

9

Summary, Conclusion and Suggestions

Poverty has diverse dimensions. Women and men experience poverty in different ways. Feminization of poverty which is due to unequal opportunities and asset ownership is a concern of development practioners all over the world. For uplifting poor women from indigence, opportunities for them for economic participation become necessary. Economic participation of poor women is, by itself, a reward for them, but also serves as a major influence for social change. As employment opportunities all over the world are decreasing due mainly to rapid technological changes, entrepreneurship is seen as the only way to lift women out of poverty. But lack of financial assets such as credit and savings prevents them from entrepreneurial ventures. It is in this context that an innovative financial arrangement for the poor—microfinance—came into being.

Finance is the lubricant which oils the wheels of development. All economies rely upon the financial intermediary function to transfer resources from savers to investors. In many developing countries, capital markets are at a rudimentary stage, and commercial banks are reluctant to lend to the poor largely because of the lack of collateral security, high transaction costs and uncertainty of recovery. As a consequence, financial institutions for providing credit in various forms emerged all over the world. Most of them deal with small numbers of customers. Microlending institutions such as Rotating Savings and Credit Associations (ROSCAs), co-operatives and credit unions constitute some typical examples of such agencies.

The beginning of the decade of 1980s saw an unprecedented growth of microfinance institutions/programmes (MFI/Ps) all over the world. The pioneer in this field was the Grameen Bank of Bangladesh which started its functioning in 1976. The success of this institution led to the emergence of various poverty alleviation and microenterprise programmes. Among them Bank Rakyat Indonesia's Unit *Desa* System (BRI), BancoSol in Bolivia, Thana Resource Development and Employment Programme (TRDEP) in Bangladesh, and Self Employed Women's Association (SEWA) in India are well-known.

There now exists a rich crop of literature on microfinance—both theoretical and empirical studies. The theoretical issues relating to microfinance may be broadly classified under categories: sustainability of microfinance institutions, their outreach to target populations and their impact. Related issues such as: sustainability vs. outreach vs. impact, transaction cost in microfinance system, efficacy of microfinance and self-employment, low absorption capacity of the poor, problem of replication and competition are also important.

The responsibility of meeting the credit needs in the rural areas of India had been primarily with the cooperative banking sector until the mid-1960s. One of the major objectives of the nationalisation of Indian commercial banks (in two spurts in 1969 and 1980) was to improve the flow of formal institutional credit to rural areas—to households, especially to the poor, thus relieving them of the burden of usurious debt. Although these measures were ambitious and laudable, they failed to reach the poor people in adequate measure. In this context, a paradigm shift was needed for reaching the poor and the needy with timely and adequate credit facilities at a fair price.

The microfinance institutions and programmes (MFI/Ps) which emerged around the globe showed the way and many Non-Governmental Organisations (NGOs) started working in this field. Viewing the success of these experiments, the National Bank for Agriculture and Rural Development (NABARD), the apex bank for rural credit in India, came forward to link the self help groups formed by the NGOs with the various banks in the country. The Government of India, while launching the various poverty alleviation programmes in urban (SJSRY) and rural (SGSY) areas also emphasised the formation of groups for reaching the benefits to the poor below the poverty line. A review of the institutional arrangements launched by the Government of India since independence and their impact on the Indian economy, especially in the field of credit to the poor, emergence of microfinance in India and the major actors involved and the various programmes initiated by Government of India for reaching the needy reveals the meandering path that microfinance has taken in this country in recent decades.

Kerala has gained international acclaim due to its unique pattern of social development achieved under the conditions of low levels of income. One of the avowed merits of Kerala's development experience is that gender difference in social development in Kerala is lower than that in many other states in India. It is sometimes argued that the Kerala model owes its genesis to Kerala women and that it has, in turn, helped women in Kerala too.

In spite of these claims, women in Kerala do face a number of problems. Some of them are discrimination in field of education, high unemployment, low work participation, wage discrimination, poverty, morbidity, violence and sexual harassment and lack of public space. Many of the problems of women were unattended and neglected by social uprisings and organisations in Kerala.

In the regions constituting the present day Kerala, formal financial institutions had come into existence, even before the attainment of independence. In 1914 itself, the Travancore state had introduced the cooperative movement. Long before nationalisation of commercial banks in India (in 1969 and in 1980), commercial banks had started functioning in the rural and semi-urban areas of Kerala. This was because of the commercial character of the state's economy. In terms of per capita deposits and average population per branch, Kerala fares well compared to the other states in the country. But in the case of credit-deposit ratio, Kerala stands far behind. This has a direct impact on the poor sections of the population in the state. Non-availability of loans for consumption purpose and procedural difficulties with the formal financial institutions make the poor dependent on informal sources of funds.

It was in this background, that the idea of microfinance gained momentum in Kerala. Microfinance is considered as a solution to many problems faced by women in Kerala, especially their low economic and social status. When microfinance was found to be a viable proposition, several microfinance institutions and programmes emerged in Kerala under different agencies. Besides, the state government was keen on forming groups among poor women for imparting benefits to them through a programme called Kudumbashree. The People's Plan Campaign (PPC) initiated during the ninth five year plan fostered women self help groups as micro level organisations for developing political participation and empowerment of women.

The major characteristics of microfinance are microsavings and microcredit. Microfinance helps the poor to mobilise their meagre savings which might, over a period of time, grow into a major source to cushion economic shocks. Likewise, microcredit enhances their economic choices and opportunities. Microfinance institutions supply credit for various needs of the poor—production and consumption. Thus, it is a means to enhance economic capacity of poor women. In Chapter 6, results of the survey of beneficiaries and self help groups are discussed. For the purpose of the present study, data regarding demographic particulars, standard of living, personal savings and loan details of the 323 members in *Samatha Vanitha Swayam Sahaya Sangham* (SVSSS) were collected and analysed.

Even though microfinance is primarily an informal institution performing financial functions, it has several linkages with formal financial institutions such as banks and local political institutions, the State Government and the Central Government. It also acts as a sub-system of these institutions and takes part in poverty alleviation and capacity building processes of women who take part in it. The way in which SVSSS helped the women in the low-income groups in the Ulloor panchayat to increase their democratic capacity building was examined on the basis of the data collected from its members.

Now-a-days, microfinance is considered a panacea for most of the socio-economic ills in the society. Hence a number of agencies, organisations and governments have taken up the idea and have popularised it. However, several issues have emerged subsequently. Various problems such as disparity in savings, problem of default, low credit absorption of the poor, problems faced by the poor in microfinance and coverage of non-poor under microfinance were observed in the case of our sample beneficiaries. Declining attendance in weekly meetings, improper record keeping, lack of incentives for leaders, laxity in enforcement of rules and problems of group activities in SHGs were also observed at the SHG level. General problems such as multiplicity of promoting agencies, long waiting period for loans, improper follow up and dropping out from the groups also existed in the sample SHGs.

Major Findings

Beneficiaries

The majority of women in the organisation belong to the middle age group. It is in this age group that women are found to be highly active and taking part in organisation. Four-fifths of the beneficiaries are married. Women from female-headed households have found that self help groups were of great support to them. Nearly one-half the members in SVSSS have education up to high school level. But, the proportion of women having some kind of technical qualification or training is only one-fourth. Thus we find that the large majority of the members in this organisation are in need of training and skill formation to enable them to take up income generating activities.

About 17 per cent of the members are the Scheduled Castes and majority of the others belong to other backward castes. More than one-tenth of the households had alcoholics. The degree of indebtedness, economic deprivation and social insecurity of these households is found to be higher than that of others.

Nearly one-fifth of the members are landless. The majority of the landed households have only tiny plots ranging from one to six cents in extent. The majority (70%) of beneficiaries have their own dwellings. Only less than one-tenth live in rented houses. The proportion of members who live with their relatives in ancestral houses or common lands is nearly one-fifth.

It is noted that not many beneficiaries are having savings with other financial institutions. The proportions of members who maintain savings with banks and co-operatives are found to be as low as three per cent and one per cent respectively. Some beneficiaries (27%) keep their savings with Life Insurance Corporation. Normally, the poor found it difficult to obtain loans from formal financial institutions. However, when such an opportunity arose through the agency of MFO they readily accepted and welcomed it.

About two-thirds of the members have outstanding loans with agencies other than SHGs. It is also observed that the proportion of members who have such loans is higher among the poor (more than two-thirds) than among the non-poor (three-fifths).

All SHG members in this MFO save Rs. 20 to 25 every week. More than 75 per cent of total members in 50 per cent of the SHGs save regularly. Decision regarding sanction of loans is taken by all members together at meetings. SHGs helped poor women to cultivate banking habits. In about one-half of the groups, the members themselves go to the bank for depositing money, withdrawing cash and other purposes on a rotational basis.

The microfinance loans are given for wide range of purposes—consumption, social necessities, festivities and production. The largest proportion of the loans was used for repayment of their earlier loans. About one-fifths of the loans were taken for education purposes. Loans were taken for maintenance and repairs of existing houses or construction of new houses also. The other purposes for which loans were taken included medical treatment, funeral expenses and marriages. Income generating activities accounted only for a minor share of the total loans released. Since most of the loans were used for unproductive purposes, repayment became difficult for most of the borrowers.

Capacity Building

This part is to assess the role played by microfinance in building up economic and political capacity of women and thereby enhancing empowerment. It was found that only about one-fifth of the beneficiaries are found to participate in political, cultural and social organisations. Participation by the poor is lesser than that of the non-poor women. While about one-fourth of them take part in such organisations, the corresponding figure for the poor is only about one-seventh.

Most of the women in the sample came to know about *Grama Sabhas* only after becoming members of SHGs. SHGs motivated many of them to take part in the *Grama Sabhas*. One-half of the beneficiaries take part in *Grama Sabha* activities in the Ulloor panchayat. Most of them received economic benefits in the form of livestock and poultry, sewing machine, house, toilet, and grants and loans for maintenance and construction of houses.

Of the 323 women studied, only 20 per cent were engaged in income generating activities. Such activities comprised: (a) trade and commercial establishments; (b) animal husbandry units; (c) production and processing activities; and (d) service enterprises. All these activities were mostly of the conventional type. Women are found in activities like petty trade and small business involving low risk.

It was observed that education was neither a hindrance nor an advantage for starting an income generating activity. Motivation, self-confidence and entrepreneurial capacity were the major facilitating factors. Most of the enterprises run by women were home-based or belonged to the extended home activity type. Hence, the majority of the enterprises were located and run in own premises and own lands. However, about one-fifth of the women engaged in income generating activities did not have any fixed place for housing their trading activities and storing their wares. They were fully mobile. They are itinerant traders vending their wares to customer households, carrying things headload or in hand-bags.

Three-fourths of the entrepreneurs among the members are doing business of their own; that is, they organise, operate and manage the enterprise themselves. Almost all of them—the exception being only seven per cent—have income other than that from the microenterprises.

Only less than 30 per cent of the entrepreneurs have found to have availed loans from self help groups for starting enterprises. The average loan amount was quite small. Nevertheless, these small loans from SHGs helped them to develop their business units; further loans were available to them as and when required. However, the amount per loan offered by SHGs was not sufficient for establishing viable enterprises. Hence, majority of the members availed loans from other sources as well, mostly from local moneylenders at exorbitant interest on daily or weekly basis.

Women are the managers of their households. They look after their children, manage household affairs and do all household chores. The entrepreneurs among them usually had to bear double (or even triple) burden. Nearly one-half of them spent six to ten hours a day on their enterprises. One woman said that she had been working for seventeen hours a day at her unit. Such overburdening takes their toll in terms of ill-health, physical and psychological. There are a few women entrepreneurs who go for odd jobs such as that of housemaid, over and above looking after their business units, just for eking out a sufficient living.

In most cases of the entrepreneurs, the business responsibilities are seldom shared with other members of the family, especially the husband. One of the reasons reported by these women for taking up low profile, less profitable business activities is that they require less attention and time.

Performance of Self Help Groups

To study the performance and stability of self help groups with *Samatha Vanitha Swayam Sahaya Sangham* (SVSSS), twelve indicators were identified and values were assigned to them. Out of the 34 groups, there were nine high performers, eighteen medium-performers and seven low-performers.

Participation in meetings of the SHGs by members is seen declining. Even among the majority of the highly performing groups, attendance of members was not high. In many of the groups, some members have quit. Dropping out of members affects the smooth functioning of SHGs. Keeping of records and registers is a tedious and laborious job. Only about one-third of the groups maintained the records systematically and correctly.

Incentives are lacking for the leader of the SHG. The secretary has to perform both organisational and financial responsibilities. The voluntary nature of leadership cften leads to indifferent performance. Therefore, institutions of financial incentives for the secretary seem to be essential for efficient management of SHGs.

Highly performing groups conduct weekly meetings which last for more than one hour. Poor women find it difficult to spend time in such meetings.

Participation of members in discussions at the meetings is not satisfactory. In the vast majority of SHGs, only less than one-half of the members participated in discussions.

Nearly three-fifths of the SHGs are found to strictly implement the sanctions and enforce discipline. The majority of high-performing groups strictly enforce the rules. Those groups which could enforce rules strictly have greater control over their members.

Self help groups are not taking up serious issues within their societies during the meetings. However, the majority of them take part in *Grama Sabhas* and discuss collective community needs. More than one-half of the SHGs have already created emergency/welfare funds for the well-being of their members.

The majority of SHGs (56%) have taken up some kind of activities—financial, cultural or economic. But low economic viability and serious marketing problems have held back some groups from taking up any of the income generating activities.

Lack of cohesion among members and marketing problems weaken group enterprises. Other problems observed are multiplicity of promoting agencies, long waiting periods for loans, improper follow up and dropping out from the groups.

Major Issues Emerging in the Field of Microfinance

More than one-half the members in the sample belonged to the target group of poor women; however, non-poor accounted for almost the same proportion.

In a mixed group (having both the non-poor and the poor) the poor would fall out of place in terms of culture, money, asset position and participation. Penalties and sanctions exert pressures more on the poor. So within a short period, they are automatically (both voluntarily and involuntarily) excluded from the group.

Reasons for inclusion of the non-poor are not far to seek. They have time to spare, as most of them are unemployed. Those persons who are immediately above or near the poverty line also find it difficult to avail of the financial facilities from formal financial institutions. When credit-deepening takes place, the non-poor are increasingly attracted to the organisation. It may also be the case that persons who had been poor at the time of starting the organisation have graduated to the category of the non-poor.

There did not exist much difference between the poor and the non-poor in the case of savings. But with higher amounts, the share of saving of the poor is found to be lower. The poor have found it difficult to save when burdened with the liability of loan repayment.

Default is found both in the case of savings and of loan repayment. More than one-third of the beneficiaries had defaulted at least one instalment of monthly repayment of loan or of remittance of savings. Most of the default was due to low-paid or irregular employment or no employment at all.

From the present study, it is understood that the contribution of microfinance to the wellbeing of the poor women in terms of mobilisation of microsavings, utilisation of microcredit and organization, management and performance of income generating activities is substantial in the study area. It also proved that microfinance helped in building up economic and political capacity of women and thereby enhancing empowerment of women.

The performance of self help groups is largely influenced by the attendance of members and participation of members in meetings. But other factors such as keeping of records and registers, implementation of sanctions and enforcement of discipline also help their performance. On the other hand, drop out of members and lack of incentives to the leaders who organize everything are weakening the organisational performance of the SHGs.

To study the level of participation of women in self help groups and examine the group dynamics that influence their participation, it was found that even if the majority of SHGs (56%) have taken up some kind of activities, low economic viability and marketing problems have held back many groups from taking up any of the income generating activities.

While assessing the extent of participation of the poor in the microfinance institution, it is found that participation of hardcore poor is declining. The reasons are varying. As many of the self help groups do not have homogeneity and as they become a mixed group, the poor would fall out of place. Penalties and sanctions also exert pressures on the poor. Hence they are automatically excluded from the group.

The study clearly proved that microfinance has surely helped the beneficiary women to enhance their resource base by improving their microsavings, microcredit and microenterprises. It has also helped them to develop banking habits. The economic, political and social empowerment of women has enabled them to improve their overall capacity building.

In the study area, networking of SHGs at the panchayat level has helped to achieve some common goals of the groups. Also linkages with local institutions such as panchayats and financial institution have improved the overall resource base of the self help groups. Thus it is proved that microfinance institutions can effectively act as a sub-system of local bodies and commercial banks for conferring inputs and services on the poor.

Suggestions

Microfinance organisations should arrange work-related training courses for the benefit of women entrepreneurs. Entrepreneurship Development Programmes (EDPs) should be tailored to suit the requirements of women entrepreneurs, to train them in specific areas such as decision making, discipline, communication skills and management without imposing much financial burden on them. A team of experts for providing counselling to women entrepreneurs at the time of difficulties may also be put in position.

At present, there exists no organisation at the government level to assist microenterprises in marketing their wares. The government should think in terms of setting up such organisation. The proposed organisation could have its own brand name for different products that it buys from the units. It could also lay down qualitative standards and could evolve a system of quality control. It could help the small entrepreneurs in their input needs. However, it will be necessary to equip the microfinance organisation with an expert body for both domestic and export markets for products exclusively of microunits. Technical advice for diversification and quality improvement of SHG products should also be made available. At present the microfinance organisations in Kerala give training only in a few activities such as soap-making and catering. Coordination and networking of self help groups are necessary on both vertical and horizontal basis.

In order to obviate the difficulties experienced by the extremely poor among the members of MFOs, it is necessary to make the terms and conditions of savings and borrowings more poor-friendly than they are at present. Penalties and sanctions need to be made less stringent. Setting up a welfare fund at the SHG level is necessary so that it can be used at times of emergency. Membership of a SHG may be kept in the range of 20 to 25. Large groups lack cohesion and effective management.

APPENDICES

APPENDIX I

Sampling Design

Ward No.	*Name of the Ward*	*Number of SHGs Formed*	*Number of SHGs Studied*
1.	Alathara	12	3
2.	Engineering College	17	4
3.	Akkulam	14	3
4.	Bappuji Nagar	10	2
5.	Pransanth Nagar	10	2
6.	Kochulloor	15	3
7.	Ulloor	6	1
8.	Pongumoodu	7	1
9.	Kariyam	16	4
10.	Karimbukonam	14	3
11.	Kattachakonam	7	2
12.	Nalanchira	12	2
13.	Chencheri	5	1
14.	Andhawalleeshwaram	6	1
15.	Mannanthala	12	2
	Total	**163**	**34**

Interview Schedule for the Self Help Groups

Date:
Schedule No.

1. Name of the group and ward it belongs to:
   Group :
   Ward :
2. Name of the President and Secretary:
3. Number of members:
   At the time of formation:
   New:
4. When does the group start?
5. When does the group meet?
6. Generally how long do the meetings last?
   (a) Under one hour (b) one to two hours
   (c) two to three hours (d) varies a lot
7. Does the group prepare agenda before the meeting?
   (Yes—1, No—2)
8. Does the group keep all the records and registers prescribed by the NGO?
   (Yes—1, No—2)
9. How is the group's leadership selected?
   (a) By consensual selection (b) By an election
   (c) By self-appointment
   (d) Appointed by the NGO
   (e) Don't know
10. Attendance in each group meeting:
    (a) 80—100% (b) 60—80% (c) 40—60% (d) 0—40%

11. Do all members aware of the relevance of group formation?
    (a) Very strong (b) Moderate (c) Not very much
12. Saving habit of members:
    (a) 50% (b) 50—75% (c) >75%
13. Who is responsible of operating the bank account and other dealings with bank?
    (a) Elected member (b) Everybody in rotation basis
    (c) Secretary (d) President
14. Members' awareness about loan rules and bank loan details:
    (a) <50% (b) 50—75% (c) >75%
15. What percentage of members availing loan to total members?
    (a) <50% (b) 50—75% (c) >75%
16. Decision on loan taken during meeting:
    (a) By all (b) By elected members (c) By leaders or others
17. Are there written byelaws? (Yes—1, No—2)
18. Members awareness about the byelaws:
    (a) Written and strong awareness
    (b) Oral but strong awareness (c) Oral and not aware
19. Participation in discussion and group functioning:
    (a) <50% (b) 50—75% (c) >75%
20. Does the group create emergency or welfare fund? (Yes—1, No—2)
21. Imposition of sanctions and enforcement of byelaws:
    (a) Strictly enforced (b) Sometimes (c) Not at all
22. Participation in community needs:
    (a) Collective action for community problems
    (b) Participation in *Grama Sabhas* (c) If others, specify
23. Place of group meeting:
    (a) Permanent place (b) Rotational basis
24. What is the total amount of group savings?
25. Besides dealing with loans and savings, does your group have any other activities? (Yes—1, No—2)
26. If yes, enumerate the major activities taken up during the last years:

27. Does the group get money from other sources?

Source	*Amount*	*Date of Avail*	*Rate of Interest*	*Remarks*
Panchayat				
Bank				
Zila Panchayat				
Any Other Source, Please Specify				

28. Profile of members

Community	*Number of Members*	*Religion*	*Numbers of members*	*Remarks*
SC		Hindu		
ST		Christian		
OBC		Muslim		
Others		Others		

Interview Schedule for the Beneficiaries

Date:
Schedule No.

I. Personal Particulars

1. Name of the respondent:
2. Name of the group you belong to:
3. Religion: (i) Hindu (ii) Muslim (iii) Christian (iv) Others
4. Caste: (i) SC (ii) ST (iii) OBC (iv) Others
5. Marital status: (i) Currently Married (ii) Never Unmarried (iii) Widowed (iv) Separated (v) Divorced (vi) Others
6. General education: (i) Illiterate (ii) LPS (iii) UPS (iv) High School (v) Hr. Sec. (vi) Graduate (vii) Post Graduate (viii) Professional Courses
7. Technical qualifications, if any:

II. Household Particulars and Access to Public Utility Services

1. Household size:
2. Type of household: male headed—1, female-headed—2
3. Nature of housing:
   - 3.1. Material used for floor: (i) Mud (ii) Cement (iii) Others
   - 3.2. Material used for walls: (i) Mud (ii) Brick (iii) Hollow blocks (iv) Others
   - 3.3. Type of material used for roof: (i) Thatched (ii) Tile (iii) Concrete (iv) Asbestos (v) Others

4. Ownership of house: (i) Owned (ii) Rented (iii) Otherwise occupied
5. Access to public services:
   5.1. Source of drinking water: (i) Public well (ii) Public tap (iii) Private well (iv) Private tap (v) Other sources
   5.2. If public source, distance (kms.) from home:
   5.3. Availability of toilet within the premises: (Yes—1, No—2)
   5.4. Source of lighting: (i) Electricity (ii) Kerosene (iii) Others
   5.5. Type of fuel used for cooking: (i) Fuelwood (ii) Kerosene (iii) L.P.G.
6. Access to health services:
   6.1. Are you availing of formal health care? (Yes—1, No—2)
   6.2. If yes, specify whether it is from: (i) Primary Health Centre (ii) Government Hospital (iii) Private dispensaries, hospital, doctors, etc. (iv) Others
   6.3. Distance of the PHC/Govt. hospital facility from home (kms.):
7. Ownership of Assets
   7.1. Land owned (in acres): (i) Cultivable, (ii) Non-cultivable, (iii) Homestead
   7.2. Livestock owned (in Numbers) (i) Cows (ii) Bullocks (iii) Goat (iv) Chicken (v) Others
   7.3. Other Assets Owned: (i) T.V. (ii) Radio (iii) Refrigerator (iv) Scooter (v) Music System (vi) Cycle (vii) Auto rickshaw (viii) Others
8. Annual family income:
9. Are there any alcoholic persons in your household? (Yes—1, No—2)

III. Level of Participation in Business/Social Organisations

1. Are you a member of any business /social organisation? (Yes—1, No—2)
2. If yes, write the name of the organisation and its activity:

3. Do you attend the meetings of the *Grama Sabhas*? (Yes—1, No—2)
4. If yes to three, then what is the level of participation? (Very regular—1, Occasional—2, Very rare—3)

IV. Level of Participation in Self Help Group (SHG)

1. When did you join this group?
2. How often do you attend the meetings? (Very regular—1, Occasional—2, Very rare—3)
3. Are you an office bearer in the group? (Chairman—1, Secretary—2, Committee member—3, Not an office bearer—4)
4. As a member of the group have you received any training? (Yes—1, No—2)
5. If yes, specify the nature and type of training

V. Savings

1. As on 31.3.2001 what is your total savings in the MFO?
2. Do you receive any interest rate from the savings?
3. Do you have savings in any other institutions? (Banks—1, Co-operatives—2, Others—3, No other source—4)
4. If yes, what is the value of savings in those institutions?

VI. Credit

1. Total number of loans taken from MFO:
2. Details on borrowing:

Date of borrowing	*Source of borrowing*	*Purpose of borrowing*	*Amount borrowed*	*Amount due at each instalment*	*Amount repaid*	*Total Repay-ment period*

3. Utilisation of loan: (fully utilised for the purpose—1, partly used for the purpose—2, diverted—3)
4. Is the loan overdue? (Yes—1, No—2)
5. If any loan is overdue what are the reasons? (Returns from enterprise is not enough—1, No source to supplement income—2, Other reasons specify—3)
6. What is the source of income for loan repayments? (Own savings—1, Savings of other household members—2, Grant from others—3, Other sources—4)
7. Are any of your previous loans (loans from other sources) outstanding? (Yes—1, No—2)
8. If yes, what was the total amount of your previous loans outstanding?
9. How did you first come to hear about the possibility of getting a loan from this institution? (Report the major source) (MFO workers—1, Family/Friends—2, Neighbours—3, Advertisement—4, Others specify—5)
10. Do you need more credit from MFO? (Yes—1, No—2)
11. If yes, specify the purpose: (Productive enterprises—1, Household expenses—2, To meet unforeseen expenses—3, Repayment of debts—4, Others—5, More than one purpose—6)
12. Do you have problem regarding obtaining credit? (Yes—1, No—2)
13. If yes, specify the reason:

VI. Entrepreneur and Enterprise Profile

1. Year of establishing the enterprise:
2. What type of enterprise is this?
3. What is the location of the enterprise? (Rural—1, Urban—2, Semi-urban—3)
4. Is your business located at the same place as your home? (Yes—1, No—2)
5. What is the ownership structure of the enterprise? (Proprietorship—1, Family partnership—2, Non-family partnership—3, Co-operative/Group—4, Others specify—5)

6. Type of business: (With fixed premises—1, Without fixed premises—2, Mixed—3)
7. Do you have any income generating activity besides the enterprise? (Self-employment in Agriculture—1, Self-employment livestock—2, Self-employment in productive enterprises—3, Salary/wage paid employment—4, Others—5)
8. Is your loan assisted enterprise your main source of income? (Yes—1, No—2, don't know—3)
9. If no, what is your main source of income?
10. What was the main source of your start up funds? (Project loan—1, Other loans—2, Household Savings—3, Gifts—4, Borrowing from other sources—5, Others specify—6)
11. How many employees are there in your business?
12. How many of your household members are engaged in your enterprise?
    Male: Female:
13. What are the average hours of operation of your business?
14. Nature of activity in the enterprise: (Perennial—1, Seasonal—2, Casual—3)
15. Over the period of the present loan have you succeeded in doing any of the following? (Increase the volume of goods/services—1, Improve the quality of goods/services—2, Purchase new tools or equipment—3, Move to better premises—4, Expand the business—5, Others—6)
16. Net average cash flow per month:

Performance Rating

Indicators of Group Stability

Sl. No.	*Indicator*	*Rating*	*Sl. No.*	*Indicator*	*Rating*
1	Attendance in meetings		7	Awareness about byelaws and whether they are written or oral	
	50%	1		Oral and not aware	1
	50—75%	2		Oral but strong awareness	2
	>75%	3		Written and strong awareness	3
2	Regularity in savings		8	Participation in discussion and group functioning	
	50%	1		50%	1
	50—75%	2		50—75%	2
	>75%	3		>75%	3
3	Recording keeping/ book keeping, etc.		9	Creation of emergency/ welfare fund	
	No	0		Yes	1
	Yes	2		No	0
4	Operation of bank account/other dealings with the bank		10	Imposition of sanctions and enforcement of byelaws	
	Secretary/president	1		Not at all	1
	Everybody in rotation basis	2		Sometimes	2
				Strictly enforced	3
5	Percentage of members availing loan to total members		11	Participation in community needs	
	50%	1		Participation in *Grama Sabhas*	2
	50—75%	2		Collective action for community problems	3
	>75%	3			
6	Decision on loan taken during meeting		12	Starting of income generating and other activities	
	By elected members	1		Financial	1
	By all	2		Cultural	2
				Economic	3

For evaluating the stability and performance of the self help groups, 12 indicators were identified and assessed. Weights were given for the indicators on their relative importance in the functioning of the groups. The indicators and the rates are given in the table.

Value of Index	*Performance Rating*
25-28 points	High
21-24 points	Medium
17 to 20 points	Low

The performance level of the SHGs was measured in terms of the composite index worked out for the purpose. If the index worked out for a particular SHG shows higher value the performance of the SHG is better. Similarly, if the value of the index is low, it is a reflection of the poor performance of the SHG.

Poverty Index

As one of the objectives of the study was to capture the involvement of the poor in the organisation, a measure of poverty was needed. For the purpose, the poverty index used by community development system (CDS) of Kerala was used for identifying poor families. The measure has a nine-point index. At first, this index was used to identify the poor families in Alappuzha town in 1993. Later it was used in all the other 57 towns in Kerala and Malappuram district. Now, the state poverty alleviation programme (Kudumbashree) is also following the same index to identify the poor and initiate action.

Variables of Poverty Index

P1	=	Family living in a thatched hut (no pucca house)
P2	=	Family with literate adults
P3	=	Family with no or only one employed
P4	=	Family with children below five years
P5	=	Household with no sanitation facility
P6	=	Household with no drinking water facility within 150 metres
P7	=	Family with two square meals or less per day
P8	=	SC/ST family
P9	=	Family with alcoholics/drug addicts

According to this index, the poor families were identified using composite criteria. It is assumed that a family should have at least four of the nine variables to be identified as poor (Oommen, 1999).

Economics of Self Help Groups and Microfinance

1. Economics of scale	A larger clientele served by a fixed investment in operating assets
2. Economics of scope	Increased capacity to deliver multiple services through the same group mechanism
3. Less information asymmetry	Through group's knowledge of potential borrower-savers
4. Reduced moral hazard	Risks through group monitoring and peer pressure
5. Joint liability	Makes up for absence of individual collateral
6. Improved local collection	Better screening and selection through peer pressure and joint liability, especially if group penalties and incentives are incorporated in the loan terms
7. Improved savings mobilisation	Especially if incentives are incorporated in the group schemes
8. Lower administrative costs	In terms of selection, screening and loan collection

Source: Yaron *et al.*, 1997.

Some Basic Features of SHGs Promoted by NGOs/Banks in India

1.	Organisation	Homogeneity in terms of economic/socio-economic status, common identity of activity, etc.
2.	Nature of target groups	Generally poor and weaker sections of the people in rural areas and particularly women.
3.	Management	Selected/elected leader and duty generally rotated. Holds meeting regularly.
4.	Financial instruments	
4a.	Common fund	Created out of saving, interest earned on loan, donation, etc.
4b.	Savings mobilisation	While in certain cases no fixed rate of savings, in some cases regular and fixed rate savings, and in some cases as per capacity of the members.
4c.	Loaning	Decided by the purpose, quantum and the resources available with the SHGs. Purpose loans for individuals include consumption, clearing outside debt, social, medical, education, business, agriculture, etc., and loans for common production activities.
4d.	Repayment period	Generally lower than prescribed by banks
4e.	Rate of interest	Varies from two to twenty per cent. In a few cases the interest rates are determined by NGOs.
5.	Linkage with banks	Banks treat SHGs as borrowers.

Source: Namboodiri and Shiyani, 2001.

Population in the Wards of Ulloor Panchayat

Ward No.	Name of the Ward	Total Population	Male Population	Female Population
1.	Alathara	2,396	1,161	1,235
2.	Engineering College	3,170	1,619	1,551
3.	Akkulam	2,677	1,274	1,403
4.	Bappuji Nagar	4,350	2,196	2,154
5.	Prasanth Nagar	4,275	2,094	2,081
6.	Kochulloor	4,304	2,066	2,236
7.	Ulloor	2,750	1,348	1,382
8.	Pongumoodu	3,020	1,532	1,488
9.	Kariyam	3,485	1,725	1,760
10.	Karumbukonam	2,387	1,181	1,206
11.	Parottukonam	4,156	2,037	2,119
12	Nalanchira	5,040	2,744	2,296
13.	Chencheri	2,376	1,198	1,181
14.	Andhawalleeshwaram	2,636	1,304	1,332
15.	Mannanthala			
	Tulal	**47,005**	**23,481**	**23,524**

Source: Ulloor Panchayat, 1997.

A Framework for Analysing Women's Empowerment

Power within or increased will for change for individual women

- Increase in women's confidence and assertiveness
- Changes in women's aspirations and consciousness to challenge gender subordination
- Increased autonomy and willingness to take decisions about self and others

Power to or increased capacity for change for individual women

- Increased access to income
- Increased access to productive assets and household property
- Increase in skills including literacy
- Increased mobility and access to markets
- Reduction in burden of domestic work including child care
- Improved health and nutrition

Power over or reduction in obstacles to change at household and community level

- Control over loan use
- Control over income from loans and other household productive activities
- Control over productive assets and household property

- Increased ability to determine parameters of household consumption and other valued areas of household decision making in favour of self
- Ability to defend self against violence in the household and community
- Enhanced perception of women's capacities and rights at household and community levels

Power with or increased solidarity with other women for change at household, community and macro levels

- Increase in networks for support in times of crisis or for chosen strategies to challenge gender inequality
- Participation in actions to defend other women against abuse in the household and community
- Participation in movements to challenge gender subordination at the community and macro level
- Ability and willingness to act as role model for other women entrepreneurs, particularly in lucrative and non-traditional occupations
- Increased expenditure on girl children and other female family members
- Higher valuation of girl children and other female family members
- Prioritisation of provision of wage employment for other women at good wages

Source: Mayoux, 1998.

Bibliography

Adams, Dale W., and J.D. von Pischke. 1992. "Microenterprise Credit Programs: deja vu." *World Development* 20(10) 1463-1470.

Adams, Dale W., and Robert C. Vogel. 1986. "Rural Financial Markets in Low-Income Countries: Recent Controversies and Lessons." *World Development* 14(4):477-487.

Agarwal, B. (ed.). 1988. *Structure of Patriarchy, the state, the Community and the Household.* New Delhi: Kali for Women.

Agarwal, K.P., V. Puhazhendhi, and K.J.S. Satyasai. 1997. "Gearing Rural Credit for the Twenty-First Century." *Economic and Political Weekly* 32(42):2717-2728.

Analyst, 1993. "Myth of Non-Viability of Rural Branches." *Economic and Political Weekly* 28(18):853-854.

Anderson, Robert T. 1966. "Rotating Credit Associations in India." *Economic Development and Cultural Change* 14(6): 334-339.

Bell, Clive. 1990. "Interactions between Institutional and Informal Credit Agencies in Rural India." *The World Bank Economic Review* 4(3):297-327.

Bennett, Lynn. 1992. *Women, Poverty and Productivity in India.* EDI Seminar Paper 43. Washington D.C.: World Bank.

Berger, Marguerite. 1989. "Giving Women Credit: The Strengths and Limitations of Credit as a Tool for Alleviating Poverty." *World Development* 17(7):1017-1032.

Besley, Timothy, Stephen Coate, and Glenn Loury. 1993. "The Economics of Rotating Savings and Credit Associations." *The American Economic Review* 83(4):792-810.

Bhatt, Ela R. 1989. "Toward Empowerment." *World Development* 17(7):1059-1065.

Bhatt, Ela R. 2006. *We are Poor but So Many: The Story of Self-Employed Women in India.* New Delhi: Oxford University Press.

Bidinger, Patricia, D.B. Nag, and P. Babhu. 1986. Factors Affecting Intra Family Food Distribution in a South Indian Village. Hyderabad: Institute for Rural Health Studies.

Binswanger, Hans, and S. Khandker. 1992. The Impact of Formal Finance on the Rural Economy of India. WPS 949. Agricultural and Rural Development Department. Washington D.C.: World Bank.

Bomda, Justin. 1999. "The MC^2 Network as an Example for Private Initiative—A Case Study from Cameroon." *Agriculture + Rural Development* 6(2):48-51.

Boomgard, James J. and Kenneth J. Anjell. 1994. "Bank Rakyat Indonesia's Unit Desa System: Achievement, Replicability." In Mario Otero and Elisabeth Rhyne, eds., *The New World of Microenterprise Finance.* West Hartford, Conn.: Kumarian Press.

Bouman, F.J.A. 1989. *Small, Short and Unsecured: Informal Rural Finance in India.* Delhi: Oxford University Press.

Buckley, Grame. 1996a. "Financing the Jua Kali Sector in Kenya: The KREP Juhudi Scheme and Kenya Industrial Estates Informal Sector Programme." In David Hulme, and Paul Mosley, eds., *Finance against Poverty.* Volume II. London: Routledge.

Buckley, Grame. 1996b. "Rural and Agricultural Credit in Malawi." In David Hulme, and Paul Mosley, eds., *Finance against Poverty.* Volume II. London: Routledge.

Chathukulam, Jos. 2002. "Survival through Social Capital Formation: the Case of Women's Self Help Groups." Proceedings of International Workshop on Research for Poverty Alleviation, Kerala Research Programme on Local Level Development, Centre for Development Studies, Thiruvananthapuram, Kerala.

Christabell, P.J. 2001. "Microfinance—Obstacles to Reach the Poor." Proceedings of the Thirteenth Kerala Science Congress held on 29-31 January, Kerala State Committee on Science, Technology and Environment, Thiruvananthapuram.

Christabell, P.J. 2002. "Role of Microfinance in Development Process." Proceedings of the Fourteenth Kerala Science Congress held on 29-31 January, Kerala State Committee on Science, Technology and Environment, Thiruvananthapuram.

Christabell, P.J. 2006. "Women Empowerment and Education" *Focus Chronicle* 6(1):62-69.

Christabell, P.J. 2007. "Poor Outreach to the Poor" *Loyola Journal of Social Sciences* 21(2):159-174.

Coleman, Brett E. 1999. "The Impact of Group Lending in Northeast Thailand." *Journal of Development Economics* 60(1):105-141.

Conlin, Michael. 1999. "Peer Group Micro-lending Programs in Canada and the United States." *Journal of Development Economics* 60(1):249-269.

Damayanthi, U.T. 1999. *Development of Women in Rural Areas: A Study of DWCRA in Thrissur District*. Discussion Paper 5, Kerala Research Programme on Local Level Development, Centre for Development Studies, Thiruvananthapuram.

Dowla, Asif Ud. 1998. Micro Leasing: The Grameen Bank Experience. PRPA WP# 21. Programme for Research on Poverty Alleviation, Grameen Trust, Dhaka.

Dreze, Jean, and Amartya Sen. 1989. *Hunger and Public Action*. Oxford: Clarendon Press.

Dreze, Jean, and Amartya Sen. 1995. *Economic Development and Social Opportunities*. Delhi: Oxford University Press.

Dreze, Jean, and Amartya Sen, eds. 1996. *Indian Development: Selected Regional Perspectives*. Delhi: Oxford University Press.

Dunkley, Graham. 1993. *People for Change: A Study of Four CAA Projects in India*. Melbourne: Department of Applied Economics, Victoria University of Technology and Community Aid Abroad/Freedom from Hunger.

Egger, Philippe. 1986. "Banking for the Rural Poor: Lessons from Some Innovative Saving and Credit Schemes." *International Labour Review* 125(4):447-462.

Franke, Richard W., and Barbara H. Chasin. 1994. *Kerala: Radical Reform as Development in an Indian State*. California: The Institute of Food and Development Policy.

Fundacio'n de la Mujer Campesina (Fundelam). 1995. *The Socio Economic Impact of Credit Programs on Rural Women: A Study in Carchi, Ecuador.* Promoting Women in Development (PROWID).

Gailey, Robert, Anton Simanowitz, Ben Nkuna and Sukor Kasim. 1999. "Overcoming the Obstacles to Identify the Poorest Families." Microcredit Summit. Draft.

Geertz, Clifford. 1963. "The Rotating Credit Association: A Middle Rung in Development." *Economic Development and Cultural Change* 10(3):243.

Getubig, I., J. Remenyi, and B. Quinones, eds. 1997. *Creating the Vision: Microfinancing the Poor in Asia-Pacific: Issues, Constraints and Capacity-Building*. Malaysia: Asian and Pacific Development Centre.

Ghatak, Maitreesh, and Timothy W. Guinnane. 1999. "The Economics of Lending with Joint Liability: Theory and Practice." *Journal of Development Economics* 60(1):195-228.

Gibbons, D.S. 1996. "Outreach to the Poor with Financial Services." Issues Paper #1 for the Bank Poor 1996 Meeting, 10-12 December, Kuala Lumpur.

Glosser, Amy J. 1994. "The Creation of BancoSol in Bolivia." In Mario Otero and Elisabeth Rhyne, eds., *The New World of Microenterprise Finance*. West Hartford, Conn.: Kumarian Press.

Gonzalez-Vega, Claudio. 1985. "Cheap Agricultural Credit: Redistribution in Reverse." In D. W. Adams, ed., *Undermining Rural Development with Cheap Credit*. London: Westview Press.

Gonzalez-Vega, Claudio, Mark Schreiner, Richard L. Meyer, Jorge Rodriguez, and Sergio Navajas. 1997. "BancoSol: The Challenge of Growth of Microfinance Organisations." In Hartmut Schneider, ed., *Microfinance for the Poor?* France: Organisation for Economic Co-operation and Development.

Government of Kerala. 2001. *Economic Review 2000*. Thiruvananthapuram: Kerala State Planning Board.

Government of Kerala. 2005. *Economic Review 2004*. Thiruvananthapuram: Kerala State Planning Board.

Government of Kerala. 2007. *Economic Review, 2006.* Thiruvananthapuram: Kerala State Planning Board.

Gulati, Leela. 1981. Profiles *of Female Poverty: A Study of Five Poor Working Women in Kerala.* Delhi: Hindustan Publishing Corporation.

Gupta, Suraj B. 2001. *Monetary Economics: Institutions, Theory and Policy.* New Delhi: S. Chand and Company Limited.

Hasanuzzaman, Al Masud. 1996. "Graduating the Poorest Women into the NGO Programme: The IGVGD (Income Generation for Vulnerable Group Development) Programme in Bangladesh." Working Paper 5. Programme for Research on Poverty Alleviation, Grameen Trust, Dhaka.

Hashemi, Syed M. 1997. "Building up Capacity for Banking with the Poor: The Grameen Bank in Bangladesh." In Hartmut Schneider, ed., *Microfinance for the Poor?* France: Organisation for Economic Co-operation and Development.

Hashemi, Syed M., and Sidney Ruth Schuler. 1997. "Sustainable Banking with the Poor: A Case Study of Grameen Bank." Working Paper 19. Programme for Research on Poverty Alleviation, Grameen Trust, Dhaka.

Holt, Sharon L. 1994. "The Village Bank Methodology: Performance and Prospects." In Mario Otero and Elisabeth Rhyne, eds., *The New World of Microenterprise Finance.* West Hartford, Conn.: Kumarian Press.

Hossain, Mahabub. 1988. "Credit for Alleviation of Rural Poverty: The Grameen Bank in Bangladesh." Research Report 55, International Food Policy Research Institute, Washington D.C.

Hulme, David, and Paul Mosley, eds. 1996. *Finance against Poverty.* Volumes I and II. London: Routledge.

Hunter College Women's Studies Collective. 2005. *Women's Realities, Women's Choices: An Introduction to Women's Studies.* New York: Oxford University Press.

Inter-Parliamentary Union. 2000. *Politics:Women's Insight.* Geneva.

Issac, T.M. Thomas. 2001. "Campaign for Democratic Decentralisation in Kerala." *Social Scientist* 29(9 and 10):2-6.

Jagajeevan, N., and Suresh. 2002. "Janakeeyasoothrana Prasthanavum Bahujanapankalithavum: Aryanad, Kanjikuzhi Blockkukale Aadharamakki Oru Padanam." In *Vikendreekaranam, Samoohya Suraksha, Susthiravikasanam.* (Mal.) Joint Committee of Panchayats, Aryanad and Kanjikuzhi Blocks and International Labour Organisation.

John, M.S., and Jos Chathukulam. 2002. "Building Social Capital through State Initiative: Participatory Planning in Kerala." *Economic and Political Weekly* 37(8):1939-1948.

Joseph, Ammu. 2000. "Unquiet Waters." *The Hindu.* August 27.

Joshi, P.N. 1999. "Banking Sector Reform—The Other Side of the Coin." *Economic and Political Weekly* 34(4):797-798.

Kabir, Royeka. 1999. "Political Empowerment of Women: Roles of NGOs in Ensuring Good Governance at the Local Levels." *Grameen Poverty Research* 5(2):11-13.

Kaladhar, K. 1997. "Microfinance in India: Design, Structure and Governance." *Economic and Political Weekly* 32(42):2687-2706.

Karmakar, K.G. 1999. *Rural Credit and Self-Help Groups: Micro-Finance Need and Concepts in India.* New Delhi: Sage.

Khalily, M.A. Baqui, Mahmood Osman, Immam, and Salahuddin Ahmed Khan. 2000. "Efficiency and Sustainability of Formal and Quasi Formal Microfinance Programmes: An Analysis of Grameen Bank and ASA." *The Bangladesh Development Studies* 26(2 and 3): 49-78.

Khandker, Shahidur R. 2000. "Savings, Informal Borrowing and Microfinance." *The Bangladesh Development Studies* 26(2 and 3):49-78.

Khandker, Shahidur R., Baqui Khalily, and Zahed Khan. 1995a. *Grameen Bank; Performance and Sustainability.* World Bank Discussion Paper 306. Washington, D.C.

Khandker, Shahidur R., Zahed Khan, and Baqui Khalily. 1995b. "Sustainability of a Government Targeted Credit Program: Evidence from Bangladesh." World Bank Discussion Paper 316. Washington, D.C.

Kumar, Shubh K. 1978. "The Role of the Household Economy in Child Nutrition at Low Incomes: A Case Study in Kerala." Occasional Paper 95, Department of Agricultural

Economics, Cornell University Agricultural Experiment Station, Cornell University, New York.

Magill, John H. 1994. "Credit Unions: A Formal Sector Alternative for Financing Microenterprise Development." In Mario Otero and Elisabeth Rhyne, eds., *The New World of Microenterprise Finance*. West Hartford, Conn.: Kumarian Press.

Mahmud, Simeen. 2000. "The Gender Dimensions of Programme Participation: Who Joins a Microcredit Programme and Why?" *The Bangladesh Development Studies* 26(2 and 3):79-102.

Manjula, B. 2000. "Voice from the Spiral of Silence: A Case Study of Samatha Self Help Groups in Ulloor." International Conference on Democratic Decentralisation held on May 23-27, Thiruvananthapuram, Kerala State Planning Board.

Matin, Imran. 1997. "Grameen and Shakti Groups: Unpacking Joint Liability Credit Conduct." Programme for Research on Poverty Alleviation, Grameen Trust, Dhaka.

Matin, Imran. 1998. "Mis-Targeting by the Grameen Bank: A Possible Explanation." *IDS Bulletin* 29(4):51-58.

Matin, Imran. 2000. "Rapid Credit Deepening and a few Concerns: A Study of a Branch of Grameen Bank." *The Bangladesh Development Studies* 26(2 and 3):147-172.

Mayoux, Linda. 1998. "Participatory Learning for Women's Empowerment in Microfinance Programmes: Negotiation, Complexity, Conflict and Change." *IDS Bulletin* 29(4):39-50.

Mckinnon, R.J. 1971. *Money and Capital in Economic Development*. Washington, D.C.: The Brooking Institution.

Mencher, Joan P. 1988. "Women's Work and Poverty: Women's Contribution to Household Maintenance in Two Regions of South India." In Judith Bruce and Daisy Dwyer, eds., *A Home Divided: Women and Income Control in the Third World*. California: Stanford University Press.

Menon, Leela. 1998. "Widowed, Abandoned, Neglected, Isolated." *Indian Express*.

Misra, Indira. 2002. "Towards Empowerment of Women through Microfinance Experience of Rashtriya Mahila Kosh." Proceedings of Workshop on Strategies for Sustainable Rural Development at the National Institute of Rural Development, Hyderabad.

Moghadam, Valentine. 1996. "The Feminization of Poverty?" In UNDP, *Human Development Report 1997*. New York: Oxford University Press.

Mohanan, N. 2002. "Sustainability of Micro Credit Systems in India: an Overview." Proceedings of Workshop on Strategies for Sustainable Rural Development at the National Institute of Rural Development, Hyderabad.

Mohiuddin, A., Hemalatha Prasad, C. Rizwana, A. Sridhar Seetharaman, Ramana Rao, D.V.V., and Yadappanavar, A.V. 2001. "Activities for Women under Cluster Approach and their Capacity Building SGSY—An Evaluation Study." Orientation Programme on SGSY for District Level Officials. Hyderabad: National Institute for Rural Development.

Montgomery, Richard, Debapriya Bhattacharya, and David Hulme. 1996. "Credit for the Poor in Bangladesh: The BRAC Rural Development Programme and the Government Thana Resource Development and Employment Programme." In David Hulme, and Paul Mosley, eds., *Finance against Poverty*. Volume II. London: Routledge.

Morduch, Jonathan. 1999. "The Role of Subsidies in Microfinance: Evidence from the Grameen Bank." *Journal of Development Economics* 60(1):229-248.

Morduch, Jonathan. 2000. "The Microfinance Schism." *World Development* 28(4):617-629.

Moser, Caroline O.N. 1993. *Gender Planning and Development: Theory, Practice and Training*. London: Routledge.

Mosley, Paul. 1996a. "Metamorphosis from NGO to Commercial Bank: The Case of BancoSol in Bolivia." In David Hulme, and Paul Mosley, eds., *Finance against Poverty*. Volume II. London: Routledge.

Mosley, Paul. 1996b. "India: the Regional Rural Banks." In David Hulme, and Paul Mosley, eds., *Finance against Poverty*. Volume II. London: Routledge.

Mosley, Paul. 1996c. "Indonesia: BKK, KURK and the BRI Unit Desa Institutions." In David Hulme, and Paul Mosley, eds., *Finance against Poverty*. Volume II. London: Routledge.

Mujumdar, N.A. 1995. "New Banking Culture and Small Borrower." *Economic and Political Weekly* 30(35):2169-2170.

Mutua, Albert Kimanthi. 1994. "The Juhudi Credit Scheme: From a Traditional Integrated Method to a Financial Systems Approach." In Mario Otero and Elisabeth Rhyne, eds., *The New World of Microenterprise Finance*. West Hartford, Conn.: Kumarian Press.

MYRADA. 1999. *The MYRADA Experience: Self Help Groups-Reading Materials and Related Literature*. Karnataka: MYRADA, Gulbarga, PIDOW Project.

NABARD. 1999. RBI and NABARD Guidelines on Linking Self Help Groups (SHGs) with Banks. Thiruvananthapuram.

Naisbitt, John. 1996. *Megatrends Asia*. New York: Simon and Schuster.

Namboodiri, N.V., and Shiyani, R.L. 2001. "Potential Role of Self Help Groups in Rural Financial Deepening." *Indian Journal of Agricultural Economics* 56(3).

Navajas, Sergio, Mark Schreiner, Richard L. Meyer, Claudio Gonzalez-Vega, and Jorge Rodriguez. 2000. "Microcredit and Poorest of the Poor: Theory and Evidence from Bolivia." *World Development* 28(2):333:346.

O'Connel, Helen. 1994. *Women and the Family*. London: Zed Books Ltd.

Oomen, M.A. 1999. *The Community Development Society of Kerala: An Impact Study*. Volume I. New Delhi: Institute of Social Sciences.

Osmani, Lutfun N. Khan. 1998. "Impact of Credit on the Relative Well Being of Women: Evidence from the Grameen Bank." *IDS Bulletin* 20(4):31-38.

Palnitker, Sneha. 2000. "Promoting People's Participation for Local Governance in Urban Areas." *Shelter* 3(2):75-85.

Panda, Pradeep Kumar. 2001. *Domestic Violence against Women in Kerala*. Project report submitted to Kerala Research Programme on Local Level Development, Centre for Development Studies, Thiruvananthapuram, Kerala.

Patil, A.S. 1997. "Innovations in the Rural Financial System in India." *Grameeya* 3(1 and 2):58-81.

Pitt, Mark M. 2000. "The Effect of Non-agricultural Self Employment Credit on Contractual Relations and Employment in Agriculture: The Case of Microcredit Programmes in Bangladesh." *The Bangladesh Development Studies* 26(2 and 3):15-48.

Puhazhendhi, V. 1995. *Transaction Costs of Lending to the Rural Poor: Non-Governmental Organisations and Self-Help Groups of the Poor as Intermediaries for Banks in India*. Brisbane: Foundation for Development Co-operation.

Quisumbing, Agnes R., Ellen Payongayong, J.B. Aidoo, and Keijiro Otsuka. 1999. "Women's Land Rights in the Transition to Individualized Ownership: Implications for the Management of Tree Resources in Western Ghana". Food Consumption and Nutrition Division, International Food Policy Research Institute, Washington, D.C.

Rajasekhar, D. 1994. *Savings and Credit Systems of the Poor: Some Non-Governmental Organisation (NGO) Experiences*. Bangalore: NOVIB and HIVOS.

Rajasekhar, D. 1997. *Savings and Credit Systems of the Poor: Some NGO Experiences from Andhra Pradesh*. Andhra Pradesh: Inter-Co-operation-NGO Programme.

Rajasekhar, D. 2000. "Microfinance Programmes and Women's Empowerment: A Study of Two NGOs from Kerala." *Journal of Social and Economic Development* 3(1):76-94.

Ratnam, V.C.V. 2001. "Self-Help Groups: Case Study of Two Districts (Trivandrum and Kanyakumari)." Paper presented in Workshop on Decentralisation in Kerala: An Assessment held on October 22-24, Kerala Research Programme on Local Level Development, Centre for Development Studies, Thiruvananthapuram.

Reskin, Barbara F., and Heidi I. Hartmann, eds. 1991. *Women's Work, Men's Work: Sex Segregation on the Job*. Washington, D.C.: National Academy Press.

Rhyne, Elisabeth, and Maria Otero. 1994. "Financial Services for Microenterprises: Principles and Institutions." In Mario Otero and Elisabeth Rhyne, eds., *The New World of*

Microenterprise Finance. West Hartford, Conn.: Kumarian Press.

Robinson, Marguerite S. 1994. "Savings Mobilization and Microenterprise Finance: The Indonesian Experience." In Mario Otero and Elisabeth Rhyne, eds., *The New World of Microenterprise Finance*. USA: Kumarian.

Sarma, R.H. 1999. "Microfinancing through Self-Help Group and Non-Government Organisations by Commercial Banks." *The Journal of the Indian Institute of Bankers* 70(3):19-23.

Seema, T.N., T. Kamala, and N. Rajamohanakumar, eds. 2000. *Vikasanathil Thulyatha* (Mal.). Thiruvananthapuram: Kerala State Planning Board.

Seema, T.N., T. Kamala, N. Rajamohanakumar, and E. Sindhu, eds. 2000. *Janakeeyasoothranavum Stree Munnettavum*. (Mal.). Thiruvananthapuram: Published by the State Institute of Languages for Kerala State Planning Board and Kerala Institute of Local Administration.

Seibel, Hans Dieter, and Uben Parhusip. 1998. "Attaining Outreach with Sustainability: A Case Study of Private Microfinance Institution in Indonesia." *IDS Bulletin* 20(4):81-90.

Sen, Amartya. 1982. *Choice, Welfare and Measurement*. Oxford: Basil Blackwell.

Sen, Amartya. 1984. *Resources, Values and Development*. Oxford University Press: Delhi.

Sen, Amartya. 1992. "More than 100 Million Women are Missing." *New York Review of Books* (December): 61-66.

Sen, Amartya. 1999. *Development as Freedom*. New York: Alfred A. Knopf.

Shah, Thushar, and Michael Johnson. 1992. "Informal Institutions of Financial Intermediation: Social Values of Vishis, Chit Funds, and Self-Help Groups." Working Paper 28. Anand: Institute of Rural Management.

Shylendra, H.S. 1999. *Microfinance and Self-Help Groups (SHGs): A Study of the Experience of Two Leading NGOs, SEWA and AKRSP in Gujarat (India)*. Anand: Institute of Rural Management.

Sinha, Saurabh, and Imran Matin. 1998. "Informal Credit Transactions of Microcredit Borrowers in Rural Bangladesh." *IDS Bulletin* 20(4):66-80.

Soni, Balbir, ed. 2001. *Reform Prospects for Rural Development.* New Delhi: Dominant Publishers and Distributors.

Sunanda, S. 1994. "Institutional Credit for Agriculture in Kerala—A Disaggregated Analysis." Abstracts of International Congress on Kerala Studies, Volume II, A.K.G. Centre for Research and Studies, Thiruvananthapuram, Kerala.

Suresh, K.A. 1998. *Organisational Alternatives for Development—A Search for an Organisational Theory and a Few Cases.* Thrissur: Kerala Agricultural University.

Tankha, Ajay. 1999. "Some NGO Dilemmas in Reaching the Poorest with Microfinance." *Search Bulletin* 14(1):73-79.

Tharakan, P.K. Michael, and Vikas Rawal. 2001. "Decentralisation and the People's Campaign in Kerala." *Social Scientist* 29(9 and 10):8-47.

Tharamangalam, Joseph. 1998. "The Perils of Social Development without Economic Growth: The Development Debacle of Kerala, India." *Bulletin of Concerned Asian Scholars* 30(1):23-34.

Tiwari, Piyush, and S.M Fahad. 2000. "Microfinance Institutions in India." *http://www.soc.titech.ac.jp/icm/concept paper-india*.html., retrieved on 29th August.

Todd, Helen. 1996. *Women at the Centre: Grameen Bank Borrowers after One Decade.* Oxford: Westview Press.

Udry, Christopher. 1990. "Credit Markets in Northern Nigeria: Credit as Insurance in a Rural Economy." *The World Bank Economic Review* 4(3):251-269.

Ukkuru, Mary P., Jyothi Agustine, L. Prema, and A. Sujatha. 1994. "Working Pattern and Nutritional Profiles of Women Engaged in Stone Breaking." Abstracts of International Congress on Kerala Studies, Volume III, A.K.G. Centre for Research and Studies, Thiruvananthapuram, Kerala.

Ulloor Panchayat. 1997. *Vikasana Rekha.* (Mal.) Thiruvananthapuram.

UNDP. 1995. *Human Development Report 1995*. New York: Oxford University Press.

UNDP. 1997. *Human Development Report 1997*. New York: Oxford University Press.

UNDP. 2000. *Human Development Report 2000*. New York: Oxford University Press.

van de Walle, Dominique. 1998. "Targeting Revisited." *The World Bank Research Observer* 13(2):231-248.

Varghese, S.K. 1983. "Profits and Profitability of Indian Commercial Banks in Seventies." *Economic and Political Weekly* 18(46 and 47):145-157.

Venkiteswaran, S. 1984. The Performance of Co-operative Banks in Kerala—A Study on the Operational Efficiency of Primary Agricultural Credit Societies. Ph.D. Dissertation. University of Kerala, Department of Economics, Thiruvananthapuram.

Vogel, Robert. 1984. "Savings Mobilization: The Forgotten Half of Rural Finance." In Dale W. Adams, Douglas Graham, and J.D. von Pischke, eds., *Undermining Rural Development with Cheap Credit*, Boulder, Colo.: Westview Press.

von Pischke, J.D. 1981. The Political Economy of Specialized Farm Credit Institutions in Low Income Countries. World Bank Staff Working Paper 446. Washington, D.C.

Wimmer, Nancy. 2000. "In Poverty Mother Knows Best." *Grameen Dialogue* 44:3-4.

World Bank. 2001a. *World Development Report 2000/2001: Attacking Poverty*. New York: Oxford University Press.

World Bank. 2001b. *Engendering Development: through gender equality in Rights, Resources, and voices*. New York: Oxford University Press.

Yaron, Jacob. 1992. *Successful Rural Finance Institutions*. World Bank Discussion Paper 150. Washington, D.C.

Yaron, Jacob, McDonald, P.B., and Piprek, G.L. 1997. "Rural Finance—Issues, Design and Best Practices." Environmentally and Socially Sustainable Development Studies and Monographs Series 14. Washington, D.C.: World Bank.

Yaron, Jacob, McDonald Benjamin, and Stephanie Charitonenko. 1998. "Promoting Efficient Rural Financial Intermediation." *The World Bank Research Observer* 13(2): 147-170.

Young, Pauline V. 1992. *Scientific Social Surveys and Research.* 4th Edition. New Delhi: Prentice-Hall of India Private Limited.

Yunus, Muhammad and Alan Jolis. 1998. *Banker to the Poor.* Dhaka: The University Press Limited.

Zaman, Hassan. 1998. "Can Mis-targeting be Justified?" *IDS Bulletin* 20(4):59-65.

Zander, Rauno. 1997. "Integrating the Poor into the Rural Financial Mainstream: Issues and Options." In Hartmut Schneider, ed., *Microfinance for the Poor?* France: Organisation for Economic Co-operation and Development.

Index